CAMBRIDGE
EXAMINATIONS
PUBLISHING

OBJECTIVE

CAE

Felicity O'Dell   **Annie Broadhead**   **Student's Book**

CAMBRIDGE
UNIVERSITY PRESS

PUBLISHED BY THE PRESS SYNDICATE OF THE UNIVERSITY OF CAMBRIDGE
The Pitt Building, Trumpington Street, Cambridge CB2 1RP, United Kingdom

CAMBRIDGE UNIVERSITY PRESS
The Edinburgh Building, Cambridge CB2 2RU, UK
40 West 20th Street, New York, NY 10011–4211, USA
477 Williamstown Road, Port Melbourne, VIC 3207, Australia
Ruiz de Alarcón 13, 28014 Madrid, Spain
Dock House, The Waterfront, Cape Town 8001, South Africa

http://www.cambridge.org

First published 2002
Fourth printing 2004

Printed in Dubai by Oriental Press

Text typeface Minion 11/13.5pt System QuarkXpress®

A catalogue for this book is available from the British Library

Library of Congress Cataloguing in Publication data

ISBN 0 521 79992 9 Student's Book
ISBN 0 521 79991 0 Self-study Student's Book
ISBN 0 521 79988 0 Workbook
ISBN 0 521 007879 Workbook with Answers
ISBN 0 521 79990 2 Teacher's Book
ISBN 0 521 79989 9 Class Cassette Set

Cover concept by Dale Tomlinson and design by Jo Barker

Produced by Gecko Limited, Bicester, Oxon.

[redacted]

Acknowledgements

The authors and publishers would like to thank the teachers and students who trialled and commented on the material: Argentina: Alicia Balsells, Liliana Luna; Brazil: Angela Cristina Antelo Dupont; France: Anne Cosker, Harry Crawford; Germany: Vanessa Coughlan, Nicole Gaudet; Greece: Christine Barton, Gaynor Williams; Poland: Anita Trawinska, Tadeusz Z. Wolanski; Spain: Henry Burke, Brendan Smith; Switzerland: Helena Lustenberger; UK: Jenny Cooper, Simon Gooch, Bernie Hayden, Sarah Hunter, Roger Scott, Clare West. The authors would also like to thank the staff at EF International Language School, in particular, Mick Davies, Simone Khairi, Amy Langmead, Andrea Southgate and Alan Wilson. Special thanks to our editors, Charlotte Adams, Sue Ashcroft, Judith Greet and Claire Thacker who all gave invaluable help and support. The publishers are grateful to Annette Capel and Wendy Sharp for permission to reproduce their original course book concept in *Objective CAE* and in all other *Objective* examination course books.

The author and publishers are grateful to the authors, publishers and others who have given permission for the use of copyright material identified in the text. It has not been possible to identify the sources of all the material used and in such cases the publishers would welcome information from copyright owners. p. 12: 'Close encounters of the British kind', reproduced from *British Shibboleths, One language, different cultures*, edited by Eddie Ronowicz and Colin Yallop, with permission of the publishers, The Continuum International Publishing Group Ltd; p. 15: extract from *The Magic Toyshop* by Angela Carter. Copyright © Angela Carter 1967. Reproduced by permission of the Estate of Angela Carter c/o Rogers, Coleridge & White Ltd, 20 Powis Mews, London W11 1JN; p. 17: adapted extract from *The Cambridge Encyclopaedia of the English Language*, 1995, by David Crystal, reproduced with permission of Cambridge University Press; p. 18: extract from *My Family and Other Animals* by Gerald Durrell, reproduced with permission of Curtis Brown Ltd, London, on behalf of the Estate of Gerald Durrell. Copyright Gerald Durrell; p. 22: interview reproduced with permission of GMTV; p. 29: extract from *How to Improve Your Memory*, used with permission of www.ehow.com; p. 35: extract from *The Writing Center Online Handouts - Ten secrets of writing business letters*, reproduced with permission of Arizona State University; p. 36: *Dian Fossey*, extract adapted from the Encyclopaedia Britannica © 2001 Britannica.com Inc; p. 38: extract from 'Kiwi Surprise', *Living etc*, May 1999, reproduced with permission of IPC Media; p. 39: *Michael Flatley* by John H. Mathews, extract from Encyclopaedia Britannica 1994-1999, reprinted with permission from the Encyclopaedia Britannica © 2001 Britannica.com Inc; p. 43: extract from 'In my opinion: hello...', from Online Connected Dotcom Telegraph 29.07.99, © Telegraph Group Limited (1999); p. 45: extract from 'Bums on seats is not the answer' by Susannah Kirkman © Times Newspapers Limited 24.03.2000; p. 46: adapted extract from 'The Psychology of Success', by Jo Gardiner, reproduced with permission of the author; p. 52: extracts from *Patently Absurd!* (http://www.patent.freeserve.co.uk), reproduced with permission; p. 59 (2): extract from *Russia: A Concise History, Revised and Updated edition* by Ronald Hingley, pages 74-75, Thames & Hudson, 1991, reproduced with permission of the publishers; p. 59 (3): extract reproduced from *The Midas Touch* by Anthony Sampson (Copyright © Anthony Sampson 1990) by permission of PFD on behalf of Anthony Sampson; p. 59 (4): extract from *Every Man's Own Lawyer* by A.Barrister (Judge Brian Galpin), Macmillan Reference Books, 1981, reproduced with permission of Macmillan, London, UK; p. 59 (5): extract from *Sense and Nonsense in Psychology*, by H. J. Eysenck, published by Penguin 1958 © Penguin; p. 70: headline 'First pupils sent home for lack of teachers', © Times Newspapers Limited, 20.03.2001; p. 70: headline 'What the public really thinks of the Royal Family', © Daily Mail 26.03.2001; p. 70: headline 'Beckham recaptures form at right moment' *Independent* 26.3.01, © The Independent 26 March 2001; p. 70: headline 'Human Cloning is closer than you think', © 2001 Time Inc, reprinted by permission; pp. 70-71: adapted article 'Talking clothes get our measure', by Paul Nuki © Times Newspapers Limited 21.03.1999; pp. 76-77: extract from *The Dream* from *Collected Short Stories Volume 2* by W. Somerset Maugham published by Heinemann. Used by permission of The Random House Group Limited; p. 83: extracts from *Titanic Trail Guided Tours*, reprinted with permission, www.titanic-trail.com; pp. 86-87: extract from *The Complete Watercolour Artist* by Jenny Rodwell, published by Pelham Books Ltd, © Jenny Rodwell, reproduced with permission; p. 89: extract from 'Evolutionary factors of language' (http://www.ling.lancs.ac.uk/monkey/the/linguistics/LECTURE4/4evo.htm), reprinted with permission; p. 91: extract from 'Why was this tutorial created'? (http://www.kumc.edu/SAH/OtED/jrade/preparing_talks/101.html), (reprinted with permission of the University of Kansas Medical Centre; p. 92 (a): extract from *Magic Carpet Theatre*, Cambridge Drama Centre leaflet, January-April, www.magiccarpet.demon.co.uk, reprinted with permission; p. 95: 'What these kids need is discipline', by Ann McFerran © Ann McFerran/Times Newspapers Limited 22.08.1999; p. 98: extract from *The Way Up To Heaven*, from *Kiss Kiss* by Roald Dahl, publisher Michael Joseph, published by Penguin Books, 1962. Reproduced with permission of David Higham Associates; p. 99: adapted extract from 'The $25,000 Levi's', *Daily Mail* 16.05.2001 © Daily Mail 2001; p. 101 (a): extract 'I stumbled on the George ...' from an article by Ingrid Kennedy first published in *The Independent on Sunday* 25th June 2000; p. 104: extracts from film review page, *Hannah and Her Sisters* and *It All Starts Today*, *Radio Times* 3–9 February 2001. Reprinted with permission of *Radio Times*; p. 110: adapted extract from *Mission: implausible*, Guardian Unlimited, © The Guardian Unlimited; p. 112: extract from *On The Outskirts* Copyright © Michael Frayn, 1964 (Collins, London: 1964), reproduced by permission of Greene & Heaton Ltd; pp. 116-117 extracted from an article by Philip Hensher 'Don't be fooled: the Queen is not speaking our language', first published in *Independent* 22nd December 2000;
p. 119 (1): extract from *Eating Out: Social Differentiation, Consumption and Pleasure*, by Alan Warde and Lydia Martens, published by Cambridge University Press 2000; p. 119 (2): extract from *Frozen Food* by Robert Uhlig & Constable Robinson Publishers, © Telegraph Group Limited; p. 119 (3): extract from *The Painter's Daughters*, The Sunday Telegraph Magazine, 18.06.2000 © Telegraph Group Limited 2000; p. 128: 'Art's old masters draw the queues' by Maev Kennedy, 10.02.2001, reproduced by permission of *The Guardian*; p. 132: extract from *Full Circle* by Michael Palin reproduced with the permission of BBC Worldwide Limited. Copyright © Michael Palin 1997; p. 137: extract from 'What's the Weather?' in *New Scientist* 16.09.2000, reproduced with permission from New Scientist magazine, the global authority on science and technology news © RBI 2000 www.NewScientist.com; p. 150: article 'If bingeing on chocolate ...' by Paul Kendall, *Daily Mail* 23.04.2000, © Daily Mail; p. 151: adapted extract from 'Beaten by a tomato...' by David Munk, *The Guardian* 24.04.2001 © Guardian 2001/David Munk; pp. 158-159: extracts from *Team Development Manual* by Mike Woodcock, reproduced with permission of Gower Publishing Company; p. 161: extracts from *Running a hotel on the roof of the world* by Alec Le Sueur, published by Summersdale, reproduced with permission; p. 163 (4): extract from 'Jacques Brel hostel', *The Rough Guide to Belgium & Luxembourg*, April 1999, written by Martin Dunford et al, published by Rough Guides Ltd, reproduced with permission; p. 167-8: extract from *A Friend In Need* from *Collected Short Stories*, W. Somerset Maugham published by Heinemann. Used by permission of The Random House Group Limited, and with permission of Kay Collyer & Boose LLP, USA, reprinted by permission of the Heirs of W. Somerset Maugham; p. 173: extract from 'Oh, what a carry on!' © The Economist Newspaper Limited, London; p. 179: extract from 'Don't criticise exams ...' © Daily Express, 28.09.2000, reproduced with permission; p. 189: extract from article 'Making the best of a good job', by Peter Baker, *The Guardian* 7.11.1999, © Peter Baker, reproduced with permission; p. 189: extract from article 'Testing...testing...testing' by Will Woodward, *The Guardian* 20.05.2000, reproduced with permission of *The Guardian*.

For permission to reproduce cartoons: p. 176: *How To Be Polite* (postcard No.2) and *Asking The Way* (postcard No.12) reproduced with permission of Lee Gone Publications. For permission to reproduce book jackets: Cambridge University Press for p. 177: *Cambridge International Dictionary of English, Cambridge Learner's Dictionary, Cambridge Schools Shakespeare: Romeo and Juliet, Hamlet, King Richard II.* For permission to reproduce photographs: © Apple; Catherine Ashmore p. 103 (D, E, F); © Associated Press p. 99; © BBC Picture Archives p. 136 (tl); DEP65969 *Bowl of Pears*, 1991 by Lara Geffen (20th century) Private Collection/Bridgeman Art Library p. 118 (bl), TOP73590 *The Painter's Daughters Chasing a Butterfly*, c. 1759 by Thomas Gainsborough (1727-88) National Gallery, London, UK/Bridgeman Art Library p. 119 (r); Camera Press/Richard Stonehouse p. 88 (cr), /SUS p. 116; © Corbis/Hulton-Deutsch Collection p. 64, /Patrick Ward p 58 (tl); Corbis Stock Market/© Ronnie Kaufman p. 121 (t); Greg Evans International Photo Library/Greg Balfour Evans pp. 13 (bc, br), 19, 65 (tr), 79 (br), 109 (A), 154 (br), 160 (utr, lbl), 166 (lc, ucr), 178 (cr), 187 (cl); © Hilary Fletcher p. 13 (bl); Format/© Jacky Chapman p 177 (tr); Gettyone/FPG International/B.P. p. 160 (ubr), /Larry Bray p. 177 (br), /Ron Chapple p. 160 (ltr), /Doug Corrance p. 154 (bl), /Rob Gage pp. 109 (C), 178 (br), /Michael Malyszko p. 154 (tr), /Ian McKinnell p. 13 (tl), /Miao China Tourism Press, Wang p. 161 (l), /Antonio Mo pp. 106 (tr), 187 (tc), /Friedhelm Thomas p. 79 (tl), /V.C.L p. 65 (tl), V.C.L/Nick Clements p. 187 (bc); Gettyone Image Bank/Cesar Lucas Abreu p. 94 (tl), /David W.Hamilton p. 109 (E), /Carol Kohen p. 23, /Ghislain & Marie David de Lossy p. 16 (c), Real Life p. 187 (bl), /Nicholas Russell p. 16 (br), /Henry Sims p. 46 (l), /Ken Tannenbaum p. 177 (bl), /David Vance p. 106 (bl), /Andrew Yates Productions p. 40 (r); Gettyone Stone/Martin Barraud p. 92, /Elie Bernager p. 94, (br), /John Blaustein p. 106 (bc), /Paul Chesley p. 130 (tl), /Stewart Cohen p. 46 (r), /Mary Kate Denny p. 94 (bl), /Julie Fisher p. 106 (br), /Jules Frazier p. 119 (tl), /Margaret Gowan p. 13 (tr), /Walter Hodges pp. 65 (c), 118 (tl), /Ed Honowitz p. 37, /Chronis Jons p. 154 (tl), /Alan Klehr p. 94 (tr), /Bob Krist p. 133, /Mark Lewis p. 160 (lbr), /Laurence Monneret p. 121 (b), /Ben Osbourne p. 79 (bl), /Penny Tweedie p. 166 (b), /Art Wolfe p. 160 (lc), /Gary Yeowell p. 10 (tl); © Granada; Ronald Grant Archive p. 103 (A, B, C), / © 20th Century Fox/Paramount p. 82, / © 20th Century Fox/Paramount/UIP p. 110; Sally & Richard Greenhill/ © Richard Greenhill p. 65 (bl); Impact/ © Alain Le Garsmeur p. 161 (r); Katz Pictures/IPG/Richard Baker p. 118 (r), /Marleen Daniels/REA p. 187 (cr), /Jeremy Nicholl p. 119 (bl), /Richard Smith p. 178 (bl); Life File/Arthur Jumper p. 166 (lcl), /David Kampfner p. 73 (c), /Ken McLaren p. 127 (r); Magic Carpet Theatre, The Magic Circus, www.magiccarpettheatre.com p. 92; Encarta box shot reprinted with permission from Microsoft Corporation p. 177 (cl); Photofusion/ © Peter Olive p. 88 (cl); Pictor pp. 10 (bl, tr, br), 38, 46 (c), 49 (b), 58 (b), 79 (tr), 88 (l,r), 106 (tl), 109 (B, D), 130 (bl, r), 160 (lbl), 166 (t), 166 (lcr), 178 (t, cl), 187 (tl); Popperfoto/Reuters pp. 39, 136 (tr), 136 (br), 149; Powerstock Zefa pp. 16 (tr), 73 (left), 160 (utl), /APL p. 127 (tl), /Benelux Press p. 73 (br, B), /A.Gin p. 10 (bc), /Index p. 58 (tr), /Ian Lishman p. 187 (tr), /Sharpshooters Dream pp. 136 (cl), 154 (c), /Visual Medi Fastforwards pp. 16 (l), 73 (br A), /Visual Medi Wild p. 160 (tc); Rex Features/Edward Webb p. 49 (t), /SIPA Press p. 136 (cr), /Ray Tang p. 22 (b); Science Museum/Science & Society Picture Library p. 40; © John Walmsley p. 65 (br), 96, 187 (br); (c)Wildlife Matters p. 127 (bl). The following pictures were taken on commission for CUP: Trevor Clifford p. 34, 40 (middle), 61, 85, 177 (upper centre right, lower centre right).

Permissions research and picture research by Hilary Fletcher.

The recordings which accompany this book were produced by James Richardson at Studio AVP, London.

The publisher has used its best endeavours to ensure that the URLs for external websites referred to in this book are correct and active at the time of going to press. However, the publisher has no responsibility for the websites and can make no guarantee that a site will remain live or that the content is or will remain appropriate.

Map of Objective CAE Student's Book

TOPIC	GENRE	MAIN EXAM SKILLS	GRAMMAR	VOCABULARY
Unit 1 **Getting to know you** **10–13** People and places	Introductions	Speaking and Listening	Conditionals	Collocations Adjective-noun, adverb-verb, adverb-adjective
Exam folder 1 **14–15**		Paper 3 English in Use: 1 Multiple-choice gap fill		
Unit 2 **Keeping in touch 16–19** Making contact	Informal letters	Writing and Speaking	Prepositions and adverbs	Multiple meanings
Writing folder 1 **20–21**		Notes and notices		
Unit 3 **The real you 22–25** Career paths	Interviews	Speaking	*Wish* and *if only* *It's time*, *would* *rather/sooner*	Idioms Verb + *the* + object
Exam folder 2 **26–27**		Paper 3 English in Use: 2 Open gap fill		
Unit 4 **Acting on instructions** **28–31** Memory techniques	Instructions	English in Use	Modals: *may, might,* *can, could*	Prefixes and suffixes
Writing folder 2 **32–33**		Informal letters		
Unit 5 **Dear Sir or Madam** **34–37** Dream jobs	Formal letters	Writing and Listening	Relative clauses	Connotation Positive, negative and neutral
Units 1–5 Revision 38–39				
Unit 6 **Speak after the tone** **40–43** Communications technology	Phone messages	Speaking	Phrasal verbs	Collocations *Have, do, make* and *take*
Exam folder 3 **44–45**		Paper 3 English in Use: 3 Error correction		
Unit 7 **Running a successful** **business 46–49** The world of work	Reports	Writing	Cause and effect	Multiple meanings
Writing folder 3 **50–51**		Formal letters		
Unit 8 **Best thing since sliced** **bread 52–55** Inventions	Describing objects	Reading, Listening and Speaking	Modals: *must, should,* *ought to, shall, will, would*	Positive and negative adjectives

Content of the CAE Examination

The Cambridge Certificate in Advanced English examination consists of five papers, each of which is worth 40 marks. It is not necessary to pass all five papers in order to pass the examination. There are five grades: Pass – A, B, C; Fail – D, E. As well as being told your grade, you will also be given a statement of your results which shows a graphical profile of your performance on each paper.

Paper 1 Reading 1 hour 15 minutes

There are four parts to this paper and they are always in the same order. Each part contains a text and a comprehension task. The texts used are from newspapers, magazines, journals, non-literary books, leaflets, brochures, etc.

Part	Task Type	Number of Questions	Task Format	Objective Exam folder
1	Multiple matching	12–18	You read a text preceded by multiple-matching questions. You match a prompt from one list to a prompt in another list, or match prompts to elements in the text.	7 (104–105)
2	Gapped text	6 or 7	You read a text from which paragraphs have been removed and placed in jumbled order after the text. You decide where the missing paragraphs fit in the text.	8 (116–117)
3	Multiple choice	5–7	You read a text followed by multiple-choice questions with four options, A, B, C or D.	8 (116–117)
4	Multiple matching	12–22	As 1st text	7 (104–105)

Paper 2 Writing 2 hours

There are two parts to this paper. Part 1 is compulsory so you have to answer it. In Part 2, there are four questions and you must choose one. Each part carries equal marks and you are expected to write approximately 250 words for each task.

Part	Task Type	Number of Tasks	Task Format	Objective Writing folder
1	• article • leaflet • brochure • notice • announcement • note • message • formal or informal letter • report • proposal • review • instructions • directions • competition entry • information sheet • memo	1 or more compulsory tasks	You are given a situation which you need to respond to. You may be given two or three different types of information which you need to use in your answer.	Notes and notices 1 (20–21); Informal letters 2 (32–33); Formal letters 3 (50–51); Reports and proposals 4 (62–63); Articles 5 (80–81); Leaflets 6 (92–93); Reviews 7 (110–111); Articles, reports and memos 8 (122–123); Descriptive writing 9 (140–141); Formal writing 10 (152–153); Informal writing 11 (170–171); Descriptive, narrative and discursive articles 12 (182–183);
2	Writing text types as for Part 1	4 tasks choose 1	You are given a choice of topics which you have to respond to in the way specified.	Exam folder 9 (134–135); Paper 2, Parts 1 and 2

Paper 3 English in Use 1 hour 30 minutes

There are six parts to this paper, which test your grammar and vocabulary.

Part	Task Type	Number of Questions	Task Format	Objective Exam folder
1	Multiple-choice gap fill, mainly testing vocabulary	15	You choose which word from four choices completes each of the 15 gaps in the text.	**1** (14–15)
2	Open gap fill, mainly testing grammar	15	You complete a text which has 15 gaps.	**2** (26–27)
3	Error correction	16	You identify mistakes in a text, either extra words or spelling or punctuation mistakes. Some lines in the text are correct.	**3** (44–45)
4	Word formation	15	You form an appropriate word, using the given prompt word, to fill each of the gaps in the two short texts.	**4** (56–57)
5	Register transfer	13	You transfer information from one text to another. The two texts are different in terms of register (formal/informal), style and/or writer's purpose. You complete the second text with suitable expressions.	**5** (74–75)
6	Gapped text	6	You read a text with phrases or sentences which have been removed and placed in jumbled order after the text. You decide where the missing phrases/sentences fit in the text.	6 (86–87)

Paper 4 Listening about 45 minutes

There are four parts to this paper. Parts 1, 3 and 4 are heard twice. Part 2 is heard once only. The texts are a variety of types either with one speaker or more than one.

Part	Task Type	Number of Questions	Task Format	Objective Exam folder
1	Sentence completion, note taking	8–10	You hear a monologue twice, e.g. an announcement, a radio broadcast, telephone message, speech, talk, lecture, etc. You write a word or short phrase to complete the sentences or notes.	**10** (146–147)
2	Sentence completion, note taking	8–10	You hear a monologue **once** from the range of text types above. There may be prompts from another speaker. You write a word or short phrase to complete the sentences or notes.	**10** (146–147)
3	Sentence completion, multiple choice	6–12	You hear a conversation between two or three speakers twice from the range of text types above as well as interviews and meetings. You write a word or short phrase to complete the sentences or choose A, B, C or D.	**11** (164–165)
4	Multiple matching, multiple choice	10	You hear a series of five short extracts twice. In multiple matching you choose the correct option from eight choices. In multiple choice there are two questions for each speaker. You choose the correct option from a choice of three.	**11** (164–165)

Paper 5 Speaking about 15 minutes

There are four parts to this paper. There are usually two of you taking the examination together and two examiners. This paper tests your grammar and vocabulary, interactive communication, pronunciation and how you link your ideas.

Part	Task Type	Time	Task Format	Objective Exam folder
1	Three-way conversation between two students and one examiner	3 minutes	You are asked to respond to one another's questions about yourself, and respond to the examiner's questions.	**12** (176–177) Complete Speaking test (Parts 1–4)
2	Two-way interaction between students	3–4 minutes	Each student in turn is given a visual prompt and must talk about the pictures for about one minute. The second student has to respond as specified.	see above
3	Two-way interaction between students	3–4 minutes	You are given some prompts for a problem-solving task. You talk about the task together.	see above
4	Three-way conversation between students and examiner	3–4 minutes	You talk about the topic area in Part 3, developing wider issues.	see above

UNIT 1 Getting to know you

Speaking and Reading

1   Look at the photos. Where would you see the landmarks?

a

b

c

d

e

2   Read the extracts (a–e) and then match each one with a city from the box below.

a
The exuberant friction of a port city marked me forever; the beautiful and the decrepit – wrought-iron balconies holding up the tottering facades of Royal and Chartres Streets. It is a densely-packed city of half a million souls, with houses of the well-to-do and the poor often side by side.

b
I walked out for a good view of the world-famous building. The Broadwalk, a promenade surrounding the Opera House, led me along to splendid vistas: to the west, that magnificent structure, the Harbour Bridge, to the east, a bay with the Manly hydrofoil ferry charging in on plumes of spray.

c
It is March, a mild late-summer day here in the Southern Hemisphere. I have spent a glorious morning hiking up Table Mountain through deep green forests, up rocky ravines and finally out into wide-open moorland at the top.

d
The twin streams of history converge just below the delta, where the greatest city in the Islamic world sprawls across the Nile towards the Pyramids, those supreme monuments of antiquity. Every visitor comes here.

e
The background music in the café sounds like a distant Fellini film score; a poster of Carlos Gardel, tango idol of the thirties, winks down from the wall. Croissants are stacked along the blond wood bar. Outside the traffic has reached total gridlock, but no one is honking.

Buenos Aires, Argentina	Cairo, Egypt
Cape Town, South Africa	New Orleans, USA Sydney, Australia

3   Read the quiz below. With a partner, choose the best response in each situation. Give your reasons for rejecting the others.

1 You are in a room with a number of people. Someone who is very near you but is not looking in your direction accidentally drops some money on the ground. You want to catch their attention in order to tell them they have dropped it. What do you say?

a Look out! You're dropping money all over the place!
b Excuse me. I think you might have dropped something.
c I hope you don't mind my mentioning it but I think you've dropped something.

2 You are in a crowded bus and, by accident, bump into someone, slightly upsetting their balance. What do you say?

a Why don't you look where you're going!
b I'm so dreadfully sorry. It was entirely my fault. I do hope you can forgive me.
c Sorry.

3 You are in a crowded bus and, by accident, bump into someone, slightly upsetting their balance, but on this occasion, you have clearly caused the person some pain. What do you say?

a I'm really sorry.
b Actually, it was the driver's fault, not mine.
c It doesn't look as though you need an ambulance so there's no need to look at me like that!

4 What does the person on the bus say as they experience the pain?

a Yippee!   b Yuk!   c Ouch!

5 Someone you do not know very well is talking to you very quickly. The person doesn't know that you have a train to catch and are desperate to leave. What do you say when you cut short the conversation by interrupting?

a Must go. Got a train to catch.
b Well, it's been lovely talking to you … .
c I know you're going to think this terribly rude of me and I must apologise in advance, but I'm afraid I have to leave you now.

6 What do you say when you answer the phone?

a Hello.
b I am (your name).
c The (family name) residence.

4 With a partner, discuss the questions below.

   a If you met someone from a different country who speaks a different language, which language would you communicate in and why?

   b How many different languages do you think you need to know and why?

   c When you meet someone for the first time, how does your language vary according to whether they are the same age as you, or older or younger than you?

   d Which questions do you think it is impolite to ask the first time you meet someone?

E xam spot

In the first part of the CAE Speaking test (Paper 5) you and your partner will only have about three minutes to talk about yourselves. You may be asked to talk about where you come from, your leisure activities, your hopes for the future and so on. Make sure you use a good range of grammar and vocabulary as well as clear pronunciation.

5 Work with a different partner and discuss these questions.

   a How do you begin a question when you are not sure if it is polite to ask it?

   b When you are listening to someone, what sort of body language, sounds and phrases do you use to show you are interested and you are listening to them?

6 Look at the Exam spot above. Prepare some questions to find out more about your partner. Now ask your partner the questions.

G ···⟶ page 190

Conditionals

1 Look at this example of the second conditional from Speaking and Reading 4.

If you met someone from a different country who speaks a different language, which language would you communicate in and why?

Now complete the table about the four basic types of conditional.

Type	Tense – *if* clause	Tense – main clause	Use
zero		present simple/ continuous	
first			
second	past simple/ continuous	*would* + infinitive without *to*	to talk about a situation which is hypothetical or very unlikely to happen
third		*would have* + past participle	

2 Now look at these examples of conditional sentences. With your partner, discuss how you could express these using the conditional structures from the table above.

   a Should you experience any difficulties, please do not hesitate to contact me.

   b Had it not been for Jane's intervention, the meeting would have gone on far too long.

   c Turn on the air conditioner if it will make you feel more comfortable.

   d If you would take your seats ladies and gentlemen, the concert will begin.

   e If you happen to see Tom, could you tell him I've gone home.

3 Look at the words below which are often used in conditional sentences.

given   if so   unless   otherwise   provided

Now complete this text about advice for visitors to Japan using the words in the box.

How not to embarrass yourself in Japan

Before you go to any country where the culture is quite different, you should get to know something about the country, **(1)** .... you might end up embarrassing yourself and those around you. **(2)** .... that for most Europeans Japanese culture is very different, there are a few tips you might like to take note of. You could be invited to a Japanese home. **(3)** ...., remember that you should take your shoes off when you enter the house or flat. Don't wear your normal outdoor shoes inside **(4)** .... you really want to offend your host. **(5)** .... you follow a few basic house rules, both you and your hosts should have a mutually interesting time.

Reading

1 You are going to read an extract from a book which examines the similarities and differences between varieties of English. Before you read the extract, discuss these questions with a partner.

   a Have you ever visited a foreign country? If so, what cultural differences did you notice?

   b What might a visitor to your country perceive to be the biggest cultural difference?

   c What is culture shock? Have you ever experienced this?

2 Now read the text below and answer the questions.

Close encounters of the British kind

An underlying principle of cultural behaviour which is closely reflected in the language is the need to avoid face-to-face conflict. Even though the British may appear unpleasantly blunt when compared with some Asian cultures, they are on the whole concerned to offer a way out whenever a potential conflict between individuals occurs. This may be compared with public confrontations in large committees or parliament where much more confrontation goes on. Some cultures are, by way of contrast to the British, much less concerned to avoid conflict in private or personal encounters.

Perhaps there is a principle of 'aggression management' here: every culture has developed some ways of letting off steam, has some areas in which people are allowed to express their true feelings.

The immediate linguistic consequence of open conflict-avoidance is that you need to know what to do and what to say, for example, when someone takes a position in a queue in front of you, accidentally stands on your toe in a bus or disagrees with you in a public gathering. In the public gathering, depending on the nature of the meeting, the British reaction may be to confront disagreement openly and respond vigorously. In the other more personal situations, the same individual may work hard at taking a middle route between doing nothing and engaging in open conflict. In doing so, he or she will expect a similar cooperative response from the other person, such as an apology like, 'Oh, sorry, I didn't realise ...'. In other cultures, behaviour might well be the opposite – a great effort to reduce conflict in a public meeting and robust responses in the private situations. Within our own cultures, we understand the conventions and know when people are being normally polite or normally outspoken. The difficulties come when we make errors in an unfamiliar environment.

   a What differences are there in the way many British people handle potential personal conflict and public confrontations? Would you say this is the same or different in your country?

   b Which phrase in the text means *expressing anger*?

   c When might a British person say, 'Oh, sorry, I didn't realise ...'?

3 Discuss these questions in small groups.

   a What are the dangers of making general statements about the characteristics of certain nationalities?

   b What generalisations are made about your national characteristics? Do you agree with them?

Vocabulary

Vocabulary spot

It is important to know which words collocate (which words commonly go together) and a good dictionary will tell you this. When you see good examples of collocation, underline or highlight them in the text.

1 Look at these examples of collocations from the reading text.

   an underlying principle (adjective and noun collocation)
   closely reflected (adverb and verb collocation)
   unpleasantly blunt (adverb and adjective collocation)

   Go through the text and highlight some more collocations to remember.

2 Complete these word 'forks' with a word which collocates.

EXAMPLE: *to make*
            to reach   a decision
            to come to

a supply a noun to make a compound noun

                   binder
.... finger
                   road

b supply three different verbs

to ....
to .... permission
to ....

c supply an adjective

                   weather
.... criticism
                   flavour

d supply three different adjectives

....
.... thanks
....

e supply a verb

to   an ambition
to .... assets
to   a dream

f supply three different verbs

to ....
to .... pain
to ....

Listening

E xam spot

In the CAE Listening test (Paper 4) you listen to five short extracts. In the multiple-matching format there are two tasks. In the test there are eight choices in each task and you match the correct five.

1 🎧 You will hear five speakers talking about meeting people. Look at the pictures below. As you listen, match the speakers to the pictures.

2 🎧 Listen again and match the speakers (1–5) to the topic headings (A–G). There are two topic headings which do not fit.

Speaker 1   **A** testing friendships
Speaker 2   **B** exchanging cultures
Speaker 3   **C** no way to get to know a lady
Speaker 4   **D** sharing experiences strengthens friendships
Speaker 5   **E** business and pleasure
                 F strangers are not so strange
                 G sharing delights of the environment

3 Which of the speakers did you find interesting to listen to and why?

Exam folder 1

Paper 3 Part 1 Multiple-choice gap fill

In Part 1 of the English in Use test (Paper 3) you must choose one word from a set of four (A, B, C or D) to fill a gap in the text. The focus is on vocabulary so you have to think about the meaning of the word. You also have to check whether the word fits the grammatical context of the sentence and the text as a whole.

Below are some examples of the types of words that are tested in this part of the paper.

Expressions

I .... sight of an old friend of mine when I went to the bank yesterday.

A saw   B caught   C set   D gained

B is the correct answer. The expression is *to catch sight of someone or something.*

Collocations

All that was left for breakfast were some .... rolls and tea.

A stale   B rotten   C sour   D rancid

A is the correct answer. We say *stale* bread, *rotten* fruit, vegetables or meat, *sour* milk and *rancid* butter.

Phrasal verbs

With all his experience he intends to .... up a computer business with his brother.

A put   B lay   C get   D set

D is the correct answer. The phrasal verb is *to set up* meaning to establish a company or business.

Linking words

He decided to go .... his family begged him not to.

A although   B despite   C otherwise   D if

A is the correct answer. *Despite* would require the construction *despite his family begging him not to* or *despite the fact that his family begged him not to. Otherwise* means *or else* and *if* does not make sense here.

Vocabulary

The child fell down and .... her knee.

A skimmed   B grazed   C rubbed   D scrubbed

B is the correct answer. *Graze* means to break the surface of the skin by rubbing against something rough. *Skim* means to move quickly just above (a surface) without, or only occasionally, touching it. *Rub* means to press or be pressed against (something) with a circular or up and down repeated movement. *Scrub* means to rub something hard in order to clean it.

Advice

- Read the title because it will help you predict the main topic of the text.
- Always read the whole text first to understand the gist of it.
- Read carefully not only the sentence where the gap is but also the sentence before and after the gap. Make sure that the word you write makes sense in the context of the text as a whole.
- Consider each alternative carefully, dismissing those which do not fit.
- Read through what you have written and see if it sounds right.

For questions 1–15, read the text below and then decide which word best fits each space. The exercise begins with an example (0).

Example:

0 **A** installed   **B** tied   **C** drawn   **D** retracted

C is the correct answer. We *draw* curtains or blinds.

Aunt Margaret's kitchen

The kitchen was quite dark because the blinds were (0) ......C....... . There was a smell of (1) .... cigarette smoke and some unwashed cups were (2) .... neatly in the sink, but the room was ferociously clean. It was quite a big room. There was a (3) .... dresser, painted dark brown, loaded with (4) ...., a flour jar, a bread-bin. There was a larder you could walk into. Melanie experimentally walked into it and (5) .... the door to on herself in a cool smell of cheese and mildew. What did they (6) ....? Tins of things: they seemed particularly (7) .... of tinned peaches, there was a whole pile of tins of peaches. Tinned beans, tinned sardines. Aunt Margaret must buy tins in (8) .... There were a number of cake tins and Melanie opened one and found last night's currant cake. She took a ready-cut (9) .... of it and ate it. It made her feel more at (10) ...., already, to steal something from the larder. She went back into the kitchen, (11) .... crumbs.

There was a long table of (12) .... pine with a tablecloth (splashed with russet chrysanthemums, the sort of tablecloth you see through the windows of other people's houses as you walk by at teatime) (13) .... back to cover crockery (14) .... out ready for breakfast, perhaps to (15) .... mice from dirtying the cups.

1	**A**	stale	**B**	rancid	**C**	ancient	**D**	musty
2	**A**	erected	**B**	stacked	**C**	ordered	**D**	ranked
3	**A**	built-up	**B**	cornered	**C**	walled	**D**	built-in
4	**A**	accessories	**B**	crockery	**C**	implements	**D**	tools
5	**A**	took	**B**	pulled	**C**	made	**D**	put
6	**A**	consume	**B**	eat	**C**	devour	**D**	use
7	**A**	crazy	**B**	loving	**C**	fond	**D**	likeable
8	**A**	lots	**B**	gross	**C**	mass	**D**	bulk
9	**A**	slice	**B**	rasher	**C**	shaving	**D**	remnant
10	**A**	comfort	**B**	place	**C**	home	**D**	rest
11	**A**	sprinkling	**B**	shedding	**C**	sowing	**D**	scattering
12	**A**	grazed	**B**	scraped	**C**	bruised	**D**	scrubbed
13	**A**	folded	**B**	bent	**C**	opened	**D**	tilted
14	**A**	sorted	**B**	set	**C**	done	**D**	let
15	**A**	have	**B**	ensure	**C**	keep	**D**	save

UNIT 2 Keeping in touch

Genre Informal letters

Topic Making contact

Speaking 1

1 With a partner, discuss these questions about keeping in touch with people.

   a Which method(s) of communication do you use with your friends – face-to-face conversation, telephone, email or letter? Which method do you think is best for different occasions?

   b Do you think it is necessary to see someone regularly, face-to-face, in order to remain friends?

   c How have recent changes in communications technology affected you? Do you feel that people are becoming more or less isolated because of these?

E xam spot

In the CAE Writing test (Paper 2), you may be asked to write an informal letter either in Part 1 or Part 2. Read the situation carefully and decide who you are writing to and why before you start the letter. Make sure you are consistent in your style of writing and that your purpose is clear.

Writing

1 Read the following letter. With a partner, discuss what the purpose of the letter is.

> *on holiday in beautiful Scotland*
> *Midsummer*
>
> Hi Sarah
>
> Well, here we are on the fantastic Isle of Skye – honestly, I can't begin to tell you how wonderful it is to spend some time away after my exams. As you know I'd been working so hard, I was beginning to think life would never be normal again (what's normal anyway?). Of course, it's the other extreme here – the only serious decision I have to make in any one day is shall I have smoked salmon for dinner or Scottish beef? Ha! What a life, eh?
>
> Anyway, what I really wanted to say was a huge thank you for the present, it's the best present ever! The colours are just amazing and I love long T-shirts that I can wear for anything – even as a nightie – no, it's too good for that. Jack's been looking at it with envy so I'll have to keep my eye on it to make sure he doesn't swipe it. Really, a big thank you.
>
> Tomorrow we're going to the north of the island, up along the coast road to an area that's known for wonderful walks and stunning views; I'll come back as fit as a fiddle. There's supposed to be a great pottery shop up there so I'll have a look at that too. Trouble is it's quite pricey now; ever since the potter featured in a national newspaper article some of his pots are now fetching astronomical sums in some trendy London gallery. Ah, well!
>
>   Must dash, Jack's just come in and looks like a man hunting lunch!
>
>   love
>   Jane
>
> PS I'll be back on Sun 8th, will give you a call then.

2 With a partner, discuss these questions about the letter to Sarah.

   a What is unusual about the address and date in this letter? What are more common ways of writing them in informal letters?
   b This letter begins with *Hi Sarah* and ends with *love Jane*. What other beginnings and endings can informal letters have?
   c What do you notice about the type of vocabulary used? Give examples.
   d What do you notice about the punctuation?
   e Is it common to use contractions in informal writing?
   f How did Jane add some information which she had forgotten?
   g Write a key sentence for each paragraph which summarises the content.

3 An English friend of yours wrote to you some time ago asking about the possibilities of working in a hotel near where you live. Here is an extract from her letter.

> ... As you know I'm studying hotel management and as part of the course, I'm expected to get a holiday job working in a hotel. You mentioned once before that there are some great hotels near where you live. Could you let me know the name of one which you think would be good to work in? It would be even better if you could find out who I should contact ...

Unfortunately you have been very busy so you have not replied to her letter until now. Write to your friend to:

- apologise for the delay in writing back
- give information about a hotel and the person to contact
- suggest suitable dates for holiday jobs
- give some information about what has been happening in your life since you were last in touch with your friend
- ask some questions about your friend.

Remember to think about the points raised in Writing 2.

Prepositions and adverbs

1 Look at this sentence from Writing 1.

*Well, here we are **on the fantastic Isle of Skye** – honestly, I can't begin to tell you how wonderful it is to **spend some time away** after my exams.*

Look at the words in bold. *On* is a preposition in this example. *Away* is an adverb in this example. Read through Jane's letter again and underline more examples of prepositions and adverbs.

2 Complete the following sentences by putting in any necessary prepositions or adverbs.

EXAMPLE: *Turn left the crossroads and then after two blocks, you will see the cinema the right.* ✗
*Turn left **at** the crossroads and then after two blocks, you will see the cinema **on** the right.* ✓

   a It's your brother the phone.
   b He got married Sarah when he was in his 30s.
   c The noise of the storm prevented me sleeping.
   d Who is that present?
   e When I was my way to London, I realised I'd left my wallet home.
   f I always suffer hay fever the summer.
   g I think I was beginning to get stuck a rut in my home town.
   h In the discount book shops near me you can get books next to nothing.
   i You can find this chain of restaurants the country.
   j I'm afraid you can't trust the trains to run time.
   k Some of the students couldn't come the pub because they are age.
   l Mary's got a job a teacher.
   m Tom's a doctor and seems to be duty most weekends.

G ⋯⟫ page 190

3   Read this extract from a book. In the extract, some family
    members are all sitting down together reading the letters which
    they have just received.

    Look at the prepositions and adverbs in italics in the first paragraph.
    Then complete the gaps with a suitable preposition or adverb.

In the crisp, heady weather the family spent most of its time *on* the
veranda, eating, sleeping or just simply arguing. It was here, once a
week, that we used to congregate to read our mail which Spiro had
brought *to* us. As we browsed *through* our letters we would frequently
pass remarks *to* one another.
     "Aunt Mabel's moved **(1)** .... Sussex. She says Henry's
passed all his exams and is going to work **(2)** .... a bank. At
least, I *think* it's a bank. Her writing is really awful, **(3)** ....
spite of that expensive education she's always boasting **(4)** ....
Uncle Stephen's broken his leg, poor old dear, and done something
(5) .... his *bladder*? Oh, no, I see. Really, this writing – he
broke his leg falling **(6)** .... a ladder. You'd think he'd have
more sense than to go **(7)** .... a ladder **(8)** .... his
age. Ridiculous. Tom's married one **(9)** .... the Garnet girls."
     Mother always left **(10)** .... the last a fat letter, addressed
(11) .... large, firm, well-rounded handwriting, which was the
monthly instalment **(12)** .... Great-aunt Hermione. Her letters
invariably created an indignant uproar **(13)** .... the family, so
we all put **(14)** .... our mail and concentrated when Mother,
(15) .... a sigh **(16)** .... resignation, unfurled the
twenty odd pages, settled herself comfortably and began to read.

4   With a partner, discuss these questions about the extract.

    a How did the confusion over *bladder* and *ladder* arise?
    b How did the family members usually react to Great-aunt
       Hermione's letters?
    c The book paints a picture of life in the 1950s. In your opinion,
       has family life changed much since then? Do family members
       communicate with each other in the same way?
    d When do you tend to receive letters or cards? Will email replace
       letters written by hand?

> **V**ocabulary spot
>
> Some words in English have multiple meanings or are used in different ways
> depending on the context. In the reading text we saw *Henry's passed all his
> exams and is going to work in a bank.* Look at the use of *bank* in these
> sentences: *We had a lovely picnic yesterday on the river bank. I haven't got
> his details to hand but they'll be in the data bank.*
> Whenever you look up a word in your dictionary, check to see how many
> different meanings and uses it has.

Vocabulary

1 Which word can fit all
   three sentences?

   a • I hurt my ....
         while I was climbing.
      • It's at the .... of
         the page.
      • I'll have to ....
         the bill.
   b • The .... I heard
         of him, he was living
         in Hastings.
      • She's awful, I hope we've seen
         the .... of her.
      • The rain is expected to
         .... all week.
   c • After the accident he was
         so shocked he lost the
         .... of speech.
      • It's not in your ....
         to cancel the project.
      • You need tremendous
         .... in your legs
         to be a good runner.
   d • Have we got time for another
         .... of drinks before
         we go?
      • There were 15 of us all
         .... the table.
      • It was disappointing to see
         the politician ....
         on his critics.
   e • She showed me a computer
         which might ....
         my particular needs.
      • Police are interviewing a man
         who is said to ....
         the description of the
         attacker.
      • Does anyone ....
         to the name of Devlan?
   f • Someone .... into
         the back of my car yesterday.
      • Halfway down the motorway
         we .... out of
         petrol.
      • Mr Jones .... the
         company single-handedly for
         many years.

Listening

1 You are going to listen to a conversation between two women, Rebecca and Amanda. Look at the picture of them. What do you think their hobbies may be and their dreams for the future?

2 🎧 Work with a partner. One of you will listen for Rebecca's answers and the other for Amanda's answers. Listen to the first part of the conversation and note down both the main idea and the extra information they give to develop the answer.

Question	Main idea	Extra information
Where are you from in England?		
Have you studied any foreign languages?		

3 🎧 Now continue to listen and make notes on Rebecca's or Amanda's answers. Make notes under the two headings.

Topic	Main idea	Extra information
hobbies		
future hopes and dreams		
living or working abroad permanently		
earliest memories of school		

4 Do you have anything in common with either Rebecca or Amanda?

Speaking 2

1 What do you think makes someone a good communicator?

2 In Listening 3 we heard Amanda develop her answer about her hobbies.

I've done a sort of Middle Eastern dancing. It's like an Egyptian belly dancing but it's not Egyptian, it's a kind of country form where your hips actually go down instead of upwards. And you're dressed in lots of clothes, you're not showing any stomach or anything. So, yeah, I did that for a little while but I get fed up with things really, get bored and move on. I did yoga and that annoyed me. It used to make me anxious.

With a partner, discuss ways of developing the answers to these questions.

a What do you enjoy about living in your city?
b Why are you studying English?
c What interesting things have you done lately?
d What are your plans for the future?

> **E xam spot**
>
> In the first part of the CAE Speaking test (Paper 5), you will be expected to talk about yourself and your life in an interesting way, showing a range of structures and vocabulary. Remember to develop your ideas by giving extra information.

3 Work in groups of three. Imagine one of you is the Examiner and the other two are candidates. The Examiner should ask the questions above and three more related questions. While the candidates are speaking, the Examiner should consider whether they are using a range of structures and vocabulary. Candidates should develop answers as fully as possible and make them interesting.

4 Apart from a range of structures and vocabulary, what other features are important when speaking?

Writing folder 1

Notes and notices

1 Look at these notes and notices. For each one decide:

- what the relationship is between the person who wrote it and the person who read it
- what the purpose of the note or notice is
- what the main content points are.

a

Hi Katy

Just a note to remind you to bring a packed lunch for the walk on Sunday. There won't be any restaurants halfway up the mountain! The forecast is for sun, so bring sun cream too. See you at 7.30 am on Sat.

love Jenny

b

LOST

I left a green file with the notes from my English classes in Room 6 on Wed 7th May. It's got all my homework assignments for this term in it so it's really important. If you have found it, please contact me, Mary, on 0654 345 085.

c

John

I called round but you're not in. I've left the CDs I borrowed with your neighbour, Mrs Bond. I'm just going to play tennis for a couple of hours. Phone me on my mobile if you fancy meeting up later.

Cheers
Martin

d

SALE OF THE CENTURY!

COMPUTER

Now is your chance to obtain this wonderful Pentium 3 computer. Only 2 years old and reliable. Lots of software included. Phone for all the technical information.

8943 983 583.

Yours for only £200!!!!

e

Dear Mr Betts

I have just heard from Bournemouth University that they have accepted me for the Media Studies course. I'm really happy as that was my first choice. I would like to thank you for all the help you gave me preparing my CV and letter of application; it worked!

Best wishes
Clara

f

Tony

We've decided to meet at that new café in Bridge St. instead of in the park It's called café Select and it's next to the music store. It might be better as the weather doesn't look too good So let's meet there at the same time, 130.

See you

Diana

2 This message is too long and there is some irrelevant information. Cut it to approximately 50 words.

Hi Mike,

I think I might have left my blue jacket at your house on Friday evening when you had your birthday party. It's the jacket I bought last summer in France. If it's there, could you phone me to let me know and I'll arrange to pick it up when I'm on my way to the gym. I go to the gym every Tuesday and do about 2 hours' training. The facilities there are really good and you meet lots of new people.

Hope to hear from you soon.

Liz

3 This notice is not clear enough. Rewrite it, giving precise information, in approximately 100 words.

COLLEGE LIBRARY

We are going to catalogue all the books in the library soon. For us to do this, we first have to ask you to return all library books – so make sure you meet the deadline.

We are also asking all students to fill out a form for a new library card. Make sure you bring everything you need to do this when you bring your books back.

As some students are taking exams in the next month or so, we are going to put all the exam books in another room so that you can continue to borrow or use these books for reference.

The Librarian

4 This notice contains several spelling mistakes. Read the notice and correct the mistakes.

> If you are interrested in getting some English books at a really low prize, come to the school hall on Wensday between 2 pm and 4 pm. We are having a sail of dictionnaries, course books and grammer books; everything to do with English. Take my advise – get there early to get the bargins.

5 This message has no punctuation or capital letters. Read it and add the necessary capital letters and punctuation marks.

> maria
>
> thank you so much for looking after my plants and feeding the cat while I was on holiday if youre thinking of going to the coast this year try rimini its great theres lots to do there and the beach has golden sand were thinking of going there again in august but it depends on whether tom starts his new job with ibm in may or not anyway thanks again for everything ill return the favour any time
>
> love
>
> sylvia

6 Choose three of the following tasks and write your answers.

A Write a note to your teacher explaining that you are unable to attend classes this week as you have to go to another city to take part in an important tennis tournament. Ask your teacher for details of the classwork and homework you will miss so that you can do some schoolwork while you are away.

Write your **note** in 50 words.

B You want to write a notice to inform other English language students that there is an English film showing at the Britannia Club. The film will be followed by a discussion in English so you want to point out that it is a good opportunity to practise English.

Write your **notice** in 50 words.

C You are going to be on holiday for a week and a friend has agreed to look after your flat while you are away. Write a message explaining what your friend should check and do in your flat and thank her/him for the help.

Write your **message** in 70 words.

D You have seen the following letter to a newspaper. Your cousin is the manager of this hotel and you know the complaints are unjustified. Write a note to your cousin mentioning where you saw this letter, why it is important that he/she should reply to the letter and that you hope business will not be affected.

Write your **note** in 100 words.

Dear Sir,

I would like to warn readers about the newly opened Zeus Hotel.

I recently stayed there with my family and found the staff rather unfriendly. When we mentioned that our room was not cleaned to a satisfactory standard, they did nothing to rectify the situation.

In addition, building work is still continuing and it was very noisy, especially early in the morning when we were still in bed.

The food and service in the restaurant were less than adequate and I cannot understand how this hotel can boast five stars.

Yours faithfully,
Mr S. Capriati

7 When you have written your note, notice or message, check through the Advice box below.

Advice

- All points must be covered.
- The register (formal – neutral – informal) should suit the situation.
- Is your writing clear?
- Make sure your note is precise.
- Does the layout of the note make it easy to read?
- Have you observed the word limit?
- Check your writing for grammar, spelling and punctuation.

Genre	Interviews
Topic	Career paths

Speaking 1

1 With a partner, discuss these questions.

a Look at the magazine covers. What would you expect to read about in these magazines?

b Which magazines or TV programmes do you know where famous people are interviewed? Do you like reading or watching interviews?

c What sort of people make good guests on TV chat shows?

d Why do you think famous people appear on chat shows or do interviews for magazines?

e Who would you most like to interview? How would you approach the interview to encourage the person to give full and honest answers?

Reading

1 You are going to read an interview with a model, Helena Christensen. What questions do you think the interviewer will ask?

2 Read the interview to check if any of your predicted questions were asked.

Interviewer: Considering you belong to one of the glitziest professions there is, along with showbiz, you seem to have your feet pretty much on the ground.

Helena: I truly believe that who you are is because of your family, you know, the way that you were brought up, the love that you get from your family, the discipline from them. It all goes back to childhood no matter what happens later in your life. And also, probably, coming from Denmark has kept me very grounded because there's not too much fuss going on there and nobody really cares too much about fame, the same way that other countries are obsessed with it. In Denmark it's who you are and you shouldn't think you are more than anybody else. And, all in all, I would really say that it has helped me coming from a country like Denmark.

Interviewer: You have a really good reputation in the industry for being very professional; you come in, you do the job, you go home. There's no baggage, no tantrums and tempers.

Helena: Well, that's nice to hear, but, for me, that was the only way to deal with the job because it's such a strange job. If I didn't do it that way, if I created problems for myself, not just coming in, showing up, doing the job and leaving, if I thought too much about it, then I don't know if I would've been able to do this job. I think the only way to do it was just actually doing it that way.

Interviewer: I know it's a difficult question but why do you think you rose to the top? Was it a mixture of talent and luck, being in the right place at the right time?

Helena: It was a mixture of all of that. You know, you can't really define your look or why your look was perfect for the time. But I was really lucky. When I went to Paris for the first time I didn't really have any intentions of working as a model. I came down to eat, basically because I was invited to a weekend of good food, and it was the show week that week, and I went to see some clients and met some of the most amazing people in the industry. But it was not really that important to me. It wasn't what I wanted to do at that time.

Interviewer: What did you want to do?

Helena: I wanted to travel the world and take photos. Most people think I'm starting photography now, but actually, I did it before and did a bit of modelling in between.

Interviewer: Did a bit of modelling in between! That's one way of putting it. Do you think that all those years that you spent in front of the cameras make you a better photographer?

Helena: Obviously, working with some of the most amazing photographers in the world, you soak it all in and get a bit of their experience. And I'm very curious about everything I see in life.

Interviewer: What kind of photographs do you take, is it glamour shots or do you tend to go more for the real person as it were, showing them as they really are, warts and all?

Helena: I'm definitely more into taking portraits of people as they really are, getting something from them deep inside out through their faces. And it's an amazing thing taking photographs, portraits, as every time it's such an intimidating sensation when you take portraits of someone, and I know it makes me feel a little shy and

3 Work with a partner and answer these questions.

   a Which two factors in particular have influenced Helena's personality?

   b How did she deal with modelling?

   c How did she get into modelling?

   d What had she intended to do instead of modelling?

   e How does she relate her own experience of being photographed to being a photographer?

   f What other business is she involved in and what is her role in it?

   g What does she say about the way men react to a female model?

4 Work with a different partner and discuss these questions.

   a What is the stereotypical image of a female model? Does Helena fit this image?

   b What did you think of the way the interviewer and Helena interacted?

   c Do you think Helena develops her answers sufficiently and appropriately for this magazine interview? Give examples to support your opinion.

   d Is there anything else you would have asked her if you had been the interviewer? Are there any questions you would have left out?

   e What do you think of magazines and newspapers which carry a lot of stories about famous people's past and personal lives?

Listening

1 You are going to listen to an interview with David Burns, a soap opera star. In it, he talks about his *troubled past*. What sort of skeletons do you think there are in his cupboard?

2 🎧 Listen to the interview and tick the areas of his life that he talks about.

brothers and sisters ☐	his working relationship with a director ☐
school life ☐	his marriage ☐
hobbies ☐	his relationship with his parents ☐
a person who helped him ☐	his daughter ☐
	his future acting roles ☐
fans ☐	

3 🎧 Listen to the interview again for the expressions below. Tick the ones you know the meaning of. Put a question mark next to the ones you are not sure about. Put a cross next to the ones you do not understand and cannot guess the meaning of from the context.

   a the public eye   **e** tuned into me   **i** obsessed

   b a bully   **f** playing villains   **j** I was hogging the limelight

   c a taunt   **g** an edgy person

   d downward spiral   **h** it can turn nasty   **k** my lips are sealed

4 Try to find other students who can tell you the meaning of the phrases you do not know. If no one can help, ask your teacher or look the phrase up in a dictionary.

5 Look again at Listening 2 and discuss with a partner the ways in which David Burns has had a troubled past.

6 To what extent do you think people's childhood experiences affect them in later life?

---

nervous, and it also makes the person that you do portraits of feel a little strange about it because it's a very naked feeling to be that close to someone, and sometimes I don't even know the people that I do portraits of. But you get to know so much about them by just looking at them through your lens.

Interviewer: And now you've really branched out, got your own magazine …

Helena: Well, we started with four issues the first year and now we're on the second year and it's ten issues.

Interviewer: Ten issues, and you're doing quite a lot of the photographs for that yourself?

Helena: Yeah, I mean the idea from the beginning was that I was the creative director, but more than anything, I write and take photographs, so it's definitely what I'm most into.

Interviewer: Now, as you are Helena Christensen, super model, how easy was it for you to meet guys, to meet men? Weren't they intimidated by you?

Helena: Well, I think it does intimidate men, and I wish it didn't, to meet women from this strange profession, because it intimidates me. It's such a strange thing, I've never gotten used to doing this job really. But it really only comes down to talking to people and then as soon as you open your mouth and speak, then people are totally fine because they realise there's nothing there that's too weird. It's not what I thought it would be, which is, I guess, one of the problems with having been in the media so much. People get a kind of different perspective of you unless you really come across as the person you really are. But I haven't really had a problem with the men thing.

Interviewer: I'm sure you haven't!

Wish and if only

When people are interviewed, it is common for them to talk about their wishes and regrets. In Reading 2, Helena Christensen said *I wish it didn't*, meaning *I wish meeting famous women didn't intimidate men*. This is just one of the structures that can be used after *wish* or *if only*.

1   Work with a partner and complete these sentences with the correct form of the verb.

   a I wish I .... (start) photography earlier.

   b I wish I .... (have) more time to spend with my family.

   c I wish my parents .... (come) to visit me more often.

   d I wish .... (inform) you of our decision.

   e We do not wish the sum of money .... (disclose)

   f If only that .... (be) true!

   g If only the weather .... (brighten up)

   h I wish you .... (ask) such personal questions.

   i If only I .... (know) what it would be like before I started this job!

2   What do you think David Burns wishes? Think about his past, present and future.

   EXAMPLE: *Perhaps he wishes he hadn't been bullied at school.*

Vocabulary spot

In Listening 2, David Burns said *I was hogging the limelight*. This is an idiom with the form: verb + *the* + object. When you learn phrases with the same pattern, try saying the phrases out loud. The repetition of the rhythm may help you to remember them. Why not try it with the phrases in this section?

It's time, would rather/sooner

1   Which phrases can be used to complete the sentences?

   It's time …
   I'd rather/sooner …

   a to go home.
   b go home.
   c going home.
   d we go home.
   e we went home.

2   Read the text below and put the verbs in brackets into the correct form.

> I wish magazines (**1**) .... (have) more in-depth interviews with people. They always seem to focus on the same things, any skeletons in the cupboard and a person's love life. I'd sooner (**2**) .... (read) about their beliefs, aims and ambitions. It's time magazines (**3**) .... (wake) up to the fact that the general public has had enough of media invasion into people's privacy. If only I (**4**) .... (be born) with the necessary talent and expertise, I'd start a magazine for the company where I work. It's time (**5**) .... (do) something instead of complaining about other magazines.

3   Work with a partner and give your opinions on magazine and radio or TV interviews with famous people. What do you wish they were like or what would you rather hear about?

E xam spot

Sometimes candidates lose marks simply because they do not speak clearly enough for the examiner to hear them. Make sure you do not lose marks in this way. In the role play in this unit, make sure all the other students can hear you loud and clear.

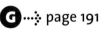 **G** ···⫶ page 191

Vocabulary

1 Work with a partner and match the verbs (a–f) with the objects (1–6). You may have to look these idioms up in a dictionary to help you. How do you look them up? In the idiom *to hog the limelight* for example, do you look under *hog* or *limelight*? Check in a dictionary.

a to take   1 the water
b to test   2 the shots
c to deliver   3 the gap
d to call   4 the biscuit
e to bridge   5 the light
f to see   6 the goods

2 Complete this text with four of the idioms from Vocabulary 1.

> She was a complete unknown when she went to Hollywood but despite her obvious beauty, film directors were unsure of her acting ability. She was given a bit part in the movie *Braveheart* so that the director could (1) .... to see if she would be a viable commercial proposition to take on for future movies. She more than (2) .... , she was an overnight success. From then on, she was the one who (3) .... Whatever part she wanted, it was hers. And at first she accepted every role that was offered. After years of working all hours and after being involved in some rather mediocre films which dented her image, she (4) .... and learnt to accept only those films which would enhance her career.

3 Which method of finding out the meaning of idioms do you prefer and why?

a guessing
b looking them up in a dictionary
c asking classmates
d asking the teacher for an English paraphrase
e asking the teacher for a sentence using the idiom
f asking the teacher for a translation into your language

4 Another form of idiom is prepositional phrase + *the* + object.

EXAMPLE: *to be in the dark* = to know nothing about something.

Match the idioms (1–5) to the definitions (a–e).

1 to be over the hill
2 to be on the spot
3 to be in the running
4 to be up to the mark
5 to be under the weather

a to have a reasonable chance
b to feel ill
c to be considered too old
d to be as good as the usual standard
e to be at a place where an event is happening or has just happened

Speaking 2

1 Look back at Speaking 1e. Work with a partner and think of a famous person you both know about. You are going to role play an interview with that person.

2 Decide which role you are going to play. One of you is the interviewer and one of you is the interviewee. Prepare some questions and answers together. In the interview, you must not say who the famous person is because the other students are going to guess.

3 Role play the interview for the class. Can the other students guess who the famous person is?

4 Now decide which interview you really liked and why. Which of your classmates do you think would make good interviewers?

Exam folder 2

Paper 3 Part 2 Open gap fill

In Part 2 of the English in Use test (Paper 3) you must complete a text by writing the missing word in the gap. You can use only one word. The focus is on structure, so you have to think about structure and meaning to fill the gaps. Check whether the word fits the grammatical context of the sentence and the meaning of text as a whole.

1 Look at these sentences and decide what kind of word would fit the gap. Is it a verb, a preposition, a determiner or a pronoun, for example? Which word completes the sentence?

   a This rolling of the letter 'r' is typical .... some Scottish accents.

   b The cold grey morning was far from welcoming and Janis pulled her dressing gown tightly round .... as she went downstairs.

   c Some people believe the only way to learn a language is to go to the country where it is spoken .... others would recommend learning the basics at home first.

   d Our teacher used to give us a vocabulary test .... single day of the week.

   e It is true that our policy may .... reviewing in the light of recent technological developments.

   f It was an epoch .... there was a true flourishing of the arts.

   g Jack was not sure .... his proposal would be accepted or not.

   h Each classroom has .... own display area, computer work station and quiet corner.

   i Anne hadn't set .... to cause such a disturbance among her colleagues.

   j .... John had had considerable success in his previous job, the new one was causing unexpected challenges.

2 With a partner, discuss what you understand by the title of the text opposite. What do you think you might read about in the text?

3 Give some examples of jargon and discuss when it might be useful and when it might cause problems.

4 Read the whole text without filling in any of the gaps. Then discuss the main ideas of the text.

5 Go through the text and decide which kind of word (verb, preposition, etc.) fits the gap. Check the sentences before and after the gap to find clues.

6 Complete the text.

EXAMPLE: 0 everyone

Jargon – the up side

The reality is that **(0)** .....everyone..... uses jargon. It is an essential part of the network of occupations and pursuits **(1)** .... make up society. All jobs have an element of jargon, which workers learn **(2)** .... they develop their expertise. All hobbies require mastery of a jargon. Each society grouping has **(3)** .... jargon. The phenomenon **(4)** .... out to be universal – and valuable. It is the jargon element, which, in a job, can promote economy and precision of expression, and **(5)** .... help make life easier for the workers.

(6) .... we have learned to command it, jargon is **(7)** .... we readily take pleasure in, **(8)** .... the subject is motorcycling, baseball or computers. It can add pace, variety and humour to speech – as when, with an important event approaching, we **(9)** .... slip into the related jargon. We enjoy the mutual showing off which stems **(10)** .... a fluent use of terminology, and we enjoy the in-jokes which shared linguistic experience permits. **(11)** .... , we are jealous of **(12)** .... knowledge. We are quick to demean **(13)** .... who tries to be part of our group **(14)** .... being prepared to take on its jargon. And we resent it when some other group, sensing our lack of linguistic awareness, refuses to **(15)** .... us in.

Advice

- Remember you must write only **one** word.
- You are never required to write a contraction. If you think the answer is a contraction, it must be wrong, so think again.
- Decide what sort of word fits the gap.
- Try to justify your answer grammatically and with regard to the meaning by referring to the text.
- Check the spelling. The spelling must be correct to get a mark in the exam.
- Try reading the sentence out to yourself to see if it sounds right.
- In the exam always write something. You never know, you might be lucky even if you are not sure of the answer!

UNIT 4 Acting on instructions

Genre	Instructions
Topic	Memory techniques

Listening 1

1 Have you ever been in situations like the ones in the pictures? What problems did you have?

2 Listen and follow the instructions.

3 Here is an example of an instruction from the listening:
Hold for three seconds and then breathe out.
Which grammatical structure is used? How else could you give this instruction?

Speaking

1 Look at these pictures which illustrate how to make an omelette. Put them into the correct order.

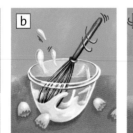
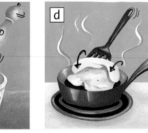
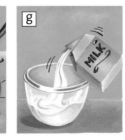

2 Now tell another student how to make an omelette.

Reading

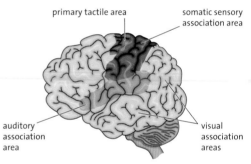

primary tactile area
somatic sensory association area
auditory association area
visual association areas

1 You are going to read some tips on how to improve your memory. Before you read, discuss these questions with a partner.

a How would you rate your memory? What evidence do you have for this?

b To what extent do you think it is possible to improve your memory with techniques or exercises? Have you ever tried to improve your memory?

c Do you think it is true that people's memory gets worse as they grow older? Why should this be the case?

2 Now read the tips below on how to improve your memory. Then with a partner discuss which recommendations you think are the most effective and why.

a Make sure you are alert and attentive before trying to memorise anything.

b Understand the material rather than merely memorising, if it is the type that requires deeper comprehension.

c Look for larger patterns or ideas, and organise pieces of information into meaningful groups.

d Link the new bits of knowledge with what you already know. Place what you learn into context with the rest of your knowledge, looking for relationships between the ideas.

e Engage your visual and auditory senses by using drawings, charts or music to aid memory.

f Use mnemonics – devices such as formulae or rhymes that serve as memory aids. For example, use the acronym 'HOMES' to memorise the Great Lakes in North America (Huron, Ontario, Michigan, Erie and Superior).

g Repeat and review what you have learned as many times as you can. Apply it or use it in conversation, as continual practice is the key to remembering things in the long term.

3 Which of the techniques would you like to try out?

4 You are going to read about three memory techniques which are recommended for language learning. Divide into three groups. Everybody should read the introduction.
Group A should read 1 (The Linkword Technique), Group B should read 2 (The Town Language Mnemonic) and Group C should read 3 (The Hundred Most Common Words).

Introduction

Learning foreign languages
Foreign languages are the ideal subject area for the use of memory techniques: the process of learning words is essentially a matter of association – associating what is initially a meaningless collection of syllables with a word in a language that we understand.
Traditionally this association has been carried out by repetition – saying the word in one's own language and the foreign language time and time and time again.
The whole tedious way of acquiring vocabulary can be eliminated by three good techniques.

1 The Linkword Technique
The Linkword Technique uses images to link a word in one language with another word in another language. For example, if an English person wanted to learn the French word for carpet – *tapis*, he might imagine an oriental carpet where a **tap is** the central design. **Tap is** has the same spelling as *tapis* so he will remember the French for carpet.
The technique was formalised by Dr Gruneborg. Linkword books have been produced in many language pairs to help students acquire the basic vocabulary needed to get by in a language (usually about 1,000 words). It is claimed that by using this technique the basic vocabulary can be acquired in just 10 hours.

2 The Town Language Mnemonic
The fundamental principle rests on the fact that the basic vocabulary of a language relates to everyday things: things that are typically found in a small town, city, or village. The basis of the technique is that the student should choose a town that he or she is very familiar with, and should use objects within that place as the cues to recall the images that link to foreign words.

Adjectives in the park
Adjectives should be associated with a garden or park within the town: words such as green, smelly, bright, small, cold, etc. can be easily related to objects in a park. Perhaps there is a pond there, a small wood, perhaps people with different characteristics are walking around.

Verbs in the sports centre
Verbs can most easily be associated with a sports centre or playing field. This allows us all the associations of lifting, running, walking, hitting, eating, swimming, diving, etc.

Remembering genders
In a language where gender is important, a very elegant method of remembering this is to divide your town into two main zones where the gender is only masculine and feminine, or three where there is a neutral gender. This division can be by busy roads, rivers, etc. To fix the gender of a noun, simply associate its image with a place in the correct part of town. This makes remembering genders so easy!

Many languages, many towns
Another elegant spin-off of the technique comes when learning several languages: normally this can cause confusion. With the town mnemonic, all you need do is choose a different city, town or village for each language to be learned. Ideally this might be in the relevant country; however, practically it might just be a local town with a slight flavour of the relevant country, or twinned with it.

3 The Hundred Most Common Words
Tony Buzan, in his book *Using your Memory*, points out that just 100 words comprise 50% of all words used in conversation in a language. Learning this core 100 words gets you a long way towards learning to speak in that language, albeit at a basic level. It is argued that if you start learning a foreign language by learning the words which occur most frequently, then your learning will be effective. However, critics of this method point out that these words alone would not allow a speaker to make sentences as the words are mainly articles, adverbs and prepositions. In order to communicate we need a range of different types of words so that we can make sentences. On the other hand there is a lot to be said for learning useful words rather than the specialised words for some particular bird or scientific process.

The first 20 basic words
The first 20 out of a list of 100 basic words used in conversation are shown below.

1. a, an	2. after	3. again
4. all	5. almost	6. also
7. always	8. and	9. because
10. before	11. big	12. but
13. (I) can	14. (I) come	15. either/or
16. (I) find	17. first	18. for
19. friend	20. from	

5 Regroup and tell the others about what you have read.

6 Would you use the technique you read about? Why?/Why not?

Modals: *may, might, can, could*

Modal verbs tell us something about the attitude of the speaker. Look at these examples from Reading 4.

*If an English person wanted to learn the French word for carpet – **tapis**, he might imagine an oriental carpet where a **tap is** the central design.*

Words such as green, smelly, bright, small, cold, etc. can be easily related to objects in a park.

In these examples, *might* expresses probability and *can* possibility.

1   Match the meaning of the modal verb *can* with its use in each of the sentences below.

> ability   negative certainty
> offer   order   permission
> request   theoretical possibility

a   Can this camera take panoramic shots?
b   Can I get you something to drink?
c   That can't be the answer. It doesn't fit.
d   Can you help me with this bag?
e   You can collate the statistics while I phone the new customers.
f   The school can take 1,000 pupils.
g   Can I borrow your camcorder until tomorrow?

2   Explain the difference in meaning between these sentences.

1   a   I could get into the house by the back door.
    b   I was able to get into the house by the back door.
2   a   She may get here by 10 if she catches the 8.30 train.
    b   May I use the office photocopier to make a copy of my passport?
3   a   She might get here on time if she leaves work early.
    b   Might I make a suggestion?

3   Look at these pictures and speculate about what might have happened to the people in them or what they might be doing.

EXAMPLE: *The man in picture a might have fallen into a river.*
           The woman in picture e might be studying for an exam.

G ⋯⋮➤ page 191

Writing

1   Write a set of instructions using imperatives and modal verbs. Choose one of the subjects below or one of your own.

How to:
- stay safe while travelling
- make a good cup of coffee
- follow a healthy diet
- make a study plan
- stay cool when you're feeling stressed out
- learn vocabulary in a foreign language.

Listening 2

1 🎧 When you phone a company, you often hear a set of instructions which tell you what to do in order to speak to a particular department. Listen to the instructions and answer the following questions.

   1 *Phoning the cinema*
   What should you do if
    a you want to make a booking for *Cast Away*?
    b you want to see a different film, not *Cast Away*, and you know what time it starts and how much it costs?

   2 *Phoning an airline*
   What should you do when
    a you want to book a flight?
    b you want a special deal?
    c you check in for a PanAir flight?

   3 *Phoning a telephone and Internet provider*
   What should you do if
    a you want information about STL's Internet service?
    b you have a problem with any STL service?
    c you do not use STL yet and would like information about their services?

2 How do you feel about hearing recorded instructions on the phone? Does it provide efficient customer service? Has the personal touch been lost?

Vocabulary

A prefix is a letter or group of letters added to the beginning of a word to make a new word. In Reading 2g you saw *Review what you've learned as many times as you can*. The prefix *re-* adds the meaning *do again*.

1 Put these words under the correct heading according to the prefix they take. Some words can go under more than one heading.

> appear   iron   believable   lead   logical   prison   mature
> accessible   polite   resistible   regular   continue   sensitive
> material   smoker   literate   trust   timely   expected   conclusive

dis-	il-	im-	in-	ir-	non-	mis-	un-

2 Complete these rules for the use of *im-*, *il-* and *ir-*.

   a We often use .... before words beginning with *m* and *p*.
   b We often use .... before words beginning with *l*.
   c We often use .... before words beginning with *r*.

A suffix is a letter or group of letters added to the end of a word to make a new word. Suffixes fall into two categories:

- those connected with the grammatical form of the word, for example, *-ly* (for an adverb), as in *carefully*, or *-tion* (for a noun), as in *recommendation*
- those connected with meaning, for example, *-less* meaning *without*, as in *careless*.

3 Put these words under the correct heading according to the suffix they take. Some words can go under more than one heading and you may have to change the spelling slightly.

> photocopy   count   judge   time   emerge   emancipate   rude
> employ   dramatise   frequent   argue   calm   recommend
> speech   deceit   care   point   respect   tend   rely

-able	-ation	-ency	-ful	-ly	-less	-ment	-ness

4 You are going to play suffixes bingo. Your teacher will give you a set of cards with suffixes written on them. Follow your teacher's instructions.

Writing folder 2

Informal letters

1 Look at these extracts from letters. For
each extract, decide who might have
written it, who it was written to and why.

a

... Then for the last week I'll have a holiday
and I'm going to spend it in Prague. I've got
a friend who went there last year and she
said it's great – a beautiful city, really
friendly people and lots to do. What could be
better after my holiday job? I'll tell you all
about it when I get back.

b

... It's just brilliant, the best thing
you could have got me. I'd tried to
get that CD the other week but it
wasn't in the shops then. I'll probably
drive the whole family mad now playing
it over and over again for days!

c

... It's a real shame you missed the party, it
was great. You know that guy who goes to
the sports club on Saturdays? Well, he was
there – gorgeous or what! I got talking to him
and he's just as nice as he looks. I hope
you're feeling better now and ...

2 What are some of the features of
informal letters? Complete the table
below. One example has been given for
the first two categories.

Choice of vocabulary:	phrasal verbs, ...
Grammatical features:	reported speech, ...
Length of sentences:	
Linking words:	
Punctuation:	

3 Look at this outline of an informal letter. What could
go in each box?

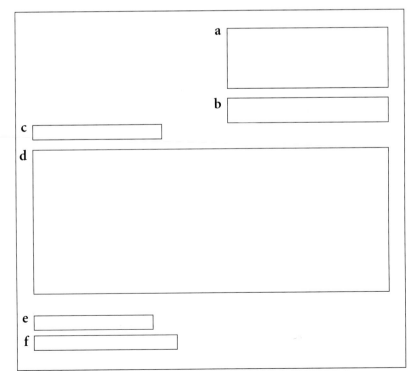

4 There are many set phrases which we can use in informal letters. Here are some examples:

Greetings

- referring to last letter: *It was wonderful to read all your latest news …*
- referring to time since last letter: *It's ages since I last heard from you. What have you been up to?*
- apologising for delay in replying: *I'm really sorry I've taken so long to get back to you but …*
- thanking for last letter: *Thanks for writing and telling me all about your plans for the summer holidays.*

Thanking

- for a present: *I really can't thank you enough for the book, it's just what I wanted.*
- for a party: *Thanks for the party, it was great. I met such a lot of new and interesting people!*
- for an invitation: *It's really kind of you to invite me to the wedding and I'd love to come.*

Now add at least two examples of set phrases to the following categories:

Refusing an invitation
Congratulating
Giving your opinion
Giving advice

Can you think of any other reasons for writing an informal letter?

5 Read the task below carefully.

A friend of yours is doing an interior design course at college and you have the same sort of taste. You have decided to redecorate your bedroom and you have saved some money to spend on it. Write a **letter** to your friend asking for his/her advice.

Now start planning. Work with a partner and discuss:

- the content – what main points do you want to include?
- the language – which phrases are appropriate for the letter?
- the organisation of the content – how can you organise the content into different paragraphs?
- linking devices – how will you link clauses, sentences and paragraphs?
- the style – remember the style features from 2.
- the opening and closing of the letter – choose an opening phrase and a closing phrase from 3.

Write a first draft of the letter. Exchange first drafts with another student and comment on the points made above.

Advice

When you check through your writing use this checklist.

- errors
- natural use of language
- good range of vocabulary
- spelling
- good range of structures
- full completion of task
- use of linkers
- appropriate and consistent style
- content – nothing relevant should be left out

The purpose of the letter should be clear and it should have a positive effect on the reader. This is what the examiners are looking for.

UNIT 5 Dear Sir or Madam

| Genre | Formal letters |
| Topic | Dream jobs |

Speaking

1 With a partner, discuss the following questions.

   a Have you ever written a formal letter? Who did you write to and what was the purpose of the letter?

   b Do you find it easier to write formal or informal letters? Why do you think that is the case?

2 Read these extracts from formal letters and say what the purpose of each letter is.

   a On behalf of everyone, I send you best wishes for a speedy recovery.

   b Please accept our sincere apologies for any distress this situation may have caused you.

   c You may have overlooked this payment but we ask that you give it your prompt attention.

   d Please confirm in writing if you wish to accept this offer and when you will be in a position to commence work.

   e Ms Wright is currently involved in a project which might be of interest to you and she will be contacting you soon to arrange a meeting.

   f If you could forward the details of the Nile Cruise, I would be most grateful.

3 Look at this outline of a layout of a formal letter in English. Complete each box with the missing information (a–g).

   a 20th March 2003
   b Yours faithfully,
   c 221 Cherry Drive
      York YK3 2FG
   d Dear Sir or Madam,
   e (signature)
      Dr C.R. Roberton
   f The University Hotel
      65 Park Parade
      Durham DH6 8HY
   g I am writing in
      connection with a
      recent visit to your
      hotel from the 12th

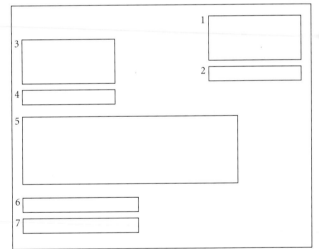

to 15th March. My wife and I stayed in room 368. Unfortunately, our otherwise enjoyable visit was spoilt by the loss of some articles from our room during our stay. This loss was reported immediately upon our discovering it to the receptionist who, in turn, contacted the duty manager. The items lost were ...

4 In the letter, *Dear Sir or Madam* is the opening phrase and *Yours faithfully* closes the letter. Imagine we had opened the letter with *Dear Mrs Simmons.* How would we close it?

Reading

1 Read through the text and match the headings (a–h) to the 'secrets' (1–8).

   a Be Professional
   b End With an Action Step
   c Get to the Point Early
   d Never Write in Anger
   e Put Yourself in Your Reader's Place
   f Start From the End
   g Say it Plainly
   h Use Active Verbs

THE SECRETS OF WRITING BUSINESS LETTERS

1 Decide what the result of your letter ought to be. List things you'd like to say, and review them. Good letters have a strong sense of purpose.

2 Don't delay. You should state your main purpose in the first paragraph.

3 If the letter came to you, how would you respond? Be pleasant; try to turn negative statements into positive ones.

4 Phrases like "in compliance with your request" and "enclosed herewith" are stilted. Write as you talk – naturally. Include just one idea. Sentences longer than two typed lines are suspect.

5 Passive voice is weak and confusing. "A decision has been reached by the committee" is inferior to "The committee has reached a decision." Also, readers can sense your evasiveness if you write: "Your order has been misplaced" instead of "I misplaced your order."

6 Emotion will evaporate; a letter won't. Devise a way to handle problems in an upbeat manner. Your chances of success will multiply tenfold.

7 The end of a letter should suggest the reader's next move, or your own.

8 The most well-written letters can't survive bad presentation. Use a clean, logical format for your letter. A crowded or over-designed page distracts from your message.

2 Work with a partner and discuss which points you agree with and which points you disagree with. Support your opinions with reasons.

Writing

E xam spot

You may be asked to write a formal letter in the CAE Writing test (Paper 2). You do not need to write any addresses in the exam. Remember:
- follow the conventions of formal letters
- use formal vocabulary
- make sure that the style is consistent
- show clear organisation
- do not use contractions
- make sure the purpose of writing is clear
- consider the effect the letter will have on the reader.

1 Work with a partner. Read the advertisement for a Business Travel Coordinator and underline all the qualities and skills the company is looking for.

BUSINESS TRAVEL COORDINATOR

Attractive salary

Our client requires an experienced travel professional to provide a planning and arrangement service for all their business travel needs.

Advising personnel on the most economical, safe and practical way to travel, you will make all the necessary arrangements and provide a proactive approach to passports, vaccinations and foreign currency. Your up-to-date knowledge on all travel options will enable you to advise the most economical travel plan, whilst with your excellent organisational skills you will manage our corporate database of travel and related medical/personal details and all liaison with external travel and hire car agencies.

As well as a thorough knowledge of the travel industry, you will need to be IT literate, including email and Internet, have good communication skills, be self-motivated, organised and have the ability to work to deadlines. You will be working with a set travel budget, therefore good numeracy is required.

2 Now plan the content of the job application.

3 Talk about your plan for the letter with another pair of students and combine the best ideas from both.

4 Write a first draft of the letter (approximately 250 words). Pay attention to organisation of ideas and formal vocabulary.

Then ask another student to read your draft and give you feedback on clarity of purpose, layout, letter conventions (opening/closing), use of formal vocabulary, sentence structure and errors.

You should comment on their first draft in the same way.

5 Write the final draft.

6 Would this type of job appeal to you? Why?/Why not?

Vocabulary

1   Read the extract below about Dian Fossey and decide if these statements are true or false.

   a   Dian had her appendix removed because she was ill.
   b   She lived alone with the gorillas.
   c   She spent all her time collecting data for research.
   d   She had no formal qualifications.
   e   She enjoyed a positive relationship with the game wardens.

Fossey, Dian 1932–1985

Six weeks after leaving hospital minus her appendix, Dian Fossey received a letter from the famous anthropologist, the late Louis S. B. Leakey. 'Actually,' he wrote, 'there was really no dire need to have your appendix removed. That's only my way of testing applicants' determination.' Louis Leakey had only somewhat facetiously suggested she have her appendix removed, but of course, he was so convinced of her determination that he offered her the job and invited her to begin field work in 1966. She lived alone on the damp misty slopes among the mountain gorillas in the Democratic Republic of the Congo until civil war forced her to escape to Rwanda. She established the Karisoke Research Centre (1967), alternating her time between her field work there and obtaining a PhD based on her research (Cambridge University Press, 1974), and writing her best-selling book, *Gorillas in the Mist* (published 1983). She was considered the world's leading authority on the physiology and behaviour of mountain gorillas, and portrayed these animals as dignified, highly social, "gentle giants" with individual personalities and strong family relationships. Her active conservationist stand against game wardens, zoo poachers, and government officials who wanted to convert gorilla habitats to farmland caused her to fight for the gorillas not only via the media, but also by destroying poachers' dogs and traps. She was found hacked to death, presumably by poachers, in her Rwandan forest camp in December 1985.

2   Look at the following words and phrases and put them under the appropriate heading. Some words can go under more than one heading.

Positive	Negative	Neutral

> shack, mansion, house
> evaluation, judgment, praise
> modern, state-of-the-art, new-fangled
> nosy, inquisitive   courageous, foolhardy
> innocent, gullible, naive

3   Choose the word with the more positive connotation to complete this text.

Leakey's judgement was (**1**) *flawed/sound* when he chose Fossey as a field researcher. She had a (**2**) *steely/feeble* character and a natural empathy with the gorillas. She would sit for days in (**3**) *solitude/loneliness* in the mountains with the animals, making (**4**) *wordy/detailed* notes about the gorillas' every move. She was a (**5**) *keen/careless* observer. But still the (**6**) *dull/intriguing* question remains: why did she give up a life of luxury in the West?

Relative clauses

1   Look at these sentences about Dian Fossey. Which type of clause is the subordinate clause; a defining relative clause, a non-defining relative clause or an adverbial clause?

   a   Dian Fossey, born in San Francisco, was interested in animals from an early age.
   b   Her active conservationist stand against game wardens, zoo poachers, and government officials who wanted to convert gorilla habitats to farmland caused her to fight for the gorillas not only via the media, but also by destroying poachers' dogs and traps.
   c   Her book, *Gorillas in the Mist*, which was published in 1983, became a bestseller.

2   Explain the difference in meaning between these two sentences.

   a   Her stand against government officials, who wanted to convert gorilla habitats to farmland, became her overriding aim.
   b   Her stand against government officials who wanted to convert gorilla habitats to farmland became her overriding aim.

3   Write four sentences, two with defining relative clauses and two with non-defining relative clauses, using the ideas below.

   • Leakey – give job to – person – show determination
   • Fossey's PhD – Cambridge University Press – based on her research in Africa
   • Fossey – live with gorillas in area – mountain slopes of the Democratic Republic of the Congo
   • Fossey – spend several years in Africa – met her untimely death there

4 Explain the omission of the relative pronoun in this sentence.

This is the region I like best.

5 If the relative pronoun is not necessary in any of these sentences, cross it out.

a Dian lived in a hut which had no electricity.

b The film of the story of her life made an impact that many people will never forget.

c The story which she told in the film made Dian Fossey a household name.

d The clothes that she wore in the jungle were old and worn.

e The place where she grew up has a different sort of beauty.

f The place that she grew up in is known to few, even in the USA.

g The people who made the film about Dian immediately realised the remarkable effect that her story has on whoever sees it.

h She had an inspirational quality which defies analysis.

i Her animals were often the only 'people' that she talked to for days on end.

j Dian had an intimate relationship with the land, which to a large extent determined the way that she lived.

6 In formal or academic English we tend to put the prepositions before the relative pronoun instead of at the end of the sentence, e.g. *There's the man to whom you were talking.* We use *which* not *that* to refer to things, and we use *whom* not *who/that* to refer to people when they are the object of the main clause. Rewrite the following sentences in formal style.

a This is the area of research that he is working on.

b Here are some new statistics that you'll be interested in.

c Is this the advertisement for the job you're applying for?

d Is this the experiment that you were reading about?

e Is this the person who you've entered into correspondence with?

f She received a reply from the editor that she sent her paper to.

g Social Sciences is the category that his work falls into.

h The college has cancelled the conference that you wanted to enrol for.

G ⋯⋮▶ page 192

Listening

1 With a partner, discuss these questions.

a How do you feel about dangerous sports like Formula One?

b Do you think there is too much money involved in sports these days?

c How do you think fame and money can affect a young person?

E xam spot

In the CAE Listening test (Paper 4), you may be asked to complete notes or sentences. When you have written your answers, reread the whole sentence to make sure that it makes sense and is grammatically correct.

2 You are going to listen to an interview with James Warton, a successful Formula One driver. What word or words do you think might complete the sentences below?

a James's mother does not like facing a .... whenever she goes out.

b James's father believes that because James has a .... character, he will be a winner.

c In Australia, James was in .... place when his car developed mechanical problems.

d James remembers the time when his father did not have enough money for ....

e According to the interviewer, there are many .... who would love to get James to sign a contract with them.

f The next thing James would like to buy is a .... even though he knows he may be criticised for it.

g Most of James's former school friends are now ....

3 🎧 Listen to the recording and check your predictions.

4 James has been successful in both his professional and personal life. Work in small groups and discuss all the things in your life that you have been successful at or can do well.

Topic review

a Which countries in the world would you most prefer to visit and why?

b If you went to stay with a British family, what would you take them as a gift from your country?

c How do you prefer to contact friends? By email, phone or by sending a text message?

d Is the art of letter writing dead?

e Would you rather work as a nurse or an artist?

f If you could have three wishes, what would they be?

g What is your earliest childhood memory?

h How may technology help you to learn a language?

i What would be your dream job?

j How interested are you in ecological issues?

Grammar

1 Read this letter from a friend who is not having a very good holiday. Fill the gaps with a verb in the correct form.

Hi Anita,

Well, I wish I (1) .... that I was having a wonderful time but that's far from the truth. For a start, it was a mistake to come here at Easter; it's too crowded, you can't move. And the second thing is I wish I (2) .... here with my sister. She's driving me mad. She always wants to go shopping and I'd sooner (3) .... for long walks along the cliffs. If only you (4) .... with me instead, it would have been so much better. As you know we're staying in a self-catering cottage and she never lifts a finger. I do all the cooking, clearing up, everything! It's time she (5) .... up and stopped acting like a baby. I don't know what to do because I don't want to have a row with her. Supposing you (6) .... with us, what would you do?

Oh well, from now on I'm going to do what I like. I'm not going to have my holiday ruined by her!

Hopefully some more cheerful news next time I write.

Lots of love
Carol

2 For questions 1–15, read the text below and decide which word best fits each space. The exercise begins with an example (0).

Example:

0 **A** provided **B** offered **C** enabled **D** presented

0	A	B	C	D

Kiwi Surprise

When a work project (0) .....*B*..... me the opportunity to return to New Zealand, I spent several weeks (1) .... a country I had left in my early twenties. I'd forgotten about the petrol stations where men in smart uniforms (2) .... to you. They fill your tank, (3) .... your oil and still (4) .... you less than one third of the British price for fuel. And the people rush to your assistance if they see you (5) .... over a map. Or the blissful (6) .... of tips. Locals simply cannot understand why anybody should (7) .... to pay extra for friendly efficient service.

Given that New Zealand has about 3,000 kilometres of coastline, it should come as no (8) .... that social life (9) .... around the sea. When Auckland office workers leave their desks at the end of the working day, they don't (10) .... home. Instead they (11) .... a beeline for the marina and spend the evening (12) .... sail on the Hauraki Gulf. There are more yachts in Auckland than in any other city in the world – no wonder it's called the City of Sails. Even those who can't afford a (13) .... of their own will always know someone who has one, or at the (14) .... least, will windsurf the offshore breezes at speeds that make the commuter ferries appear to stand (15) ....

1	**A** regaining	**B** recapturing	**C** refamiliarising	**D** rediscovering
2	**A** assist	**B** attend	**C** supply	**D** serve
3	**A** control	**B** measure	**C** check	**D** calculate
4	**A** charge	**B** ask	**C** require	**D** demand
5	**A** pointing	**B** doubting	**C** clamouring	**D** puzzling
6	**A** absence	**B** shortage	**C** removal	**D** neglect
7	**A** accept	**B** insist	**C** expect	**D** respond
8	**A** wonder	**B** surprise	**C** amazement	**D** news
9	**A** centres	**B** revolves	**C** turns	**D** gathers
10	**A** move	**B** aim	**C** head	**D** divert
11	**A** have	**B** do	**C** get	**D** make
12	**A** under	**B** by	**C** with	**D** on
13	**A** vehicle	**B** hull	**C** vessel	**D** receptacle
14	**A** simple	**B** single	**C** hardly	**D** very
15	**A** still	**B** dead	**C** afloat	**D** upright

Vocabulary

1 Complete these 'forks' with a word which collocates.

a to ....
  to .... an exam
  to ....

b to .... a room
  to .... a competition
  to .... information

c the ....
  the .... of nature
  the ....

d a ....
  a .... thinker
  a ....

e to ....
  to .... debts
  to ....

2 Choose the correct form of the word in brackets to complete these sentences. Each new word will be formed with either a prefix or a suffix.

a It was thought that the lawyer had .... the jury into believing the accused had been in trouble with the police on a previous occasion. (lead)

b This type of .... windscreen enables the driver to have a clear view even when it is smashed. (shatter)

c The manager's .... can be put down to his people skills. (popular)

d Andrew's .... was idyllic, as he was brought up in a tight-knit family with three sisters, a doting mother and caring father. (boy)

e I can't eat this steak, it's .... I don't like seeing the blood in it. (do)

f A great deal of work has been done to .... land from the sea in order to build a new airport. (claim)

g That was a .... remark to make. I'm sure you've hurt Suzanna's feelings. (heart)

3 With a partner, discuss how you would express the words in the box in a negative way.

| simple | house | eat | assertive | evaluation |

How would you express the words below in a positive way?

| a problem | cheap | nosy | childish | gullible |

4 Write a paragraph about someone you know or a place you know in either a positive or negative way. Make your attitude very clear.

5 Read this extract from a biography about Michael Flatley, who is famous for his modern interpretation of Irish dancing, and fill the gaps with a suitable word.

Flatley, Michael

At the 1994 Eurovision Song Contest, held at the Point Theatre in Dublin, the most successful act was not even entered (**1**) .... the competition. An intermission entertainment entitled *Riverdance*, starring American dancer Michael Flatley, captivated the audience (**2**) .... a modern interpretation of traditional Irish dancing. His arms flying, Flatley leapt (**3**) .... the stage, transforming Irish dance (**4**) .... a rigid, tradition-bound art form that placed a premium (**5**) .... discipline and control (**6**) .... an expressive, buoyant celebration. The jubilant response (**7**) .... the seven-minute performance was overwhelming, and the producers of *Riverdance* soon expanded it (**8**) .... a feature-length spectacle that thrilled audiences in London and Dublin. Following a bitter creative dispute (**9**) .... the show's producers, however, Flatley was fired (**10**) .... October 1995. His response was to develop *Lord of the Dance*, a spectacular Las Vegas-style Celtic dance show that featured Flatley (**11**) .... his most flamboyant.

Flatley was born (**12**) .... July 16, 1958, in Chicago (**13**) .... Irish immigrant parents. Flatley, whose grandmother was a champion Irish dancer, began taking dancing lessons (**14**) .... the age of eleven. His first teacher told him he had started too late to achieve real success, but Flatley persevered. When he was seventeen, he became the first American to win the all-world championship (**15**) .... Irish dancing. Flatley was also a Golden Gloves boxer and a champion flute player. None of these skills, however, seemed likely to help him earn a living, so he went to work (**16**) .... his father's contracting business and performed with local Irish dance groups (**17**) .... his spare time.

UNIT 6 Speak after the tone

Speaking 1

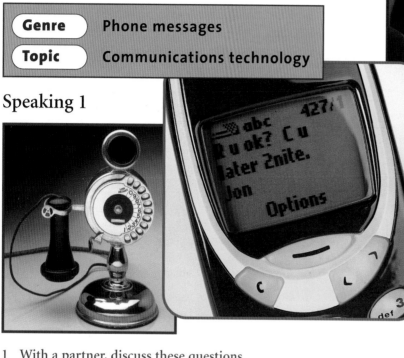

1 With a partner, discuss these questions.

a What is the difference between an answering machine and voice mail? How do you feel about recording a message on a machine? How do you think that suddenly having to speak to a machine affects the way you express yourself?

b Do you have an answering machine? If so, do you ever leave it on when you are actually at home? If so, why?

c List the advantages that answering machines and voice mail offer.

d A lot of additional telephone services and equipment are available now. What are each of the following and when are they useful?

- a mobile
- a videophone
- text messaging
- a ring back service
- the speaking clock
- a bleeper
- a WAP phone
- a call waiting service
- dialling 1471 in the UK or *69 in the USA or 10 # in Australia

e Add to the list any other examples of telephone services or new communications equipment that you can think of.

Listening

1 🎧 Listen to this anecdote which mentions the speaking clock and answer the questions which follow.

a Why did the woman want revenge?
b How did she take revenge?
c Was it an effective way of taking revenge? Why?

2 🎧 You are going to hear six messages on an answering machine. Complete the notes below.

1 For:
  From Name:
        Number:
  Message:

2 For:
  From Name:
        Number:
  Message:

3 For:
  From Name:
        Number:
  Message:

4 For:
  From Name:
        Number:
  Message:

5 For:
  From Name:
        Number:
  Message:

6 For:
  From Name:
        Number:
  Message:

Phrasal verbs

1 Your teacher will give you the tapescripts of the phone messages. Note down any phrasal verbs that you find in them.

2 Look at the sentences below which contain phrasal verbs that can be useful when phoning people. Which particle is needed to complete each sentence?

  a You have to stop talking to someone from a public phone box if your coins run ....

  b Sometimes it can be difficult to get .... to distant or remote places on a mobile phone.

  c If you can't hear the person you are trying to talk to, you may ask them to speak ....

  d You ring a large business and the receptionist there will put you .... to the person you want to speak to.

  e You ring a friend but he wants you to wait a moment while he answers the door bell. He may ask you to hang ....

  f You ring home and talk to your dad for a while. After a few minutes, he says, 'I'd better pass you .... to your mum now'.

  g If you ring someone from a mobile and the signal begins to disappear, you may say, 'Oh dear, we're breaking .... '.

  h You were making a phone call and suddenly you lost contact with the person at the other end of line; in other words, you were cut ....

  i When you have finished talking to someone on the phone you ring .... or you hang ....

3 Match a sentence from A with one from B.

A says:	B says:
a I can't hear you very well.	1 I'll just put you through.
b Can I speak to the Finance Department, please?	2 OK, I'll try to speak up.
c We're going to have to stop talking soon. My money's about to run out.	3 Yes, we're going through a tunnel. I'll ring back in a few minutes.
d Well, I guess I'd better go. It's getting late.	4 No problem.
e Hang on a moment. I'll just turn the TV off.	5 That'd be great. I'll check with my parents and call you back.
f Is it easy to get through to Beijing from here?	6 Would you like me to call you back?
g I hate to say goodbye to you, darling.	7 No, don't ring off now – there's something I've got to tell you first.
h What's happening? We seem to be breaking up.	8 OK, bye then. Thanks for ringing.
i I think we've only got a few seconds left. We're going to be cut off in a moment.	9 Me too. You hang up first. Please.
j Do you want to come round to my house this evening?	10 It's usually OK but I had some problems last night.

 page 193

Vocabulary

1 Put the words in the box under the correct headings, *have, do, make, take,* and *both have and take.*

> a baby   a bath   a cake
> a chance   a go   a mistake
> a nap   a party   a phone call
> a photo   a shower   an effort
> an excuse   dinner   fun
> hold of   part   the cooking
> someone a favour   your best
> someone seriously
> someone's word for it
> the housework   your homework

2 Choose one of the collocations from Vocabulary 1 to complete the following sentences.

  a Just .... your best at the interview. No one can ask for more than that!

  b It's easy to .... mistakes when you're tired.

  c My grandfather always .... a nap after lunch.

  d I have to go and .... some important phone calls.

  e I don't remember you giving me back the money you borrowed but I suppose I'll have to .... your word for it.

  f That looks like a great game. Can I .... a go?

  g You must .... your homework before you go out with your friends.

Speaking 2

E **xam spot**

In the CAE Speaking test (Paper 5), you will be given a mark for pronunciation, so try to work on any aspects of English pronunciation that are problematic for you.

1 Read the tapescript below of the anecdote about revenge from Listening 1.

> **Oh, talking of revenge, I read about a great one once. There was this girl, she'd been dumped by her boyfriend, cos he'd decided he'd gone off her and he told her to move her things out of his flat before he got back from a business trip. I think he was going to the States for a month or something. Anyway, she moves her stuff out straightaway but before she leaves, she picks up the phone and dials the speaking clock. Then she leaves the phone off the hook while the clock goes on speaking the time to an empty flat. 'At the third stroke, it'll be ten twenty-five and thirty seconds…' So the boyfriend finds it when he returns four weeks later. You can imagine what the bill was like after a solid month of phone calls. Even at local rates, it'd be huge! That must have been really satisfying for the dumped girl!**

a Highlight all the schwas.
b 🎧 Listen to the tape again to check your answers.
c Practise reading the text aloud, taking care to pronounce all the schwas as the speaker did.

Reading and Speaking

1 Read the article opposite from a newspaper and answer the questions below.

a Why is the first paragraph written in such a strange way?
b What had the writer intended to write in the first paragraph?
c What sort of new technology does the writer tell us that he has and how does he feel about it?
d How has communications technology changed in the writer's lifetime?
e Why do you think capital letters are used for the phrase *a Very Long Telephone Lead*?
f What drawback does the writer see to these advances in communications technology?
g What is the point of the story about President Carter?

2 With a partner, discuss these questions. Then compare your answers with those of other students.

a In what ways might modern communications technology make people feel more harassed? List as many examples as you can.
b What do you understand by the expression *information overload syndrome*? Have you had any personal experience of it?
c At the beginning of the unit you considered the uses of a number of other developments in communications technology. Can you think of any disadvantages that each of these might also have?
d Can you give any examples from your own experience of people using sophisticated communications technology for trivial ends?
e What sorts of things do you think people spend most time talking about these days? List as many popular topics as you can.
f Do you think the topics you have listed are equally popular with men and women? Discuss what differences you think there are between male and female communication.
g In what ways do you think what people talk about has/has not changed over the last 100 years?
h All things considered, do you think modern communications technology has improved our quality of life?

Hello, this is me calling to say hi

Life in the Information Age leaves less and less time for thought, thinks Michael Bywater.

I AM wroting tgis on the train. I am wruting this, not jyst on thr train, but on ny telepjone on thr train. My teleohone is sumiltameously pixking up ny email and I habe just orderwd a book frim the Cambrudge Iniversity Librart, via their websute. – All on ny trlrphone! – Ism't techmology winderful?

I am not on the train any more. I am at home, on my new Macintosh PowerBook G3, which is also wonderful. I emailed the first paragraph of this column to myself, from my telephone, on the train, and it all worked perfectly. Admittedly the keyboard on my telephone is a bit small, as you can probably tell, but the idea of a telephone even having a keyboard is so exciting that I feel strangely proud of myself.

Actually, I am old enough and vulgar enough still to be impressed by the idea of a telephone that works on a train at all. When I was a child, telephones were made of black Bakelite, and had a dial, and a little drawer which slid out to reveal a small piece of card on which there was plenty of room to write down the telephone numbers of everyone you knew who had a telephone. Far from being able to take your telephone on the train, you couldn't even take it out of the room; if you wanted to make calls somewhere else in the house, you had to call in a GPO engineer and wait a month or two for him to turn up, whereupon he would drill huge holes in the walls and run transatlantic-style cabling around the place, and install a whole other telephone somewhere else on a very short cord, in case you had the un-English idea of walking round the room while making phone calls. Those were the days when a Very Long Telephone Lead was the height of sophistication; rich men had them in American films but they weren't for the rest of us.

As for the calling process itself, there were three possibilities. (1) The other person answered and you had your conversation. (2) Nobody answered and you tried later. (3) The line was engaged and you tried later.

Now we save time and keep in touch and, above all, communicate. My mobile telephone-cum-fax-cum-Internet-cum-diary-cum-notebook has even decided it's not a telephone at all: it is a Nokia Communicator. But do we really have that much more to communicate – and to communicate now – than our grandfathers did? And are we really saving time and being more efficient?

No; and no. Most of our hi-tech communications are communicating nothing more than the fact that we are communicating ("Hello? Hello? I'm on the train"). And as for time-saving and efficiency, well, isn't the greatest source of stress nowadays caused by the sense that none of us have any time?

Time is like computer memory: the more we have, the more stuff rushes in to fill it. In the communications game, we have overshot. "Personal productivity tools" haven't made us more productive, just more harassed.

A journalist told me, some years ago, that he had been sent to interview former President, Jimmy Carter. He worried about Carter at first; every time he asked a question, there was a long silence. Had Carter's mind started to fail? Then the journo realised. Carter was doing something extraordinary. Every time he was asked a question, Carter was stopping to think about it.

Perhaps that's the secret of surviving the Communications Era. Ensure brain is engaged before setting mouth in motion. I promise to give it a try but only if you do, too.

Exam folder 3

Paper 3 Part 3 Error correction

In Part 3 of the English in Use test (Paper 3), you must proofread a text. You will be told what you have to check the text for. This could be unnecessary words, wrong punctuation or misspelt words.

Some lines in the text will be correct and you must tick these lines. In the lines where there is an error, you must indicate the correction in the space at the end of the line.

The point about proofreading is that you have to read very carefully, checking every detail and correcting any errors.

1 Here are some texts which have already been corrected. Explain the mistake in each case.

a Unnecessary word

Do after-school programmes actually improve ~~the~~ ....the..........
educational standards? Inspection ~~by~~ evidence ....by..........
suggests that the critical factor is how ~~much~~ effectively ....much..........
time is used within the school day. But ~~if~~ there has ....if..........
been ~~a~~ very little rigorous examination as to whether ....a..........
a longer school day really benefits ~~from~~ pupils. ....from..........

b Punctuation

I (dont) know about you but my favourite day of the week ....don't..........
is (friday) You have all the pleasure of being able to ....Friday..........
look forward to the weekend and (its) the day when you ....it's..........
can go out without worrying about homework ⊖ getting ....?..........
up in the morning or anything like that. It's great ⊙ ....!..........
Do you agree with me ⊖ Jane? ....?..........

Here the misspelt words have been marked for you.
Write the correct spelling on the lines provided.

c Spelling

I am <u>writting</u> to tell you about all the different ....
things which have been <u>happenning</u> at school ....
this term. Firstly, we've had new <u>bycicle</u> sheds ....
built. We can now keep books and <u>stationary</u> ....
in our lockers though I'm <u>embarassed</u> to say ....
I've <u>allready</u> lost the key for mine! ....

2 Which punctuation marks are required in the cases (a–h) below?

a to mark the end of a sentence

b to mark the end of a question

c to indicate the exact words that someone said

d to separate two items in a list

e to indicate that a letter is missing in, for instance, a contraction like *isnt* or *theres*

f to mark the end of an exclamation

g to indicate possession as in *Johns car* or *my sisters husband*

h to indicate that something is additional information, as in the sentence *The WHO the World Health Organisation is based in Geneva.*

3 Write down five cases where capital letters are required in English. Compare your answers with those of other students in the class.

4 Create a page in your file or vocabulary notebook and head it *Difficult spellings*. Then look through all your recent homework and write down any words that you misspelt. Add to the page regularly.

5 Now try this exercise which is a continuation of the text in 1a. In most lines, there is one unnecessary word. It is either grammatically incorrect or does not fit in with the sense of the text. For each numbered line, find the word and then write it on the corresponding line. Some lines are correct. Indicate these with a tick on the line. The exercise begins with two examples.

0	At Thomas Telford secondary school, which had the best	......✓......
00	exam results of any state school in the other country last year,	<u>other</u>
1	the commitment to an extended school by day was based	....
2	partly on a research into successful American schemes. The	....
3	school has a teaching week of between 31 and over 35 hours,	....
4	up to 10 hours time longer than the 24–25 teaching hours	....
5	recommended by the Government for secondary schools.	....
6	But it is not just a question why of spending extra time in the	....
7	classroom, says the Headmaster. 'The longer day gives	....
8	pupils a wider range of enriching activities like a sport,	....
9	music and the performing arts, raising their self to esteem	....
10	and boosting academic outcomes', he says us. But the	....
11	Telford pupils also benefit from a very high standard	....
12	of teaching. 78 of per cent of the school's lessons received	....
13	the most highest grades in a recent inspection. The school	....
14	was also lucky enough for to be able to build in the longer	....
15	day from its opening, rather than the relying on the goodwill of	....
16	teachers to run after the extra activities.	....

Speaking 1

1 You are going to read a report about research into young people's attitudes to work. Before reading, discuss these questions in groups.

   a In what ways do you think your own experience of work differs (or will differ) from that of your parents' or grandparents' generation?
   b Do you think your attitudes towards work differ from those of your parents?
   c List three advantages and three disadvantages of being an employee in a large company and of running your own business.
   d If you could run any business of your own, what would it be and why?

Reading

1 Read the report then answer these questions.

   a Who exactly was studied in the research?
   b What factors were found to lie behind young people's enthusiasm to set up their own businesses?
   c What problem is identified at the end of the report?
   d What is the significance of the different words written on the brain in the picture in the article?

2 Now read the report again and fill the gaps with a suitable word.

The psychology of success

The need to be challenged. The need to be valued. A desire (1) .... financial independence. These are all powerful motivating factors for young people, an increasing number of (2) .... are setting up their own businesses and (3) .... a success of it.
But (4) .... drives young entrepreneurs? The Industrial Society has researched the views of 10,000 young people, aged 12 to 25, on attitudes on (5) .... from work to the family. Its study, published under the Society's 2020 Vision campaign, found a number of factors.

The first is the legacy of the buoyant 1980s where people (6) .... encouraged to take risks. The youngest people in our survey will have only caught the tail end of Thatcher's Britain but will have grown up watching (7) .... elders strike out on their (8) .... A second factor is the change in the nature of work – the decline (9) .... long-term employment prospects and the rise in contract and freelance work. No more jobs for life. Many people have realised that the few real advantages of 'employment' – occupational pensions, sick pay, company cars – are (10) .... eroded. They have seen people around them struggle to adjust (11) .... their lives in line with their changing work circumstances. And they have felt the pain it causes.

Ironically, the targeting of 'youth' culture by everything from drinks companies to Nike is also influencing their attitudes. Young people are realising that they are the (12) .... placed people to exploit these media and leisure markets because they are living in them – they are in the thick of it. Some of the most successful young entrepreneurs exemplify this – they own companies which have grown out of their hobbies and leisure activities, (13) .... as computer games.

We also identified a new 'work ethic'. It appears that many young people don't believe (14) .... buckling down to trade their time and skills for pay; they are unwilling to make someone (15) .... rich. They have a broader definition of 'work' which includes doing something productive or beneficial. And for many young people their 'ethic' includes not exploiting others. Yes, there (16) .... those who make their money from drugs – but there are far more who want to build a business doing something they enjoy.

They will put (17) .... with initial hardship in the hope that they will reap the benefits (18) .... a later stage. They are driven by their belief in their enterprise, their love of the industry or field in (19) .... they work, and their determination to have more control over their lives than they (20) .... as an employee.

It's time business realised that the very people it needs in order to compete and survive – creative, entrepreneurial youngsters – are choosing to work on their own, because they prefer it and because they can.

3 Mark each of the following statements true or false. If the statement is false, change it so that it is true.

a The report says that one reason why young people start up their own businesses is that they want to make a lot of money.

b The survey was carried out by the Industrial Society and investigated young people's attitudes to work.

c The 1980s was a time when it was particularly risky for people to start up their own businesses.

d Before the 1980s, many people were attracted to being employed rather than self-employed because of the security it provided.

e Large companies have tended to ignore the existence of young people and their interests.

f Young people's moral values are also one reason why they prefer to be in charge of their own working lives.

g Young people don't mind it being tough at first if they believe in what they are doing.

h The report says that established businesses ought to realise that new businesses founded by young people are going to provide serious competition for them.

Vocabulary

Vocabulary spot

Many words in English have more than one meaning. For example, the word *field* is used in the text to mean area of interest but it can also mean an area of land on a farm, a category of sporting event or a category in a computer database program. It can even be a verb meaning to catch or retrieve a ball in a game like baseball or cricket, or to deal cleverly with difficult questions.

1 One word can be used to fill the gaps in each of these pairs of sentences.

EXAMPLE: *The farmer has decided to sell off the large* **field** *next to the wood.*
The Prime Minister successfully managed to **field** *most of the interviewer's questions.*

1 • .... the table before dinner is the children's daily task.
• Streaming and .... are used by some schools as ways of dividing pupils into able or less able groups.

2 • Most computers have at least two .... – one for a hard disk and one for CDs or floppies.
• The boss .... his workers very hard, begrudging them even a coffee break.

3 • Worsening conditions for the work force led to a major .... last year.
• Did anything .... you as strange about Hilary's behaviour last night?

4 • I'm afraid I am going to have to .... your invitation.
• Letters to newspapers regularly complain about a .... in standards of English.

5 • A lot of young people would like to go on the .... but it is a very risky career.
• I'd like to leave this question now and return to it at a later .... in my lecture.

6 • Her success owes at least as much to .... as to talent, as she has never shirked hard work.
• Rod's main aim is to get a job in the film .... and he really doesn't mind what he has to do.

2 Some words in the reading text are used not so much with a different meaning as with a metaphorical meaning. Here are the literal and metaphorical meanings of some of the words used in the text. Which words are being defined?

1 • money or possessions that a person is left after someone's death
• something that remains as a result of something that happened previously

2 • floating on water
• going through an effortlessly successful time

3 • worn away by the weather (e.g. of rocks)
• gradually reduced or destroyed (e.g. confidence)

4 • aiming at something with a gun or a bow and arrow
• aiming at something with an advertising campaign

5 • fastening something down with a metal clasp
• starting to work hard

6 • cut and collect crops
• receive something as the benefit of your own actions

Cause and effect

1 Read the text below about Pat and her business success. Underline any expressions that relate to the language of cause and effect.

What do you think is the reason for Pat's success?

Well, I think there are many reasons why she has done so well. Firstly, her boss had a profound influence on her. More importantly perhaps, her years of hard work have resulted in considerable financial rewards. Recently, her increased sales could be said to be a consequence of an improved marketing campaign. I think her interest in retail stems from a childhood passion for playing shops. It may also have its roots in her ancestry as both her grandfathers were shopkeepers.

2 Now read the rest of the text and fill each of the gaps with a suitable word.

It was Pat's sister who inspired her (1) .... open her own outlet although her teachers also encouraged her (2) .... a career in sales. Her experience in a Saturday supermarket job while she was still at school had a considerable effect (3) .... her later approach to selling. Studying for an MBA brought (4) .... a change in her attitude to business. She started a mail order service so (5) .... to gain a wider customer base. Many potential customers had complained that, because (6) .... work commitments, they could not get to her shop during opening hours. (7) .... a result of this new mail order service, her sales tripled. All these factors taken together then probably explain (8) .... Pat has been so successful in business.

3 🎧 Here are some more common words and expressions which can be useful to talk about cause and effect. Listen to someone talking about why he became an actor. Tick the expressions from the list that he uses.

(as a) consequence	accordingly	affect	aim	basis of
be based on	consequently	correspondingly		explanation
generate	give rise to	grounds for	lead to	motive
objective	originate	outcome	owing to	produce
purpose	reason	repercussion	so	thanks to	therefore

Ⓖ ⋯⋮⋗ page 193

Writing

1 Read the report below. It was written by a group of 17-year-olds who took part in a work experience programme organised by a local supermarket during the summer holidays. Their head teacher asked for the report to find out whether it was worth encouraging similar programmes in the future.

2 Now answer the following questions.

a List the main points of each paragraph.
b Are the headings for each paragraph appropriate and useful? Do you think that this report follows a standard pattern?
c Underline all the words and expressions in the report which are used to link ideas within the text.
d Write headings for a report about a work, study or holiday experience that you have recently had. Your report should be for the benefit of someone who is considering embarking on a similar experience.

Work experience programme

Ten students took part in this year's work experience programme, which took place from July 4th to August 4th. We were all employed in the main branch of the supermarket and had the opportunity to experience different types of jobs; during our four weeks there we spent a week each as checkout cashier, shelf stacker, office junior and kitchen hand.

Usefulness of the programme

We all found the programme useful in a number of ways. Firstly, we learnt a great deal about what life is like behind the scenes in such a large supermarket. None of us had any previous experience of shop work and we found it much more demanding than we had expected. By the end of the month, we all felt that we had gained much more respect for people who do the routine tasks required in such an organisation and feel confident that we will never again get impatient with a slow checkout cashier. Secondly, we enjoyed the chance to learn about the supermarket business as a whole. We had two days' induction before starting work and this taught us a great deal about the complexities of

the international operation of which this supermarket is part. Thirdly, we believe that we have benefited from the experience in that it served to highlight the importance of being able to deal effectively with the general public and people of all ages and backgrounds. Finally, and perhaps most importantly, we feel that we gained a lot of confidence from the opportunities we were offered. At the beginning of the month we thought that we would never be able either to do the jobs expected of us or to fit in with the regular staff, but we quickly managed both to get to grips with our duties and to make friends. We now feel much more prepared for life in the 'real world'.

Drawbacks to the programme

At times we felt as if we were being exploited as cheap labour by the supermarket. We worked at least as hard as the regular staff but only received about a quarter of their wages. Nor were we allowed any of their discounts on purchasing supermarket products. Moreover, although we enjoyed the experience, we all finished the month convinced that we never want to work in a supermarket again. We felt that it might have been even more useful if we could have had the opportunity to work in the kinds of environments that we hope to be in one day ourselves. Might it not be possible, for example, to arrange work experience in the health service for pupils who plan to become doctors or nurses or in hotels for people planning a career in tourism?

Conclusion

In conclusion, we would recommend continuing with this programme. However, we would also like the school's work experience programme to be expanded to include a wider variety of job opportunities in a range of different organisations.

Speaking 2

1 Look at these jobs. Which of them do you think are most valuable to society?

airline pilot	astronomer	car mechanic
chef	computer programmer	dentist
English teacher	footballer	lawyer
newsreader	plastic surgeon	plumber
poet	pop singer	Prime Minister
refuse collector	psychiatrist	soldier
stockbroker	vet	waiter/waitress

2 Work with a partner. Choose the three jobs which you think are most valuable and the three which you think are least valuable and put them in order. Be prepared to justify your choices and your ordering.

3 Regroup so that you are now working with a different partner. Compare your decisions.

4 Here are some features which might attract people to particular jobs:

being your own boss	occupational pension
company car	opportunity for creativity
flexitime	opportunity to travel

Work with a partner and add at least eight other things to this list.

5 Take one aspect of work from the list and prepare some questions to conduct a survey about this aspect of work. Keep notes of the answers which each student gives you.

6 Present the information which you collect to the rest of the class.

7 Discuss how you would present the information gained in your survey in the form of a report. What headings would you use? What kind of language would be appropriate?

Listening

1 🎧 Listen to eight people talking about their jobs.

a Which job is each person talking about? How do you know?

b What does each person like and dislike about their job?

c Why is the speaker in each job?

2 Which of the jobs described appeals to you most? Why?

Writing folder 3

Formal letters

1 Here are some statements about writing letters. If the statement refers to formal letters, write F. If it refers to informal letters, write I.

   a You write your own name and address in the top right hand corner of the page.

   b You write the addressee's name and address on the left hand side of the page above the salutation.

   c You begin the letter *Dear* (*name*).

   d You indent each new paragraph.

   e You use contracted forms (*I'm, you'd,* etc.).

   f You end the letter *Love from.*

   g You sign your name by hand and then print it in brackets underneath in case your signature is illegible.

2 Much of the skill of writing formal letters is being able to use the typical phrases of such letters accurately and appropriately. Here are some examples of typical sentences from formal letters with some words missing. The first letters of the missing words are provided to help you. Complete the sentences.

   a I a _ _ _ _ _ _ _ _ for the d _ _ _ _ in
      r _ _ _ _ _ _ _ to your letter of 15th May.

   b I s _ _ _ _ _ be g _ _ _ _ _ _ _ if you c _ _ _ _
      send me f _ _ _ _ _ _ information about …

   c Please could you a _ _ _ _ _ _ _ _ _ _ the
      r _ _ _ _ _ _ of this letter.

   d I e _ _ _ _ _ _ a s _ _ _ a _ _ _ _ _ _ _ envelope.

   e I w _ _ _ _ very much a _ _ _ _ _ _ _ _ an early
      r _ _ _ _ _ _ _ to my letter.

   f I look f _ _ _ _ _ _ to h _ _ _ _ _ _ from you at
      your e _ _ _ _ _ _ _ c _ _ _ _ _ _ _ _ _ _.

3 Writing formal letters at CAE level often requires you to be firm while remaining tactful and diplomatic. Grade the sentences below in accordance with the key.

Key	
✗	likely to antagonise reader
✓	firm and tactful
?	might be OK but could be improved (if so, how?)

   a Your hotel did not live up to the claims made in the brochure.

   b Someone as stupid as you should never be allowed to run a hotel.

   c Your newspaper is usually full of rubbish but today it outdid itself.

   d Unfortunately, there were a number of errors in today's article on …

   e You must give me full compensation for all the inconvenience.

   f I feel that some compensation would be appropriate.

4   Look at tasks A and B and choose which one to respond to.

A You recently went on the holiday advertised below. However, many of the promises made in the advert did not match the reality of the holiday. There were a number of problems with the accommodation and some of the excursions offered were not available. Write a **letter** to the holiday company, putting your case for some kind of compensation.

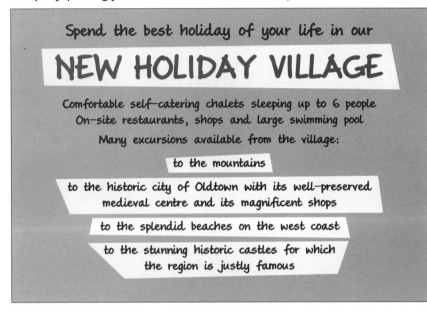

Spend the best holiday of your life in our

NEW HOLIDAY VILLAGE

Comfortable self-catering chalets sleeping up to 6 people
On-site restaurants, shops and large swimming pool
Many excursions available from the village:

to the mountains

to the historic city of Oldtown with its well-preserved medieval centre and its magnificent shops

to the splendid beaches on the west coast

to the stunning historic castles for which the region is justly famous

B This article recently appeared in a British newspaper about the town where you live. There are a number of things that you object to strongly in the article. Read the article, then plan a **letter** to be published in the newspaper so that readers are not left with a false impression of your town.

. . . is the town which I had the misfortune to visit last week. Although I had heard and read many good things about the beauties and facilities of this town, it was an extraordinary disappointment to me. There was nothing historic or architectural that seemed to me to be of any interest. The nightlife was poor and I certainly didn't find a restaurant that I could recommend. In short, if you have the chance to go there, don't bother!

5   Now write your letter which should be firm but tactful. Exchange your letter with a partner. If you were the person to whom the letter was addressed, would it have the desired effect on you? Tell your partner how you feel.

Genre	Describing objects
Topic	Inventions

Speaking 1

E xam spot

Inventions are sometimes the topic of a text in the CAE Reading or Listening tests (Papers 1 and 4) and you may also be asked to write or speak about them.

1 Look at the pictures. Then, with a partner, name each object, put the objects in the order in which they were invented and name the correct decade in which they were invented. There is one invention for each decade of the twentieth century.

Reading

1 Work with a partner. Which of these inventions do you think is the best and which is the worst? Give each invention a mark out of ten (10 = best, 0 = worst).

a **A glove** for courting couples who wish to maintain palm-to-palm contact while holding hands. It has a common palm section, but two separate sets of fingers.

b **A ladder** to enable spiders to climb out of the bath. It comprises a thin flexible latex rubber strip which follows the inner contours of the bath. A suction pad is attached to the top edge of the bath.

c **A horse-powered minibus**. The horse walks along an endless conveyor belt treadmill in the middle of the bus. This drives the wheels via a gearbox. A thermometer under the horse's collar is connected to the vehicle instrument panel. The driver can signal to the horse using a handle, which brings a mop into contact with the horse.

d **An umbrella** for wearing on the head. The support frame is designed so as not to mess up the wearer's hair.

e **A portable seat** which you wear on a waist-belt. The seat cushion is pivotable between a stowed position and a seating position in which it hangs down so that you can sit on it.

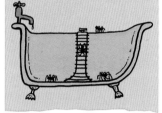

2 Why do you think the inventors thought these inventions might be successful?

3 Why do you think each invention failed to catch on? Can you suggest any ways in which each of these objects might be changed to make them more successful?

Vocabulary

1 Answer these questions about the vocabulary used in the texts.

a What do you think these words mean? In each case, the context should give you some clues.

courting	contours
suction pad	treadmill
mop	pivotable

b What is the significance of the prefix *mini-* in *minibus*? Give more examples of nouns using this prefix.

c What is the significance of the suffixes *-able* (in *pivotable*) and *-less* (in *endless*)? Give more examples of adjectives using these suffixes.

d Suggest opposites for these words as they are used in the text.

common	flexible
inner	drives
mess up	stowed

Vocabulary spot

Words can suggest whether the speaker or writer has positive or negative feelings about what is being described. If you called one of the inventions *brilliant*, it would be obvious that you admired it, whereas calling it *ill-conceived* would show that you thought it was inadequate in some way.

2 Put the adjectives below into the appropriate column.

absorbing	breathtaking	brilliant	delightful	enchanting
engrossing	grotesque	hackneyed	hideous	ill-conceived
impractical	ingenious	inspired	monstrous	pointless
ravishing	repulsive	ridiculous	stunning	trivial

Positive	Negative

Which of the words above could be used to describe any of the inventions in the reading texts?

3 Choose the best word to complete each sentence.

a The view from our hotel window was *inspired/engrossing/breathtaking*.

b I saw her grandmother in town wearing a *pointless/ridiculous/ill-conceived* hat.

c This is a very *enchanting/ingenious/ravishing* device for crushing garlic without having to peel it first.

d This kind of painting is very *hackneyed/grotesque/monstrous* – there's nothing original about it at all.

e Esther was wearing a(n) *absorbing/stunning/inspired* scarlet dress and jacket.

f I find films with gratuitous violence totally *trivial/impractical/repulsive*.

g Although the basic plot of the film is rather *ill-conceived/brilliant/hideous*, the locations are *delightful/trivial/engrossing* and the acting is first class.

Listening

1 🎧 You are going to listen to a radio programme in which people discuss things they could not live without. Which of the things in the pictures are mentioned by each speaker? Which other things are mentioned?

Speaker 1: ....
Speaker 2: ....
Speaker 3: ....
Speaker 4: ....

2 List the positive and negative adjectives used by the speakers.

Modals: *must, should, ought to, shall, will, would*

1 Underline the modal verbs in these sentences.

a Someone really ought to invent a machine to do the ironing for you.

b This key ring bleeps when you whistle – that should help you next time you lose your keys.

c You must get yourself a mobile phone – they're invaluable.

d My hair dryer's missing – my flatmate must have borrowed it again.

e You should have kept the instructions for the video recorder!

f He submitted his request for a patent ages ago – he must be going to hear from the department soon.

g You shouldn't have pressed that button before switching the power off.

h The design has been approved and we should be starting production next week.

i Even when he was still at school, he would spend hours in the shed designing weird and wonderful inventions.

j You will accept this design or else.

k We must light a fire somehow but no one's brought any matches – what shall we do?

2 What do the modals in these sentences convey? Choose from the possibilities in the box.

advice	deduction	obligation
offering	past habit	requesting

a You must help me.
b Will you help me?
c You ought to help him.
d She must be in her fifties.
e I think you should help him.
f Shall I answer the door?
g They must have left by now.
h He would walk down to the river every day.
i Would you close the window?
j You should consult him first.

3 Complete the sentences below using the modals in the box.

> must   mustn't   must have   ought to
> ~~shall~~   should   shouldn't have
> should have   will   would

EXAMPLE: ***Shall** I carry some of your heavy bags for you?*

a All pupils .... wear school uniform at all times in school and on their way to and from school.

b We're going to be doing a lot of hill-walking and so you .... bring strong outdoor shoes.

c I wonder where they can be. They .... been here by now. They .... missed their train.

d After school we used to go to the sweet shop on the corner where everyone .... buy a penny's worth of sweets or liquorice.

e You .... smoke in the garage forecourt.

f He's always late for work. He .... catch an earlier train.

g .... you take this man to be your lawful wedded husband?

h Jo looked very upset. You .... criticised her in public like that.

4 What kind of invention would you like an inventor to design for you? Write some instructions for the inventor, using modals.

EXAMPLE: *I'd like you to design a machine which will do the ironing for me. It must be able to recognise what type of material the clothes are made of and it should be able to adjust the temperature accordingly. It shouldn't cost more than £500 but it must be totally reliable …*

Ⓔxam spot

When someone is speaking to you, you need to show that you are listening and appreciating what is being said. In other words, you need to have a range of exclamations and fillers to use in different circumstances.

Speaking 2

1 Below is a list of common exclamations.

a Absolutely!
b Fantastic!
c How extraordinary!
d Oh dear!
e So do I!
f That's terrible!
g Brilliant!
h What a coincidence!
i Me too!
j Poor you!
k Surely not!
l What a surprise!
m What a shame!
n You must be joking!

Match the exclamations (a–n) with the appropriate language function from the box below.

> expressing agreement   expressing admiration
> expressing surprise or disbelief   expressing sympathy

2 Which of the exclamations do you think would be appropriate responses to the following?

a I've been offered a fantastic job in New York but if I take it, I have to start next week!

b I've failed my driving test. Again!

c Jackie and I turned up at the party wearing identical outfits!

d I'm going to have to have a small operation next week.

e Would you like these free tickets for tonight's concert?

f I'm sure the government will hold on to power at the next election.

g I love that amazing painting!

h I don't think we're going to be able to come to your party at the weekend.

Ⓔxam spot

Fillers such as *Yes*, *Right* and *Mm* are also useful to indicate that you are listening attentively as someone is telling you something. They can be said with different intonation in order to convey different reactions.

3 🎧 Listen to some snippets of speech on the tape. Respond in an appropriate way to each of them.

4 Can you think of any other useful fillers? Practise saying the fillers using different intonation to indicate enthusiasm, doubt and surprise.

5 Tell a partner about an interesting experience that you have recently had. Your partner should use some of the exclamations and fillers practised in this section while listening.

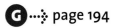 **Ⓖ ⋯⋗ page 194**

Exam folder 4

Paper 3 Part 4 Word formation

In Part 4 of the English in Use test (Paper 3), you have two short texts. Most of the lines in these texts contain one gap. At the end of the line is a word in capitals. You have to form a word from the same root as the word in capitals to fit the gap in that line.

EXAMPLE : *India gained its .... from Britain in 1947.* **DEPEND**
It should be clear from the context that the gap has to be filled by a noun, i.e. *dependant, dependence* or *independence.* In this case, the noun required is an abstract noun with a negative prefix. The answer is, therefore, *independence.*

1 Look at the gaps in the text. What part of speech is needed to fill each gap – a noun, a verb, an adjective or an adverb? When you have identified the parts of speech, can you suggest what the missing words might be?

THE school where pupils once fought and (**1**)...................... attacked a teacher during a visit by senior inspectors has been transformed and is now in the top 12 per cent for its teaching. Pupils were described as "polite, (**2**)................... and helpful" by the latest (**3**)................... of inspectors to visit The Ridings school in Halifax, West Yorkshire. Four years ago the Government (**4**)...................... an emergency inspection after a teachers' (**5**)................... voted to back members refusing to teach its (**6**)................... pupils. Union leaders described a school descending into chaos and said the situation could be (**7**)................... only by the permanent exclusion of around one in 10 of the 610 (**8**)................... .

2 Bear in mind that sometimes the words will need to have a prefix added to them. Add a negative prefix to the words below.

Verbs	Adjectives	Nouns
wrap	safe	appearance
ice	loyal	security
spell	sane	ease
tie	comfortable	comfort
entangle	European	mobility
understand	responsible	balance

3 List as many words as you can based on the words below.

a law ....
b hope ....
c act ....
d press ....
e centre...
f head ....
g office ....
h spoon ....
i place ....
j broad ....

4   Here is some more of the article from question 1. Fill each gap with a word related to the word in capitals at the end of the same line.

An **(1)** .... of the school carried out in 1996 was disrupted by	INSPECT
pupil **(2)** .... In their subsequent report the inspectors said	VIOLENT
poor teaching and weak **(3)** .... by the then head teacher had	LEAD
contributed to the poor behaviour. In 1997 "the **(4)** .... and	OUTRAGE
(5) .... behaviour of a few pupils" was said to create a hostile	CONTROL
atmosphere. A **(6)** .... report blamed the local authority for	LATE
failing to support its schools **(7)** .... and highlighted political	PROPER
interference by local **(8)** .... After that, the head of a	COUNCIL
(9) .... school in the same local authority was brought in to turn	SUCCESS
around the failing school. No **(10)** .... teaching was observed	SATISFY
by the most recent team of inspectors who were **(11)**	REMARK
impressed by the rapid turnaround the school has undergone.	

5   Here is different text for you to practise with. Again, fill each gap with a word related to the word in capitals at the end of the same line.

Nine years ago Philip Fletcher was a normal, **(1)**	HAPPY
married man with three children working as a highly **(2)**	SKILL
chemical worker. Then an accident changed his life beyond **(3)**	RECOGNISE
He was plunged into a surreal and **(4)** .... world as a head	FAMILIAR
(5) .... meant he could remember nothing of the previous	INJURE
15 years. In the accident a metal pole became **(6)** .... and	LODGE
fell on his head. He survived only thanks to his **(7)** .... helmet.	SAFE
He was **(8)** .... from hospital after only 4 hours. He seemed	CHARGE
normal at first but was soon having **(9)** .... He suffered	CONVULSE
for a number of years but his **(10)** .... breakthrough came	PSYCHOLOGY
when he learnt to accept his own **(11)** .... A few years ago he	LIMIT
and his wife accepted that their **(12)** .... could no longer continue	MARRY
but, **(13)** .... , they have both succeeded in building new lives.	FORTUNE

Genre	Academic texts
Topic	Further study

Speaking 1

1 With a partner, discuss the following questions.

a Have you ever used English to study another subject? If you have, how easy did you find it?

b Some people say that one of the best ways of learning English is to study another subject through English. Do you agree with this? Why?/Why not?

c How likely do you think you are to use English for studying other subjects in the future?

Reading

1 The extracts opposite come from textbooks about economics, history, law, sociolinguistics and psychology.

a Match the extract with the subject.

b Match each extract with one of the pictures.

c Suggest a heading summarising each text.

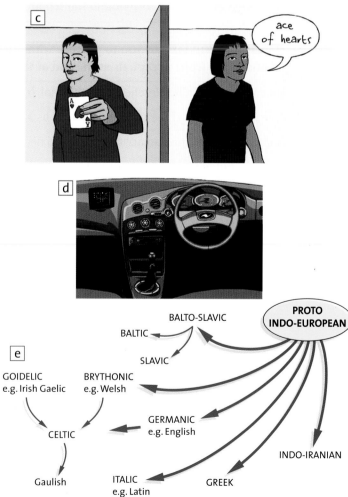

ace of hearts

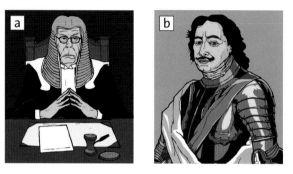

1

Recent work in sociolinguistics has raised once again a long-standing question: can linguistic change be observed while it is actually occurring? In modern linguistics, the answer to that question has usually been a resounding negative. Following the example of two of the founders of the modern discipline, de Saussure (1959) and Bloomfield (1933), most linguists have maintained that change itself cannot be observed; all that you can possibly hope to observe are the consequences of change.

2

As a further symbol of his determination to haul Muscovy kicking and screaming into the eighteenth century, the Tsar refused to let his boyars kow-tow to him in traditional oriental style, and took scissors, cutting off their beards and snipping the capacious sleeves of their traditional robes as a prelude to making shaven chins and European dress obligatory for all Russian gentry and officials. Along with robes and beards, the ancient title of boyar was soon to disappear as well. Peter also greeted the eighteenth century by adopting the Julian Calendar, an important symbolic change since Muscovy had hitherto reckoned time from the notional beginning of the world. For so backward a state to have been, as it were, 6,508 years ahead of western Europe was absurd, and the Julian Calendar put it, more appropriately, eleven days in arrears.

3

The immediate crisis of 1968 soon passed and the marketing experts dismissed it as a spasm, an intellectuals' fantasy. Students went back to business schools, consumers went on consuming and the car – with the help of gadgetry, computers and improved engineering – soon became once again an object of glamour, status and sexiness. East Asians did their bit to promote Western spending by producing gadgetry, music-machines and glamorous electronics which could be replaced by still more novelties every year; while their own spending power created new opportunities at home. 'I don't think saturation will ever happen,' Akio Morita of Sony told me, 'because our technology can create new products which give new joy to the public.'

4

English law now fixes the age of majority at eighteen, all persons below that age being minors. A minor attains his majority on the day of his birthday – not, as formerly, on the beginning of the day before his birthday. A minor is incapable of holding office as a Member of Parliament or a Local Authority. He cannot be a priest or deacon, or a barrister or solicitor. Minority is no defence in an action in tort – that is for a wrong done independently of contract. Where an undergraduate, who was a minor, had hired a horse for riding, on the express condition that it was not to be used for jumping, but took it out with a friend to whom he lent the horse, and allowed it to be used for jumping various fences and ditches with the result that the horse staked itself on a fence and was fatally injured, he was held to have committed an 'independent tort' for which he was liable to the owner apart from any question of contract, just as if he had ridden the horse without hiring or the leave of the owner.

5

Experiments on both these lines have shown that both clairvoyance and telepathy must be presumed to exist. It has also been found that, while many people who possess the one type of ability tend to possess the other, this is by no means necessary and in certain cases individuals may obtain high scores by telepathy but not by clairvoyance and vice versa. The great majority of experiments, however, do not attempt to differentiate between these two abilities and must simply be taken as evidence of some all-round parapsychological or extra-sensory perception capacity on the part of individuals.

2 Academic language often uses rather unfamiliar vocabulary. Match the words and phrases (a–l) from the texts with their meanings in the box.

a a resounding negative (text 1)
b as a prelude to (text 2)
c hitherto (text 2)
d in arrears (text 2)
e spending power (text 3)
f saturation (text 3)
g attains (text 4)
h formerly (text 4)
i leave (text 4)
j obtain (text 5)
k vice versa (text 5)
l differentiate (text 5)

before   behind   a firm no
get   make a difference between
permission   previously (×2)
reaches   spare money
stage where nothing more is needed
the other way round

3 Choose one of the words or phrases from the list in Reading 2 to fill the gaps in the following sentences.

a It is estimated that the demand for mobile phones will soon reach .... point in this country.
b People who are colour blind cannot always .... between shades of red and green.
c Student A should look at Student B's composition and ....
d You cannot go out of the school during the day without getting .... from the head.
e I am afraid you are .... with your mortgage payments.
f These nineteenth century stamps are almost impossible to ....
g Mr Peter Tomlins, ... Sales Manager at XYZ Ltd., joins us on April 1st.
h Teenagers these days tend to have much greater .... than used to be the case.

Vocabulary

1 Many words used in academic texts are of Latin or Greek origin. They are often part of a set of words formed from the same root. Complete the following table based on words used in the reading texts.

Verb	Noun	Adjective
occur		
	founder	
✗	consequence	
		obligatory
disappear		
	glamour	
	authority	
		various
presume		
	perception	

2 Rewrite the sentences using the word in brackets.

a All pupils must wear school uniform. (obligatory)
b There are a great many different animals which are indigenous to Australia. (variety)
c Burglaries happen every day in this part of town. (occurrence)
d Most people think that the mountaineer must have died in the blizzard. (presumed)
e Giving up work to bring up a child and the loss of income which happens as a result is difficult for many women. (consequent)
f What is the opinion of people in your country on the role of the United Nations? (perceive)
g Cambridge University Press has been in existence since 1534. (founded)
h Modern films tend to make violence seem more glamorous than it really is. (glamorise)

Participle clauses

Participle clauses are clauses beginning with either a present or past participle. Look at these examples from the texts.

Following the example of two of the founders of the modern discipline, de Saussure (1959) and Bloomfield (1933), most linguists have maintained that change itself cannot be observed …

the Tsar … took scissors, cutting off their beards and snipping the capacious sleeves of their traditional robes …

Participle clauses can be expanded to make full clauses. This may be done by expanding the phrases into clauses beginning with conjunctions like *when, if, because* or *and* or into relative clauses beginning with *who, which* or *that*.

1 Expand the phrases in italics in the extracts above.

2 Here are some more examples of participle phrases. How can each of these sentences be expanded?

a Hoping to gain a speedy victory, the army invaded.
b They killed many people living in the border areas.
c It being a Sunday, most of the shops were shut.
d Generally considered a weak king, Charles I was eventually beheaded.
e Having previously learnt their language, Picton was able to communicate with the tribe.
f Having measured the wood carefully, cut as indicated.

3 Rewrite these sentences using a clause beginning with a present or past participle.

a While I was walking round the exhibition, I caught sight of an old school friend at the far end of the gallery.
b Because Marti had made so many mistakes in her homework, she had to do it all over again.
c As she is only a child, she can't fully understand what is happening.
d As Jack didn't know anyone in the town to spend the evening with, he decided to have an early night.
e When all the inequalities of life before the revolution are considered, it is surprising that a revolution did not happen sooner.
f When you have climbed to the top of the church tower, be sure to walk right round and admire the view from each of the four sides. (Use two participles here.)
g We set off at midnight and hoped to avoid the rest of the holiday traffic which would be heading for the coast. (Use two participles here.)
h When he saw me, he stood up and knocked his glass to the floor. (Use two participles here.)

It will create a good impression in your answers in the CAE Writing test (Paper 2) if you occasionally make use of appropriate participle clauses.

4 Work with a partner and complete the sentences below. Compare your sentences with those written by other students.

a Having been a major news item last week, …
b Having become successful at quite a young age, …
c Being one of the largest cities in our country, …
d Not daring to interrupt him, …
e Starting this CAE course, …
f Having worked hard all his life, …

G ⋯⋮ page 194

Speaking 2

Exam spot

In the CAE Speaking test (Paper 5), you may have to contrast pictures. Using the stress patterns practised here can help you to do this.

1 Read the dialogues and underline the words which Speaker B would be most likely to stress.

1 A Did you go to the cinema last night?
  B No, but I went to the theatre.
2 A Did you go by bike to the theatre last night?
  B No, Marco was using my bike last night.
3 A Did you go to the theatre by bus last night?
  B No, I went to the theatre by taxi last night.
4 A Did you go home by taxi last night?
  B No, I went home by taxi two nights ago.
5 A Anne's wearing a lovely green dress.
  B It's a green blouse and skirt, actually.
6 A Did you have a good time at the party last night?
  B Yes, we had a brilliant time.
7 A Are you hungry yet?
  B I'm not hungry, I'm starving.
8 A Are you hungry yet?
  B I'm not hungry but Tina is.
9 A Are you tired?
  B Yes, I'm exhausted!
10 A Are you feeling a bit cold?
  B Yes, I'm freezing!

2 🎧 Now listen to the tape and check whether your predictions were correct.

3 Practise reading the dialogues with a partner.

4 Write three more two-line dialogues like those in exercise 1.

5 Look at the pictures below and notice the differences between them. Work with a partner taking turns to suggest sentences about them. Make sure that you use contrastive stress in the appropriate way.

EXAMPLE: *There's a **red** fountain pen in picture **a** and there's a **blue** fountain pen in picture **b**.*

Writing folder 4

Reports and proposals

1 With a partner, discuss these questions.

   a Name five possible kinds of reports or proposals, e.g. *A scientific report of an experiment.*
   b Have you had any experience of writing reports or proposals?
   c What do you think is going to be characteristic of the format and language of a report or proposal?
   d How is an article about some interesting scientific research likely to differ from a report of the same research?

Reports and proposals are similar in many ways. They both aim to set out information in a formal and clear way, often so that someone else can take a decision based on the information provided.

The differences between a report and a proposal are largely:
- a report looks backwards while a proposal looks forward
- a proposal always presents the writer's viewpoint whereas a report focuses more on facts; although a report may have a persuasive element to it, this is not always the case.

2 **Work with a partner and choose one of these pairs of tasks that interests you.**

   A Write a **report** for your teacher on the work experience and aspirations of other students in the class.

   Write a **proposal** for your college principal in which you ask for money to travel to an English-speaking country to gain some work experience there. Explain what you would like from the college and why it would be of benefit to you.

   B Write a **report** for your teacher on the most popular Internet sites among the class. Describe what they are, why they are popular and comment on any trends that you observe.

   Write a **proposal** to your college principal suggesting that your college set up its own website. Explain why it would be a good idea and what it should contain.

   C Write a **report** for your teacher on the physical fitness activities done by the students in your class. Describe what people do and how much time they spend on it and comment on any interesting tendencies that you observe.

   Write a **proposal** for your college principal about improvements to your college's sports provisions. Describe what you would like and give reasons why it would be of benefit to the college.

3   With a partner, discuss the questions below.

   a What information do you think it would be useful to include in the **report** you have chosen?

   b What questions will you ask the other students in the class in order to get the information you need?

   c What trends do you think you might observe from the information you collect?

   d Why do you think your requests in the **proposal** would be a good idea?

   e Remember that the college principal is likely to be more concerned than you are about costs, potential organisational problems and college prestige. How will you address these issues in your **proposal**?

4   Collect the information you need for your **report**.

   a Ask the other students in your class the questions you prepared in 3b.

   b Discuss the information you collected with a partner. Did you observe the trends you predicted in 3c? Did any other particularly interesting points emerge from your questions?

   c What headings would it be appropriate to use for your report?

5   Discuss the presentation of your **proposal**.

   a It is important to open with a clear statement of what the proposal contains. How will you do this in your proposal?

   b It is also important to close effectively. How will you do this in your proposal?

   c What headings are appropriate to use for your proposal?

6   In pairs, decide which of you should write the **report** and which the **proposal**.

   a Write the report or the proposal.

   b Give your work to your partner for comments and suggestions.

   c Make any improvements suggested by your partner.

UNIT 10 I have a dream

Genre	Speeches
Topic	Social change

Speaking 1

1 Who makes speeches? On what occasions? Have you ever had to make a speech? If so, why, and how well did the speech go?

Exam spot

You are not asked to write or to make a speech in the CAE exam. However, you might hear an extract from a speech in the CAE Listening test (Paper 4). You can learn from studying famous speeches, as they use language in a clever and powerful way. This can help you to write more effectively yourself.

2 Who is the man in this photo? What do you know about him? How do you think the other people in the picture are feeling?

3 Have you heard of a famous speech which is often referred to as *I have a dream*? If so, what do you know about it? Who made it, when and why?

Five score years ago, a great American, in whose symbolic shadow we stand today, signed the Emancipation Proclamation. This momentous decree came as a great beacon light of hope to millions of Negro slaves who had been seared in the flames of withering injustice. It came as a joyous daybreak to end the long night of their captivity.

But one hundred years later, the Negro still is not free. One hundred years later, the life of the Negro is still sadly crippled by the manacles of segregation and the chains of discrimination. One hundred years later, the Negro lives on a lonely island of poverty in the midst of a vast ocean of material prosperity. One hundred years later, the Negro is still languished in the corners of American society and finds himself an exile in his own land. So we have come here today to dramatize a shameful condition.

In a sense we have come to our nation's capital to cash a check. When the architects of our republic wrote the magnificent words of the Constitution and the Declaration of Independence, they were signing a promissory note to which every American was to fall heir. This note was a promise that all men, yes, black men as well as white men, would be guaranteed the unalienable rights of life, liberty, and the pursuit of happiness.

It is obvious today that America has defaulted on this promissory note insofar as her citizens of color are concerned. Instead of honoring this sacred obligation, America has given the Negro people a bad check, a check which has come back marked "insufficient funds". But we refuse to believe that the bank of justice is bankrupt. We refuse to believe that there are insufficient funds in the great vaults of opportunity of this nation. So we have come to cash this check – a check that will give us upon demand the riches of freedom and the security of justice. We have also come to this hallowed spot to remind America of the fierce urgency of now. This is no time to engage in the luxury of cooling off or to take the tranquilizing drug of gradualism. Now is the time to make real the promises of democracy. Now is the time to rise from the dark and desolate valley of segregation to the sunlit path of racial justice. Now is the time to lift our nation from the quicksands of racial injustice to the solid rock of brotherhood.

Reading

1 Read the first part of the speech. Which of the sentences (a–e) sums up each paragraph? There is one extra sentence that you do not need to use.

   a A century after their emancipation, black Americans are still not truly free.

   b America has behaved unjustly to its black people.

   c Black people must fight to be treated equally.

   d Lincoln brought hope to Negro slaves with his proclamation of emancipation in 1863.

   e The march has come to Washington to claim the rights that all were promised.

2 How do you think people felt when they were listening to this speech?

Listening

1 🎧 Now listen to the rest of the speech. Which of the techniques below does Martin Luther King use to help to create a powerful effect on the audience? Tick all the appropriate techniques.

- repetition
- mixing short and long sentences
- shouting
- addressing the audience directly
- humour
- making use of metaphor
- drawing attention to the location where the speech is taking place
- exaggeration
- quoting famous lines
- alliteration
- making analogies or comparisons
- asking rhetorical questions
- making dramatic pauses
- appealing to the audience's emotions
- appealing to the audience's senses
- using gestures or visual aids
- presenting interesting or surprising facts

2 🎧 Listen to some more extracts from speeches. What do you think the occasion was in each case? Match the speakers (1–5) with the pictures (a–e).

3 🎧 Now listen again and note down any examples of the techniques referred to in Listening 1.

Vocabulary

Martin Luther King makes powerful use of metaphor in his speech. The metaphors are often based around the themes of light, heat, punishment, economics and the natural environment.

1 Here are some examples of metaphors he uses. Match each one to the appropriate theme.

a The life of the Negro is still sadly crippled by the manacles of segregation and the chains of discrimination.

b It came as a joyous daybreak to end the long night of their captivity.

c This momentous decree came as a great beacon light of hope to millions of Negro slaves …

d We have come to our nation's capital to cash a check.

e … who had been seared in the flames of withering injustice.

f We refuse to believe that the bank of justice is bankrupt.

g Now is the time to rise from the dark and desolate valley of segregation to the sunlit path of racial justice.

h Even the state of Mississippi, a state sweltering with the heat of injustice, sweltering with the heat of oppression, …

i … will be transformed into an oasis of freedom and justice.

> **V ocabulary spot**
>
> Sometimes metaphors are so commonly used that they become fixed as idioms. People no longer notice the metaphorical associations of the expression and think of the idiom simply as a fixed expression in its own right.

2 Here are some idioms based on the five metaphorical themes listed in Vocabulary 1.

- light: *shed light on; light dawns*
- heat: *go up in smoke; get your fingers burned*
- punishment: *be tied up; be pilloried*
- economics: *foot the bill; put your money where your mouth is; in debt*
- the natural environment: *feel (all) at sea; common ground*

Choose one of the idioms above and use it to complete the sentences (a–k) below. Make any necessary changes, such as putting the verb into the correct form.

a The washing machine is broken but we're hoping our landlord .... for a new one.

b Hopes of union and management reaching agreement finally .... yesterday.

c I .... all day but could meet you in the evening, if you like.

d I hate the first day in a new job, ...

e Thank you for .... this very complex issue for us.

f Jack was teasing her but it was ages before .... !

g We found some unexpected .... at the meeting with the opposition.

h The MP .... by the press for the foolish remarks he made in his speech.

i I am .... to my first schoolteacher for the invaluable advice she gave me.

j If the government is interested in improving the health service, it should ....

k You .... if you go on trying to interfere in their private lives.

Future forms

Look at this sentence from Martin Luther King's speech.

One day even the state of Mississippi, a state sweltering with the heat of injustice, sweltering with the heat of oppression, will be transformed into an oasis of freedom and justice.

In this sentence the future is conveyed by the word *will* and the sense is of a confident prediction.

1 Identify the words used to express the future in the sentences (a–j) and match them to the uses (1–10) below.

a What are you doing this evening?
b What will you be doing this time tomorrow?
c What are you going to do for your next holiday?
d What are you going to do when this course finishes? (two uses)
e What will you do if you pass the CAE exam?
f What would you do if you passed the CAE exam?
g What time does this English lesson finish?
h Which student in the class do you think is most likely to be very successful in business?
i Is there anyone in the class who might eventually become internationally famous, in your opinion?
j What do you hope you will have achieved by the time you are 60?

1 focus on one moment in future time
2 focus on looking forward to the future in order to then look back
3 future probability
4 future after time conjunction
5 intention
6 plan (with stated time)
7 something fixed by a timetable
8 talking about the future using the first conditional
9 talking about the future using a less confident, more hypothetical conditional
10 tentative prediction

2 Choose the best form for each of these sentences.

a *I go/I'm going/I'll go* to the cinema on Saturday to see that new Brad Pitt film.

b I'll call you as soon as I *get/will get/will have got* home.

c This time next week *we're going to lie/we'll lie/we'll be lying* on a tropical beach.

d If he got the job, *he'll leave/he'd leave/he'll have left* for Paris next month.

e Melissa is very likely *getting/to getting/to get* a good job as she is fluent in three languages.

f My flight *is going to leave/leaves/is leaving* at 10.20 tomorrow morning.

g When we *will be/are going to be/are* in London, *we are spending/we spend/we are going to spend* the first day doing a sightseeing tour.

h If Penny *gets/will get/is getting* a place at Oxford University, *she's studying/she's going to study/she studies* philosophy and politics.

i In ten years' time perhaps people *set foot/are going to set foot/will have set foot* on Mars.

3 Work with a partner asking and answering the questions in Future forms 1. Make sure you answer using the correct verb forms.

4 Think back to the speeches in Listening 2. Work with a partner and write about what the future holds for Johnny and Megan, baby Maria and Fiona.

What do you think will happen to them in the short term and the long term?

EXAMPLE: *This morning Johnny and Megan got married. In a few moments, everyone is going to drink a toast to them. Then first thing tomorrow they fly off for their honeymoon in Greece. So this time tomorrow they'll be swimming in the Aegean. Let's hope that by the time they get back they'll have got over the stress of planning the wedding.*

Compare your ideas with those of other students.

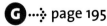 ⋯⋮ page 195

Speaking 2

1 Work with two or three students. Choose an issue that you all feel strongly about. Use the words below to help you.

canteen food

homework   local transport

the environment   taxes

leisure facilities

2 Now discuss the following questions.

a Why do you feel strongly about it? List as many points as you can think of.

b What would you like to be changed? Be as precise as you can.

c Who would you need to persuade for changes to be made?

d How would you try to persuade them to make the changes? What action could you take and what arguments could you use?

3 You are going to report your discussion back to the rest of the class. How could you do this? Decide what to say and who should say it.

4 Listen to each group's reports of their discussions in turn. Write down how many changes each group proposed and briefly note what each of these changes were.

5 After listening to each speech, discuss with a partner which of the changes would be for the better and which for the worse.

Topic review

a Which telephone services do you use most?

b How do you feel when someone hangs up on you?

c What factors can give rise to an increase in unemployment?

d What are possible grounds for sacking an employee?

e Which modern invention could you not live without?

f Do you think wearing cycling helmets ought to be compulsory?

g What are some of the rewards and challenges of studying abroad?

h What subject have you always wanted to study?

i What do you hope you will have achieved by the year 2020?

j How do you feel about public speaking?

Grammar

1 Think about last year and next year and answer the questions below. Write at least one full sentence in answer to each of the questions.

a What changes are going to take place in your life next year?

b What must you try to do next year?

c What special things did you have to do last year?

d What should you do next year if you possibly can?

e What should you have done last year but were unfortunately unable to?

f What do you think will have happened by the end of next year?

g Think about something that happened last year and the effects it has had or is likely to have. Write a sentence to link what happened with its effects or likely effects.

EXAMPLE: *Last year there was an election and this has resulted in more money being spent on the health service this year.*

h Now write a sentence using a participle clause about the events from last year that you thought about above.

EXAMPLE: *Having won last year's election, the Labour Party now has to try to implement its pre-election promises.*

Reading

1 What is teleworking? With a partner, discuss what you think would be its advantages and disadvantages.

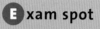 **xam spot**

Both the CAE Reading test (Paper 1) and the English in Use test (Paper 3) have questions which test your ability to see how paragraphs hang together in a text. The following exercise helps you to see what kinds of links there often are between paragraphs.

2 The article below about teleworking has the paragraphs (A–G) in the wrong order. With a partner, put them in the right order and discuss what clues there are in the text to help you do this.

WHEN THE OFFICE IS YOUR BEST BET

A He likes to tell the story of the painter Magritte, whose studio was at home. Each morning Magritte would rise and put on his suit. He would then go out through the front door of his house, walk once around the block, re-enter the house and enter his studio, where he would change into his artist's smock and spend the day painting. At the end of the day he would change back into his suit, leave the house again and go once round the block in the opposite direction, and return home for the evening.

B My score: zero out of three. Dedicating a room to work is not feasible in a small flat, and has all sorts of complicated tax implications anyhow. I didn't have a separate business line. And although I had a separate fax line, my fax machine, like my computer, was squeezed into a corner of the living room, which made drawing a line between home and work even harder: even when I was relaxing, all that equipment would be glowering at me from across the room. I'd pick up my e-mail in the evening, and half of it would be work-related.

C Technology makes it easier than ever to work from home, but unless you know what you're doing, it's still a terrible idea. Like Superman and kryptonite, home and work are meant to be kept apart.

D John, a friend who used to work from home, had a separate phone line, but he didn't have a separate room, so he couldn't get away from his work either. "At one stage," he says, "I had to go through my 'office' to get to the loo."

E I look back on my days spent working at home with mixed feelings. Sure, it was great not to have to fight through the rush-hour throng to get to my desk. The trouble was, once I'd started working, I couldn't stop. When there was more work to do, I just kept doing it. Then I spoke to Alan Denbigh of the British Telecottage Association, who explained the three laws of teleworking.

F "First of all, you should ensure that you have a self-contained office," he said. "Next, you should have a separate phone line, both from a business point of view and also from a psychological point of view. And you need to have a rule for the family."

G Magritte probably didn't have a separate phone line. But it seems he had the right ideas about working from home successfully. Unless you can stick to the three laws, stick to the office.

3 In most of the lines of the following text there is one unnecessary word. It is either grammatically incorrect or does not fit in with the sense of the text. Read the text and put a line through the unnecessary word. Then write the word in the space provided at the end of the line. Some lines are correct. Indicate these lines with a tick in the space. The first two lines have been done as examples.

GADGETS: ANYWHERE HE GOES, THE GIZMO GOES TOO

0	FRED Finn's electronic organiser has been just about ~~in~~	....*in*....
00	everywhere. Mr Finn is listed in the *Guinness Book of Records* as	....✓....
1	the world's most travelled man, and that where he goes, his	....
2	organiser goes too. "The forthcoming *Guinness Book of Records*	....
3	gives up my total distance travelled as eleven million miles," Mr Finn	....
4	says. "I have made over seven hundred of flights on Concorde."	....
5	His career racing around the globe began it when he was setting up	....
6	factories in the Third World, when his working day week regularly	....
7	involved flying right round the world, taking in South America, Africa	....
8	and the Middle East. Now he works mainly as if a travel consultant,	....
9	and has written a book which called *Don't fly … until you have read*	....
10	*Fred Finn's Guide to Air Travel*. Before he leaves from home, Mr Finn	....
11	loads his itinerary from his desktop computer to his electronic	....
12	organiser, so he has in his pocket an appointments for diary, his list	....
13	of business phone contacts, a world map and list of dialling codes	....
14	for phoning every country. Recently, however, he added so an	....
15	impressive new capability to his organiser – a program that tells	....
16	about him how to get anywhere in the world, on whatever airline. "It	....
17	has one or two gaps in places like the Albania, but for the average	....
18	traveller it is a very good idea, and I use the program by myself," he	....
19	says. It has an additional boon: because of his fame as an air	....
20	traveller, smart alecs often have try to catch him out by asking him	....
21	such questions as how often to get to Ulan Bator via Alaska. "They	....
22	expect me to know whole the world's airline timetables off the top of	....
23	my head," he says. "With this, I can give to them an answer."	....

ⓔxam spot

In the word formation exercise in the CAE English in Use test (Paper 3), it is important to understand what the missing word is likely to mean as this will help you to put the word in the right form.

---

4 Make a word from one of the words in the box below in order to fill the gaps (1–10). The first one has been done for you as an example.

late	extend	cover
obsess	proud	expense
survive	edit	~~happy~~
addict	alphabet	

Objects of desire
A BOY THING

WHAT is it about boys and toys? Men will spend hundreds of pounds and waste hours fiddling so that they can, say, dictate letters to their PCs, or they will
(0) ......*happily*........ spend a whole weekend putting their CDs in
(1) .... order – or, worse, typing their titles into a database. This
(2) .... behaviour is reflected in an ever-increasing number of men's magazines that combine buying advice with techno-fetishism and a dash of new laddism. More and more
(3) .... is being given to gadgets in an attempt to satisfy men's
(4) .... to gizmos. "Men love gadgets – it is an (5) .... of their manliness," says Adam Porter, Net
(6) .... of the lads' magazine *Loaded*. "Gadgets are toys – men can't buy Action Men when they are 30, so they go and buy something electronic and a lot more (7) ...." James Lawrence, editor of *FHM* magazine's hardware section, agrees: "There is a macho male (8) .... in gadgets – it's like it's my toy, and I know how to use it, and if you ask me nicely then I just might show you how to use it. Women don't seem to need that kind of one-upmanship." Andy Clarke, editor of *Stuff*, the
(9) .... men's glossy to hit the shelves, thinks it has something to do with the much-hyped male (10) .... instinct. "Men feel like Indiana Jones, like they are out there in the wilds if they've got a gadget in their pocket," he says.

Genre	Magazine and newspaper articles
Topic	Fashion

Speaking 1

1 Discuss these questions with a partner.

  a How often do you read a newspaper? When do you read it? Which parts do you read first?

  b Do you think people read newspapers more or less often than before?

  c Do you ever read newspapers or magazines on the Internet? Which do you think is better, reading 'real' newspapers or newspapers on the Internet? Why?

  d Look at these front-page headlines and decide what sort of newspaper you think each one is.

BOOST YOUR METABOLISM FOR LIFE!

HUMAN CLONING IS CLOSER THAN YOU THINK

First pupils sent home for lack of teachers

EXCLUSIVE: What the public really thinks of the Royal Family

Beckham recaptures form at right moment

2 What sorts of articles do you enjoy reading and which articles do you avoid reading?

Reading

1 Work with a partner. Discuss what you like and dislike about shopping for clothes.

2 Read the newspaper article below and choose which of the paragraphs opposite (A–G) fit into the gaps (1–6). There is one extra paragraph which does not fit in any of the gaps.

Talking clothes get our measure

They could be the trousers that will not belt up. Customers in some of Britain's top clothing stores may soon find their prospective purchases telling them whether they would be a good fit.

The system, which can also be applied to jackets, skirts and almost any other garment, is heralded as the most exciting innovation in retailing in years. It could cut the hours spent trying on clothes that will never fit and, once perfected, could mean the end of the changing room.

[1]

A version of the technology is already being worked on by Marks and Spencer, whose next big sizing survey, the first in more than 10 years, will make use of the latest three-dimensional scanning technology. M&S will use the information to determine the shapes of its future clothing and to run a trial in which selected customers can use the cards to order bespoke suits and other clothes.

[2]

The technology has already been taken further in the United States, with smart cards holding an individual's scan details being designed to plug into a portable device that shoppers carry round the store with them.

[3]

The beauty of scanning systems, as opposed to conventional tape measures, is that they detail an individual's shape as well as their size. "A tape measure may tell you that a lady's hips are 36 inches, but it tells you nothing about where on her hips the bulk of those inches lies," said Jerry Dunleavy, specialist clothing manager at M&S. "With a scanner you can see exactly."

[4]

"The most likely scenario, and one which is already possible, is that the shopper, once scanned, would be given a smart card holding all the information about their body type," said Stephen Gray, head of the computer clothing research centre at Nottingham Trent University.

[5]

According to Gray, it will be possible for shops to go a step further and allow customers to use their smart cards to order made-to-measure clothing. "Translating three-dimensional images into two-dimensional clothing patterns is a skill we have lost as traditional tailoring has disappeared," said Gray. "However, it is something clothing manufacturers are going to have to relearn and then automate."

[6]

Instead of loudspeakers, customers can opt for a small ear-piece, so that their potential trousers, suit or even underwear would not need to talk. They could just whisper softly in the ear.

3 How did you select the missing paragraphs?

Vocabulary

1 Use the words in the box to complete the text below.

aubergine	browsing	fake	wear	look
pencil	sleeveless	slim	suede	tailored

What's in store?

Wool, fur and tweed, new lengths and simple shapes were all over the international catwalks but have they found their way to a shop near you? Sarah McDonell previews the season's shopping.

Phew! After months of waiting, the fashion faithful here welcome the Spanish label *Mango* and rejoice in the great good fun to be had in an afternoon (1) .... through rails of clothes that combine edginess and classic, continental looks. Sharp, (2) .... trouser suits; tunics; (3) .... tops; straight (4) .... skirts in plum and (5) .... and grey. For weekend (6) ...., twinsets and T-shirts; (7) .... leg trousers; (8) .... and leather, shoes and bags. Even evening wear with (9) .... fur and lace finish, all brilliantly priced so a total (10) .... is easy to achieve.

A
As they pass racks of clothing, tags programmed with a selection of pre-recorded responses interact with the device and talk to the customer, advising on the garment's likely fit.

By doing so, the device will also enable customers to shop by mail order more satisfactorily. This is something which customer groups have been pressing for.

C
Any garment, from a top-of-the-range suit to underwear, could be programmed to chat to its buyer, with warnings such as "This is nice but not quite right for you" or encouragements along the lines of "I'm a perfect fit" or "Suits you, Sir".

"That card could then be used to guide the customer automatically to the clothes which fitted them best."

For some customers the prospect of successive pairs of trousers – in sizes that once might have fitted – loudly announcing that they are far too small could turn shopping into a humiliation – but the system is likely to be designed with them in mind.

Customers who agree to take part will be led to a scanning booth by M&S staff, who will ask them to strip off and stand still while intense beams of white light are played over their bodies. A computerised scanner will turn the results into a "virtual reflection" – an electronic recording of their exact shape.

G
He expects scanning booths about the size of a normal changing room to become available to all his customers in the next five years.

Listening

Exam spot

In the CAE Listening test (Paper 4), you will hear a monologue. You must complete the sentences. Make sure that the completed sentences are grammatically correct and spelled correctly.

1 Do you have a dress code where you work or study? If you do, are you happy with it? If you do not have a dress code, would you like one?

2 You are going to hear the manager of a company. She is not at all happy with the way some employees dress. What do you think she is going to mention?

3 ∩ Listen to the recording. Complete the sentences (a–i) with the missing information.

a The manager first singles out those who work in .... for criticism.

b Men in this department have to wear ....

c Clients may come in to see .... at any time so dress is especially important for them.

d The dress code is relaxed on what is called ....

e When the dress code is relaxed, the style of clothing accepted is referred to as ....

f The manager is particularly unhappy about the way employees dress when they are on ....

g The manager was appalled to hear that a man had worn .... when he went to a management college.

h The manager recognises that some employees may complain on the grounds that this is a .... issue.

i She suggests employees take further complaints to the .... department.

4 What do you think of the company's dress code and the way the manager addresses the staff?

Direct and reported speech

1 Change these sentences from Listening 3 into reported speech. Start each sentence with the words given.

EXAMPLE: Now, it's been brought to my attention that certain members of staff have been flouting the dress code. She said that *it had been brought to her attention that certain members of staff had been flouting the dress code.*

a I want to make it crystal clear to everyone just exactly what's expected in terms of attire.
She clarified ....

b Those of you who work in reception must be businesslike, at all times.
She insisted that ....

c Don't forget in many people's eyes sloppy clothes means sloppy work.
She reminded ....

d I'm not at all happy about the way some people dress for training days.
She pointed out that ....

e It seems as though some of you have got the idea into your head that when you're on a training day you can dress like a student.
She said that ....

f I've even heard remarks about a certain man who turned up to a management college wearing a nose ring.
She criticised someone ....

g What I want to emphasise is that it's a matter of professional pride, the way you dress.
She stressed that ....

h You have to toe the line.
She said ....

i If anyone feels particularly aggrieved by any of this, all I can suggest is that you take it up with the Human Resources department.
She said ....

j I hope I won't have to refer to this again.
She hoped ....

2 You are going to interview your partner about fashion. Here are some questions to ask. Add another two questions of your own.

a Where do you buy most of your clothes?
b Do you prefer dark or light colours?
c Have you ever bought something quite expensive which you later regretted buying?
d Do you prefer going shopping for clothes alone or with a friend?
e Have you got any brothers or sisters? Do you borrow each other's clothes?

Now interview your partner and make notes of the answers.
Write a summary of what your partner said using reported speech.

3 Match the verbs (a–n) with the appropriate structure (1–4). More than one structure may be possible.

a He promised
b She suggested
c We agreed
d They told
e She asked
f He offered
g She advised
h He recommended
i He denied
j She invited
k They warned
l I insisted
m He threatened
n I regretted

1 doing it
2 to do it
3 me (not) to do it
4 that I (should) do it

4 Choose the correct alternative to complete these sentences.

a She suggested *to buy/buying* the black jeans.
b He suggested *us another style/ another style to us.*
c *I promised myself / I promised to myself* that I would save more money.
d Your assistant promised *us to refund/ that she would refund* the money.
e He agreed *on being/to be* the one to make the speech.
f I asked her what *was her name/her name was.*
g You asked if *I was/was I* the owner of the red car.
h It is *recommended/recommend* to book well in advance.
i I recommend *you to pay/you pay* by credit card.
j He offered *to help me/to me to help.*
k I can recommend *to you the Isa Hotel/the Isa hotel to you.*

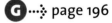 page 196

Speaking 2

E xam spot

In the CAE Speaking test (Paper 5), you will be given the opportunity to speak for about one minute without interruption. You are usually asked to comment on or react to a set of photographs or pictures. After you have finished speaking, your partner will be asked to comment briefly.

1 In order to compare (find similarities) and contrast (find differences), you will need to use appropriate linking devices. Add as many words or expressions as you can to these lists.

Comparing	Contrasting
similarly	whereas
both pictures show	but

2 Look at these plans for comparing and contrasting two photos.

Plan A Compare the photos in general terms and then in detail. Contrast the photos in general and then in detail.

Plan B Start in the foreground of each photo and compare and contrast each point as you come across it. Work towards the background.

Plan C Make a general comment about the photos being mainly similar or different. Then compare and contrast each point you find in the picture.

3 🎧 Look at these pictures and listen to two students, Angela and Luciano, doing a speaking activity.

a Which plan does Angela use?

b Tick the linking devices you hear Angela use.

but	and	on the other hand	then	in contrast	whereas

c What does Angela think about the suit the man is wearing in picture a?
  1 it's conventional   2 it's flamboyant   3 it's inappropriate

d What does Angela think might be the job of the man in picture b?
  1 a banker   2 a naturalist   3 a teacher

4 Sometimes one of the hardest things to do when you have to speak on your own is to get going. If you have some phrases that you can use to start with, you will feel more confident. Here is an example you might be able to use. Add to it by thinking of other opening lines Angela could have used to talk about her photographs.

EXAMPLE: *Well, obviously both pictures have the same theme: fashion.*

5 Work in groups of three. One of you is the Examiner and should ask the Examiner's questions, one is Student A and one is Student B.

a Examiner's question for Student A:
  Look at the two pictures and compare and contrast them saying what sort of people follow fashion.
  Examiner's question for Student B:
  Do you think that young people follow fashion whereas older people don't?

b Examiner's question for Student B:
  Compare and contrast two students in the class saying what their clothes tell us about their personalities.
  Examiner's question for Student A:
  Do you think your choice of clothes reflects your personality?

Exam folder 5

Paper 3 Part 5 Register transfer

In Part 5 of the English in Use test (Paper 3), there is a register transfer task which tests your awareness and control of style and register. There are two texts which are different from each other in terms of register, writer's purpose and/or style.

You have to:
- transfer the information from one text to the other
- change the grammar and vocabulary of one text into suitable expressions (formal or informal) which will complete the second text
- make sure your answers are grammatically correct as well as stylistically appropriate according to the reader and the writer's purpose
- complete 13 gaps with no more than two words per gap.

1 Can you think of a less formal way of saying the following words or phrases?

   a correspondence
   b annually
   c a great deal of
   d endeavour
   e retail outlet
   f require

2 Can you think of more formal ways of expressing these phrases?

   a Please send all letters to …
   b Pay your bill.
   c If you lose …
   d To get your money back …
   e She will phone you back.
   f He is leaving his job.

3 Read the writing task below and then read the advertisement and the extract from an informal letter. Underline the information in the advertisement which you need to complete the letter. Then change the formal language of the advertisement into informal language and complete the letter.

You have seen this advertisement for a job which you think is exactly what your friend is looking for. Use the information in the advertisement to complete the informal letter.

IT DEVELOPMENT MANAGERS

The role
This is a pivotal role providing a vital link between the commercial and technical aspects of the business. Responsibilities encompass management of a wide array of unique business projects combined with all aspects of day-to-day web management.

The person
Vision, adaptability and flexibility encapsulate the essence of the people we are looking for. Team management and excellent communication skills are essential and an understanding of publishing or the media would be advantageous.

I saw an advert for IT managers and I know that's just the sort of job you're looking for. It's an (0) .....*important*..... job because you'll have to be the link between the commercial and technical (1) .... of the business. The responsibilities (2) .... management of a (3) .... of business projects and day-to-day web management. The advert says what they are (4) .... looking for in the person are flexibility and adaptability. You (5) .... be good at team management and have fantastic communication skills, and it's (6) .... if you've worked in the media before. I think this describes you. Go for it!

Advice
- Identify which text is formal and which is informal.
- Read the first text carefully.
- Read the second text and go back and underline in the first text the information which you have to transfer.
- Find synonyms or paraphrases for the words and expressions you have underlined in the first text.
- Do not use the same words as in the first text.
- Check through what you have written to make sure the sentence and whole text make sense.

4 Read the writing task below and then read the email and formal notice. Underline the information in the email which you need to complete the notice. Then change the informal language of the email into formal language and complete the notice.

You have received this email from a colleague. Use the information in the email to complete the notice for the conference.

As you know I'll be away on holiday for 2 weeks from tomorrow and I've only just got all the information we need about the conference at Hull University. Could you put together the notice to send out to all the delegates? The conference is on 14th and 15th July and people need to know that it's all happening in the Scott building. Dr Douglas is going to get things rolling by talking about 'The role of online education'. Various companies who are interested are going to have all their stuff out in the lobby between the Scott building and the cafeteria. In the afternoon there will be lots of specialist workshops where people can find out more about particular online courses. People will be able to get a list of these from reception when they check in. Don't forget to mention practical things like there'll be coffee for them when they arrive on Sat am. Oh, yes, and people have to tell us if they are vegetarian so that we can let the cafeteria know for the lunches. They can only park in car park B, the other one will be in use for the university staff. As for money matters, it's £500 for everything, accommodation for one night and meals. Ask them to make sure they write Hull University Conference Centre on the cheques. And last but not least they can get a Conference Certificate if they tell us beforehand.

HULL UNIVERSITY

Conference: Online education
Dates: 14th and 15th July

CONFERENCE CENTRE

The conference will (1) .... in the Scott building, situated on the main University campus. After the Welcome and Introduction, Dr Douglas will give a (2) .... 'The role of online education'. After the morning lecture programme you may wish to visit the (3) .... of related material offered by a range of companies working in the field.

In the afternoon there will be (4) .... workshops where delegates can (5) .... more information on online courses. A list of these will be (6) .... at reception.

On arrival, coffee will (7) .... in the cafeteria. Please (8) .... us if you require vegetarian meals so that we can advise the caterers.

Parking will be (9) .... to Car Park B.

The (10) .... of the conference is £500, (11) .... accommodation on the Saturday night and all meals. Please make cheques (12) .... Hull University Conference Centre.

Delegates requiring Conference Certificates, please advise us (13) .... These can be collected from reception on the Sunday.

Genre	Short stories
Topic	Dreaming

Speaking 1

1 Work in small groups and discuss these questions.

a Why do you think we dream?
b Do you believe dreams carry significance?

2 According to the book *Dreams and their Meanings,* dreams do have significance. Match the dreams (a–f) to their possible significance (1–6).

Dream	Significance
a cage full of birds	1 an omen of success
b lightning	2 difficulties to overcome before arriving at your goal
c cats	3 solutions to your money problems
d apples	4 be careful who you trust
e milk	5 good luck
f barefoot	6 health, prosperity and rewarding work

3 Have you ever heard of someone having a premonition in a dream? Do you believe in premonitions?

4 If you dreamed of something that you thought was an omen of good or bad luck, would you change your life accordingly?

Reading 1

1 Read the first part of this story and answer the questions.

a Who is telling the story?
b Why was the narrator in Vladivostok?
c How did the narrator get into conversation with the Russian?
d What impression do you get of the Russian?
e What is the narrator's profession?

The Dream

It chanced that in August 1917 the work upon which I was engaged obliged me to go from New York to Petrograd, and I was instructed for safety's sake to travel by way of Vladivostok. I landed there in the morning and passed an idle day as best I could. The trans-Siberian train was due to start, so far as I remember, at about nine in the evening. I dined at the station restaurant by myself. It was crowded and I shared a small table with a man whose appearance entertained me. He was a Russian, a tall fellow, but amazingly stout, and he had so vast a paunch that he was obliged to sit well away from the table. His hands, small for his size, were buried in rolls of fat. His hair, long, dark, and thin, was brushed carefully across his crown in order to conceal his baldness, and his huge sallow face, with its enormous double chin, clean-shaven, gave you an impression of indecent nakedness. His nose was small, a funny little button upon that mass of flesh: and his black shining eyes were small too. But he had a large, red, and sensual mouth. He was dressed neatly enough in a black suit. It was not worn but shabby; it looked as if it had been neither pressed nor brushed since he had had it.

The service was bad and it was almost impossible to attract the attention of a waiter. We soon got into conversation. The Russian spoke good and fluent English. His accent was marked but not tiresome. He asked me many questions about myself and my plans, which – my occupation at the time making caution necessary – I answered with a show of frankness but with dissimulation. I told him I was a journalist. He asked me whether I wrote fiction and when I confessed that in my leisure moments I did, he began to talk of the later Russian novelists. He spoke intelligently. It was plain that he was a man of education.

2 Find words in the text which mean the following:

a quite fat and solid-looking, especially around the waist

b a fat stomach, especially on a man

c yellowish and looking unhealthy

d looking old and in bad condition because of wear or lack of care

e boring or annoying; causing a lack of patience

f concealment of the truth

Listening 1

1 You are going to listen to the next part of the story. What do you think will happen?

2 As you listen, note down any new information you find out about:

a the Russian
b the Russian's wife
c the narrator's reactions to the Russian

3 What are the key words in this sentence?
She was, however, of a jealous temperament and unfortunately she loved me to distraction.

4 How do you think the story will continue?

Reading 2

1 Read on and then discuss these questions with a partner.

a What new information do we find out about the Russian's wife?
b How would you describe the relationship between the Russian and his wife?
c What do you think is the significance of the dream?
d How do you think the story will end?

'I do not pretend that I was faithful to her. She was not young when I married her and we had been married for ten years. She was small and thin, and she had a bad complexion. She had a bitter tongue. She was a woman who suffered from a fury of possession, and she could not bear me to be attracted to anyone but her. She was jealous not only of the women I knew, but of my friends, my cat, and my books. On one occasion in my absence she gave away a coat of mine merely because I liked none of my coats so well. But I am a man of an equitable temperament. I will not deny that she bored me, but I accepted the acrimonious disposition and no more thought of rebelling against it than I would against the bad weather or a cold in the head. I denied her accusations as long as it was possible to deny them, and when it was impossible I shrugged my shoulders and smoked a cigarette.

'The constant scenes she made did not very much affect me. I led my own life. Sometimes indeed, I wondered whether it was passionate love she felt for me or passionate hate. It seemed to me that love and hate were very near allied.

'So we might have continued to the end of the chapter if one night a very curious thing had not happened. I was awakened by a piercing scream from my wife. Startled, I asked her what was the matter. She told me she had had a fearful nightmare, she had dreamt that I was trying to kill her. We lived at the top of a large house and the well round which the stairs climbed was broad. She had dreamt that just as we arrived at our own floor I had caught hold of her and attempted to throw her over the balusters. It was six stories to the stone floor at the bottom and certain death.

Listening 2

1 You are going to listen to the end of the story. As you listen, make notes to answer the questions below.

a In what way did the dream prey on the Russian's mind?
b Had the Russian previously thought of murdering his wife?
c Did the dream change his wife's behaviour?
d What was the second dream about?
e Why do you think the Russian was sweating when he told the story?
f According to the Russian, how did his wife die and who found her?
g What caused the narrator to doubt the Russian's story?
h How do you think the Russian's wife died?

2 Did you enjoy this short story? Why?/Why not?
Do you prefer short stories to have clear happy endings or do you prefer mysterious endings so that you have to come to your own conclusion about what happened?

Past tenses and the present perfect

1 In the short story you saw a variety of past tenses being used. Look at the extract below and underline the verbs in past tenses.

He called a waiter who was passing with a tray full of dishes and asked him, I suppose – for then I knew hardly any Russian – how much longer we were going to wait for the next course. The waiter, with a rapid but presumably reassuring exclamation, hurried on, and my friend sighed.

2 Correct the sentences below if necessary.

a I read many other stories by this author before I had read *The Dream*.

b Kate bought a new computer because she had been accepted on a Creative Writing course.

c The short story had been made into a TV drama last year.

d The author was owning an interesting collection of antiquarian books.

e We were still trying to decide on a title for our short story while the other group was finishing their plot.

f Harry asked if he could borrow my laptop to do his essay.

g I finished the short story just as Karen came in from work.

h In the story the villain was almost getting away with it but the body was being discovered.

i The end of the story left you feeling let down.

j He worked on the story for two years.

k The first page of the book was seeming very boring, that's why I didn't read it.

l He had been writing for magazines for years before he was being discovered by Hollywood.

m It's the first time I write a short story.

n Since we started the course, I've only seen John once.

o Are you sure the Russian committed the murder? I thought it had been the lodger.

3 Work with a partner. Look at the pictures and say what you think the person has done or has been doing.

Is her name Angela?

G ⋯⋗ page 196

Vocabulary

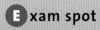
Look at this example.

a tall Russian fellow

The most usual order of adjectives is opinion, size, age, colour, origin, material, purpose. We usually only use one, two or three adjectives to describe a noun.

1   Put these adjectives in the most usual order.

Jumbled adjectives	Noun
wooden small	table
extensive new exciting	menu
red beautiful silk	dress
black shabby	suit
sallow huge	face

2   Describe these photos using a variety of adjectives.

Speaking 2

The *-ed* ending can be found in the past simple and past participle of regular verbs, e.g. *walked*. The past participle form can also be used as an adjective, e.g. *crowded*. There are three different pronunciations of *-ed*: /t/, /d/ and /ɪd/.

1   Underline the words with an *-ed* ending in this extract from *The Dream* and then put them under the correct heading in the table.

> It chanced that in August 1917 the work upon which I was engaged obliged me to go from New York to Petrograd, and I was instructed for safety's sake to travel by way of Vladivostok. I landed there in the morning and passed an idle day as best I could. The trans-Siberian train was due to start, so far as I remember, at about nine in the evening. I dined at the station restaurant by myself. It was crowded and I shared a small table with a man whose appearance entertained me. He was a Russian, a tall fellow, but amazingly stout, and he had so vast a paunch that he was obliged to sit well away from the table. His hands, small for his size, were buried in rolls of fat.

walked /t/	loved /d/	started /ɪd/

2   🎧 Listen to the words on the tape and check your answers.

3   Complete these sentences about the pronunciation of *-ed*.

   a We pronounce *-ed* .... after unvoiced sounds /f/, /k/, /p/, /s/, /ʃ/, /tʃ/ or /θ/.

   b We pronounce *-ed* .... after voiced sounds /b/, /g/, /l/, /m/, /n/, /v/, /ʒ/, /dʒ/ or /z/.

   c We pronounce *-ed* .... after /d/ or /t/.

4   Put these words under the correct heading, /t/, /d/ or /ɪd/.

asked	called	discovered	enjoyed
helped	invited	jumped	lived
looked	missed	rained	reached
needed	rented	saved	travelled
visited	worked		

Writing folder 5

Articles

1 Analysing an authentic newspaper article can help you write a good article yourself. Read the article below, and then discuss the following questions with a partner.

  a What type of publication would you expect to find this article in?

  b Who is the intended reader of the article?

  c Is the article written in informal, neutral or formal register?

  d What would you define as the overall purpose of the article? More than one answer may be possible.

  - to give information
  - to give an opinion
  - to provoke a debate
  - to entertain
  - to describe a process
  - to shock

  e Identify the purpose of each paragraph.

  EXAMPLE: *Paragraph 1: to attract the reader's attention by talking about something new*

Machines sell movies while you wait for your cash

1 Not long ago, customers at Wells Fargo Bank in San Francisco just had to put up with mechanical faults and quirky operating hours when trying to extract cash from its dispensing machines. Now they have to put up with film trailers and advertisements too.

2 Starting this week, Wells Fargo is operating three hi-tech automated teller machines in and around San Francisco which, as well as passing out banknotes, sing the praises of Ridley Scott's movie *Gladiator*. 'The general who became a slave. The slave who became a gladiator. The gladiator who defied an empire,' reads the screen on Montgomery Street. What was the outstanding checking account balance again?

3 Wells Fargo said 800 of its bank machines would be wired for commercials and news headlines by the end of the year.

4 The idea is to eventually tailor the adverts to the buying habits of the consumer trying to extract cash.

5 This may be the banking wave of the future, but the first customers to undergo the hi-tech experience were less than enthusiastic.

'I just want to get my money,' complained one of them, Brandon Hemley.

6 Yesterday's *San Francisco Chronicle* was equally unimpressed. It said: 'Even before you extract your cash, the machine tells you how to spend it … that's a lot of gall, even for avaricious bankers, who should junk the commercials in favour of machines that work, that spit out bills and transaction records – even on weekends – with no charge for retrieving our own money.'

7 Wells Fargo retorted that marketing tests showed that their customers found the idea 'cool'. The *Gladiator* commercial features spear fights, axe fights and tiger fights as well as a passionate kiss. Entertaining stuff, perhaps – just as long as nobody is waiting in line for cash behind you.

---

2   You are going to write an article of about 250 words for the same newspaper giving your opinion about the introduction of this type of advertising at cash dispensers. First, work with a partner and discuss the advantages and disadvantages of this type of advertising. Keep notes of the ideas you come up with.

3   Plan your article.

Consider the following:
- Who is going to read the article and therefore what style are you going to adopt?
- Are you basically for this kind of advertising or against it?
- Is your article going to have a headline and subheading?
- How many paragraphs is it going to have?
- What is the main idea of each paragraph?
- How are you going to round off the article?

4   Which of these pieces of advice for writing a good article do you think you will be able to use?

Advice

- Give the article an attention-grabbing headline.
- Make sure the first paragraph interests the reader and keeps their attention.
- Involve the reader by asking questions.
- Include direct speech/quotations.
- Be emphatic in your opinion.
- Vary the length of the sentences.
- Use a variety of grammatical structures.
- Use parallel expressions to avoid repeating the same words or expressions.
- Round off the article with a thought-provoking statement or question.

5   Here are some phrases which can be used to express opinion. What do they mean? Could you use any of them in your article?

a   vent my frustration
b   escalation of advertising
c   companies rely heavily on
d   lay my cards on the table
e   attach great importance to
f   conspicuous by its absence
g   I concede that
h   it surpassed my expectations
i   at a stroke
j   I would hazard a guess that
k   I envisage
l   for those unacquainted with

6   Write the first draft of your article and then give it to another pair of students to comment on. Do you agree with their suggestions?

Genre	Leaflets
Topic	Leaving home

Speaking 1

1 Work with a partner and answer the questions below.

   a Match the words in the box to the pictures (a–d).

a leaflet   a flier   a brochure   a prospectus

   b What exactly is a leaflet? What different purposes can a leaflet have?

   c Do you think a leaflet is an effective means of communication?

2 With a partner, discuss these questions.

   a Have you seen the film *Titanic*? If you have, what do you remember about it?

   b Where do you think most of the passengers on board the *Titanic* were going and why?

   c What do you think it was like to emigrate to a new country in 1912?

Reading

1 Read the leaflet about the Titanic Trail. Are the following statements true or false?

   a You can go on the Titanic Trail at any time of the year.

   b Michael Martin built the Heritage Centre.

   c The full-day *Titanic* tour allows you to reflect on the final sight of dry land that the passengers would have had.

   d Sea angling is included in the traditional Wake Special.

   e The *Titanic* sank in 1911.

Titanic Trail

Cobh (Queenstown), Ireland
"Last Port of Call" RMS Titanic

Titanic Trail *Guided Tours*

> Guided walking tours covering the main features of the 1¹⁄₂ mile trail take place daily at 11 am from the Commodore Hotel, Cobh.
>
> Afternoon tours arranged on request.

Special arrangements can be made for bus tours and other groups. Whenever possible the tour will be introduced by **Michael Martin, author and creator of the Titanic Trail, Cobh**. Additional activities such as boat trips to the anchorage, traditional wakes and evening entertainment can be arranged for groups. See below. www.titanic-trail.com

TITANIC TRAIL OPTIONS

CULTURAL AFTERNOON Ref. No. CA 10
A guided walk of the Titanic Trail with Irish Coffee being served in an authentic emigrant pub. This is followed by a visit to the Queenstown Story at Cobh's beautiful Heritage Centre.

TITANIC FULL DAY EXPERIENCE Ref. No. TF 21
A morning boat trip to the area of Cork Harbour where the Titanic anchored on the morning of April 11th, 1912. Experience for yourself the last images of Ireland that passengers would have seen from the decks of the great ship. This is followed by a cultural afternoon.

ACTIVITY AND ATTRACTIONS IN OR NEAR COBH

- Marlogue Woods
- Fota Wildlife Park
- Barryscourt Castle
- The Old Middleton Distillery
- Blarney Castle (40 minutes drive)
- Waterford Crystal (1½ hours drive)
- Lakes of Killarney (2 hours drive)
- Tralee, Co. Kerry (home of the Rose of Tralee, 2½ hours drive)
- The Famine ship, Blennerville (2½ hours drive)
- Horse riding
- Sea Angling
- Golf
- Bird watching
- Sailing
- Windsurfing

TRADITIONAL WAKE SPECIAL

Day 1 Arrival and check in to accommodation. Introduction to Cobh and guided tour of Cobh's famous Titanic Trail with Irish Coffee being served in authentic emigrant establishment
Dinner

Day 2 Breakfast
Boat trip in Cork Harbour to area of Titanic anchorage
Afternoon shopping
Dinner
Evening in authentic rural Irish bar where you can experience first hand the fun, sadness and music of a typical party afforded to the parting emigrants.

Day 3 Breakfast
Visit Queenstown Story at Cobh Heritage Centre, reliving the history of the 4 million Irish emigrants who departed this port

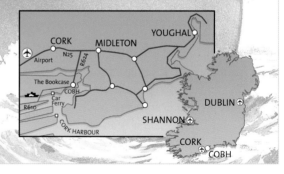

---

2 Answer these questions about the leaflet.

  a What information is provided in the leaflet?
  b What is the purpose of the leaflet?
  c How does the layout contribute to the communication of the information?
  d How does the writer try to interest the reader? Do you think he succeeds?
  e How would you describe the style of the leaflet?

3 What would you include in a leaflet for visitors to your town or a famous town in your country? Choose three points to write about. Give each paragraph a heading and write a contribution to the leaflet.

Listening

Exam spot

In the CAE Listening test (Paper 4), you will hear a monologue **once** only in Part 2. The information you need for your answers is usually repeated within the recording. You will either have to complete sentences or take notes.

1 You are going to listen to a recording for visitors to the Titanic Heritage Centre. Tick the words from the list below which you think you will hear.

a embarked   g quay
b microchip   h data
c crew   i setting out
d berthed   j diesel fuel
e hi-tech   k on board
f iceberg   l struck

🎧 Now listen and check your answers.

2 🎧 Listen again and complete the sentences below.

a The leaving party for those emigrating was known as
....

b The building of the
.... made Queenstown an easy place to reach.

c At the height of emigration, ... people left Queenstown every week.

d A .... was an immigration requirement.

e Local goods, such as .... , were taken to the liners to be sold.

f In total the number of people on board the *Titanic* was
....

3 In what ways would living in a different country from the rest of your family be easier now than in 1912?

-ing forms

In the listening text, you heard some examples of the use of -ing forms.

EXAMPLE: *Passengers on the Titanic were no doubt looking forward to **travelling** on the brand-new luxury liner.*

1 There are several different uses of the -ing form. Match the sentences (a–g) to the statements (1–7) about the use of the -ing form.

a Learning keeps the mind active.
b I avoid travelling on a Monday morning if possible; the trains are so crowded.
c I'm interested in seeing the new Heritage Centre.
d If you keep on searching the Internet, you're bound to find some information on the *Titanic*.
e It's worth making a detour to the west coast; it's spectacular.
f I hope you don't mind my asking but …
g I can't imagine being paid that much money.

1 We can use the -ing form after phrasal verbs.
2 We can use the passive -ing form.
3 The -ing form can be the subject of the sentence.
4 We can use the -ing form after some common expressions.
5 We can use the -ing form after certain verbs.
6 We use the -ing form after prepositions.
7 In formal English, possessives are used with the -ing form.

2 You are going to read an extract about a family who emigrated to the USA in the middle of the nineteenth century. The first and last sentences are in the correct order, but the other sentences have been jumbled up. Put the sentences (b–f) in the correct order, then underline all the -ing forms.

a I often recall the delightful stories my grandmother used to tell of the days when our family crossed the plains to seek a new life in the West; how must she have felt?
b He never tired of tending the horses and encouraging us all with wondrous images of our destination.
c Travelling West must have been a great adventure for the children but a tremendous undertaking for the parents.
d She told us how grandfather packed the wagon and then left without even taking one final glance back; he was so convinced that it was worth making the trip.
e Although she conjured up vivid pictures of the trip, I can't really imagine setting out in 1864 with six children and all your worldly possessions on a wagon.
f My grandmother remembered feeling a sense of excitement tinged with concern.
g My grandmother said that towards the end of the trip she used to look forward to waking up in a bed in a house, knowing that that day she didn't have to move on.

3 Correct the sentences (a–j) if necessary.

a He burst out laughing when I told him what had happened.

b Since he started his new job, he's got used to get up very early.

c Have time to spend talking with friends is very important.

d I'm looking forward to see you soon.

e I can't help thinking this is all a waste of time.

f It's no use to tell me now that you can't finish the report. You should have told me last week.

g What I miss is not to be able to have lunch with all my family every Sunday.

h I'll look into replacing the existing computers with something more up-to-date, but don't hold your breath!

i I'm fed up with not to have all the facilities I need to do the job properly.

j Having a positive outlook on life is very important.

G⋯⋮ page 198

Speaking 2

Here are two ways of linking spoken English.

Type 1
When a word ending in a consonant sound is followed by a word beginning with a vowel sound, the words run together. *Get up* is pronounced /getʌp/.

Type 2
When a word ending with a vowel sound is followed by a word beginning with a vowel sound we insert the sound /j/ or /w/.
We insert /j/ as in *he is* (/hiːjɪz/) when the mouth and lips are in a spread position.

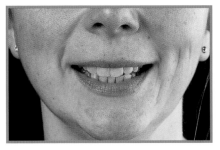

We insert /w/ as in *do it* (/duːwɪt/) when the mouth and lips are in a rounded position.

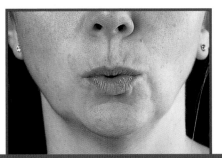

1 Which linking sounds can be used in the phrases below?

a start off

b she eats

c blue ink

d here at the centre

e We are leaving the quay at 9 am.

⌂ Now listen and check your answers.

2 Write /w/ or /j/ as necessary in the place in these sentences where linking occurs.

EXAMPLE: *I'm going to /w/ Ireland next week.*

a If you are part of a group, it's much more fun.

b So I'm going to start off by telling you about the conditions on board.

c You'll see it in the film.

d When I'm asked about that, it's difficult to answer.

e You can do it too.

f Book through our agency, which is open from 9 am to 6 pm.

⌂ Now listen and check your answers.

Exam folder 6

Paper 3 Part 6 Gapped text

In Part 6 of the CAE English in Use test (Paper 3), there is a text from which six phrases or short sentences have been removed. They are at the bottom of the text along with some additional phrases or short sentences (ten in total), including the example. You have to choose the phrases or short sentences which complete the text. This tests whether you understand how a text is structured in terms of syntax and meaning.

Advice

- Read the title of the text. It will help you know in advance what the subject is.
- Read the whole text quickly to get a general impression of the content.
- Think about the sentences immediately before and after the gap and throughout the text as a whole.
- Clues may lie in the grammar, punctuation and/or vocabulary.
- When you have chosen a phrase to fill the gap, read the text again to make sure it makes sense.
- Check any phrases/short sentences which you have not used to see if they could fit in the gap.
- Finally, read the whole text again to make sure it fits together grammatically and that it makes sense.

1 Look at the text below and answer the questions.

  a What does the title suggest about the content of the text?
  b What does *their* refer to in line 1?
  c What does *From this time onwards* refer to in line 3?

  d Which type of linking device is *however* (line 5); is it adding something, listing, giving a result, contrasting something, summing up or giving an example?
  e What does *Since then* refer to in line 6?
  f What does *they* refer to in line 6?
  g What does *their* refer to in line 7?

The Watercolour tradition

Watercolours are one of the oldest artistic mediums known. Physical evidence of their use by Stone Age people still survives – hidden in the darkness of caves that, for reasons unknown, were decorated by the world's first artists. From this time onwards, watercolours added their own particular flavour to artistic history.

5 It was not until the 18th century, however, that watercolour paintings became recognised as works of art in their own right. Since then, they have enjoyed enduring popularity among amateur, as well as professional, artists. Two of their chief qualities, freshness and versatility, have been constant factors in the development of the watercolour tradition from earliest times to the present day.

2   For questions 1–6, read the following text and then choose from the list A–J the best phrase given below to fill each of the gaps. Each correct phrase may only be used once. **Some of the answers do not fit at all.**

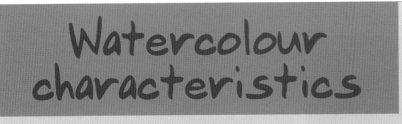

Watercolour characteristics

What makes the medium seem daunting to the beginner is the fact that watercolours are transparent; this means that you cannot paint a light colour over a dark one [0] [J]. Once you have made a dark mark on the paper, you are committed, and you can alter the effect only by painting an even darker colour on top of it. This is the chief difference between watercolours and oil paints. You cannot simply paint over a picture in layers, [1] [ ], literally covering up mistakes.

Other differences affect the way you actually paint. With oils, for instance, the addition of "highlights" – the lighter, sometimes pure white, tones [2] [ ], can sometimes be left until the final stages. With watercolours, however, the colours are conventionally applied from "light to dark". Therefore the highlights are often simply areas of the picture [3] [ ]; the white is the paper itself. When colours are applied, the lighter tones go on first, the darker ones are built up on top of this. This means that you need to know which areas of the picture are going to be the lighter ones, [4] [ ]

Moreover, oils can be manipulated [5] [ ]; the paint can be actually moved around on the surface of the canvas, and the colours will not adhere properly to the surface [6] [ ]. Watercolours, however, cannot be used in this way, since, as their name implies, they are mixed with water.

It is usually water that governs the tone – the more diluted the colour, the lighter the tone will be.

A   that usually depict the reflections of light onto objects in the picture

B   for they will be left with less paint or none at all

C   as they tend to 'bleed' into each other when wet

D   that have been left unpainted

E   which can work well in a carefully structured painting

F   as you can do with oils

G   while they are being applied

H   which can be turned to an advantage

I   until they are dry

J   because the darker colour will show through

Genre	Lectures
Topic	Language development

Listening and Reading

Exam spot

In the CAE Listening test (Paper 4), you may be asked to listen to a talk, lecture or speech. The more you understand about the style and delivery of these forms of speaking, the easier it will be to answer questions about the speaker's standpoint and attitude.

1 🎧 Listen to Speakers (1–4) and match them to the speech (a–d) they are giving.

Speaker 1	**a** a sermon
Speaker 2	**b** a eulogy
Speaker 3	**c** a summing up
Speaker 4	**d** an official statement

2 What is the difference between a lecture, a seminar, a talk, a presentation and a briefing? Match the words (a–e) to the definitions (1–5).

a a lecture   **d** a presentation
b a seminar   **e** a briefing
c a talk

1 the information that is given to someone usually just before they do something
2 a formal talk on a serious or specialist subject given to a group of people, especially students
3 a talk which presents information often with audio-visual aids
4 a speech to a group of people
5 an occasion when a teacher or expert and a group of people meet to study and discuss something

Listening

1 You are going to hear a lecture on evolutionary factors of language. Before you listen, see how many of these questions you can answer.

1 When do you think human beings began speaking?
   a 1.3 million years ago   **b** 50,000 years ago
   c 6,000 years ago

2 Why do you think humans developed language?
   a The population expanded.
   b They needed to communicate more effectively.
   c It is an innate ability.

3 Human babies need their mother and other adults to look after them for quite a long time compared with other animals. Why do you think this is?
   a Human babies are more complex.
   b The gestation period of humans is half that of other animals.
   c The father provides food for the mother and baby.

4 What physical features of human beings enable them to speak?
   a They have fewer teeth than other animals.
   b The human tongue is more flexible.
   c The larynx is simpler.

How do you think children learn their first language?

2 🎧 **Listen to the first part of the lecture and complete the notes.**

a People began writing .... years ago.

b It is estimated that people began speaking between .... and .... years ago.

c Tools from .... BC show people recognised the concept of space.

d Tools .... years old show people were capable of abstract thought.

e People first used .... to communicate.

f Pettito and Marentette concluded that manual language (sign language) is more .... , ... and .... than spoken language.

g People stopped communicating with sign language because they started using .... and wanted to communicate ....

Now let's turn to the biological constraints.

If we assume that all humans are able to speak a language, a number of biological facts fall into place, suggesting that the human body is partially adapted to the production of language.

Human teeth are different to those of other animals – being even and forming an unbroken barrier, they are upright, do not slant outwards and the top and bottom set meet. This is not necessary for eating. Yet evenly spaced equal sized teeth which touch are useful for the articulation of the sounds /s/, /f/, /v/, /ʃ/ and /θ/ as well as several others.

Human lips have well-developed muscles which are more intricately interlaced than those of other primates. The mouth is small and can be opened and closed rapidly, allowing the sounds /p/ and /b/ to be made.

The human tongue is thick, muscular and mobile. This means that the size of the mouth cavity can be varied, allowing a range of vowel sounds to be produced.

The human larynx is simpler in structure than that of other primates; air can move freely past and then out of the mouth without being hindered by other appendages. The 'stream-lining' of the larynx may be a sign of adaptation to speech – however, a disadvantage of this is that we cannot breathe while we eat, unlike monkeys. If food becomes trapped in our windpipe we could choke to death.

Our breathing is well adapted to speech; during speech we are able to alter our breathing rhythm without noticing discomfort.

Humans have a prolonged childhood compared to other animals – if factors like size, lifespan and gestation are taken into account, compared to other animals humans appear to be born prematurely; for humans to conform to the general trend, they would have to have an 18 month gestation period. Thus, with other factors taken into account, the human gestation period is only half as long as the gestation periods of other animals. This means that less information is inherited genetically. In effect the genes are given more opportunity to 'ask the questions' and the environment provides the answers. Perhaps humans are biologically disposed towards language, but they need the environment to make use of the structure of their brains.

Reading

1 Now read the next part of the lecture and answer the following questions.

upper lip — / upper teeth
tongue
lower lip —
lower teeth
larynx —

1 The importance of the shape of human teeth is that they

 A form a barrier to the throat.

 B allow certain sounds to be produced.

 C make chewing food easier.

 D allow the lip muscles to develop.

2 The structure of the human larynx means

 A the mouth cavity has space for the tongue.

 B it blocks air exiting from the mouth.

 C humans cannot breathe and swallow at the same time.

 D breathing requires effort in humans.

3 Why is it suggested that the human gestation period is so short?

 A to allow humans to learn more from the environment

 B to limit the size humans grow to

 C to take full advantage of our genetic make-up

 D to ensure children learn speech

2 Work in small groups and discuss these questions.

a Did you learn anything new from the lecture? If so, what?

b Do you think animals 'talk'? Give examples of how animals communicate.

c Do you think humans are more intelligent than other animals? Why?/Why not?

d Why do you think it takes such a long time for babies to learn their first language and for adults to learn a foreign language?

The passive

1   In Listening and Reading 1 you heard the following phrases:

Goods were taken from the warehouse.
The theft was discovered by Mr White when he arrived on the morning of February 15th.
His fingerprints were found on the window.

How is the passive formed?

It is common for the passive to be used in statements, lectures and so on because the action is often more important than the person who carried it out. The passive is also commonly used when we do not know who did something.

2   Match the sentences (1–9) to the statements (a–i) about the form and use of the passive.

1   A man has been arrested.
2   The lecture will be given by Dr Tomlinson.
3   Delegates will arrive at the centre at 6 pm.
4   The lecture room ought to be air-conditioned.
5   The lecturer should have been given more time.
6   He enjoys being recognised in the street.
7   She was awarded an OBE for her services to the community.
8   It is considered impolite to jump a queue.
9   Several people are said to have been injured in the accident.

a   Passive constructions can be made with *it* + passive + clause.
b   Intransitive verbs cannot usually be made passive.
c   When a verb has two objects, it is more usual to make the 'person object' the subject of the passive verb than the 'thing object'.
d   This is an example of the passive *-ing* form.
e   We use the passive when the action is more important than the agent or the agent is unknown.
f   We can use the construction subject + passive + *to* + infinitive.
g   This is an example of the passive of a past modal.
h   We use *by* + the agent when this provides useful information.
i   Modals can be followed by the infinitive passive.

3   Rewrite the underlined sentences in this lecture in the passive.

Recent studies have revealed three important areas in the study of the evolutionary factors of language. 90% of humans are right-handed and have language in the left hemisphere of their brain. The second is that humans freed their hands in order to make and use tools, which meant having to find a method of communication other than sign language. Thirdly, syntax developed which increased the quality and quantity of the message.

People say that we can teach chimps to speak but there are several biological factors which make humans more predisposed to speech. You should note that the form of the human teeth, lips, tongue and larynx are all important when it comes to speech.

4   Look at these two pictures. Picture a shows a sitting room before a burglary and Picture b shows the same room after the burglary. What has happened?

EXAMPLE: *The painting above the fireplace has been stolen.*

To have/get something done

We use *to have/get something done* when we talk about arranging for things to be done by other people. The past participle has a passive meaning.

I'm going to have my car serviced at that new garage down the road.

1 Look at these pictures and say what the person has had done or is going to have done.

2 Work with a partner.

  a Explain the difference in the use of *had* and *got* in these two sentences:
  I had my handbag stolen while I was on holiday.
  She got her fingers trapped in the door.

  b Explain the use of *won't* in this sentence:
  I won't have you staying out so late at night.

  c Explain the meaning of the second sentence:
  Put your money somewhere safe. We don't want it stolen.

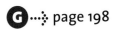 **G** ···⟶ page 198

Vocabulary

> ## **V**ocabulary spot
>
> When you learn a word, you can increase your vocabulary even more by learning all the forms of the word, e.g. the noun, verb, adjective, and adverb. This will help you in the CAE English in Use test (Paper 3) where in Part 4 you have two texts and you need to put the correct form of a word in the gap, just like in the exercise below.

1 In the extract below, use the words in capitals on the right of the text to form a word that fits in the gap.

Oral communication

Effective oral communication is an important – but often (1) .... and	**LOOK**
(2) .... – skill in scientific and academic endeavours. This tutorial has been developed to serve as an	**PRACTISE**
(3) .... guide and general	**INTRODUCE**
(4) .... for use when formulating a talk. The principles should be applied whenever you are faced with making a public presentation, whether it's an informal or a more formal talk, such as a conference presentation or interview. There are very few people who have a natural talent for delivering	**REFER**
(5) .... presentations. On the other hand, foresight, hard work, and practice can carry most of the rest of us into the 'very good' level of presentation skills. The standards for public speaking in the	**EXCEL**
(6) .... and academic realms are (7) .... low, so a good presentation is often	**SCIENCE** **RELATE**
(8) .... I've attempted to compile a short summary of skills needed to make a good presentation so that a user can learn these skills, then apply them in professional settings.	**MEMORY**

Speaking

1 You will be given a card with information about a topic. You are going to give a short talk about this topic. On the card there is one piece of information which is not correct. Read your card and check with your teacher which piece of information is incorrect. Prepare your talk.

2 Work in groups of three. One person in the group gives their talk and the others should listen and note down the piece of information which they think is incorrect.

3 After each talk, check which piece of information was incorrect.

Writing folder 6

Leaflets

1 Look at these extracts from leaflets and discuss who the leaflet is designed to attract and which techniques are used to attract the readers.

a

Cambridge Drama Centre

Events for Children

January – April

book now on 01223 322748

Saturday 29th January   Age 5 – 11

Magic Carpet Theatre: The Magic Circus

The Magical Ringmaster has planned a show full of acrobats, elephants, and tightrope walkers ... but the acts have disappeared and the Clowns have taken over! As you might expect they make a fantastically messy job of it. Packed full of audience participation, this is a colourful, exciting and funny show full of crazy circus capers and marvellous magic. Another hit from the company who enthralled us with **Mr Shell's Seaside Spells**.

11 am at Cambridge Drama Centre £3.75 (£1.75 unwaged)

3.30 pm at Impington Village College £3.50 (£1.50 unwaged)

Running time: 70 minutes

b

Lloyds TSB online wherever you are

at your *leisure*

Wouldn't it be useful to be able to pick up the phone and know how much you have in your account, be able to transfer money between accounts or confirm if a payment has gone through?

These are just some of the ways PhoneBank Express, our telephone banking service, can make everyday banking more convenient – wherever you are.

c

SOUTH WEST TRAILS

1 All roads lead to Sarum

A journey through 5,000 years of history from Stonehenge, following the footsteps of the Celts, Romans, Saxons and Normans at Old Sarum, then on to the superb medieval cathedral at New Sarum – Salisbury.

◎ Stonehenge, 2m W of Amesbury on the junction of A303 and A344/A360

2 Battlements and boats

A memorable tour of Devon's most historic towns, Totnes and Dartmouth, linked by a river cruise through the beautiful scenery of the Dart Valley.

◎ Totnes Castle, on hill overlooking the town.

3 Forts and ferries

Explore the coastal fortifications that protected the Fal estuary for 450 years.

2 Which of these features do you think we are **not** likely to find in leaflets?

- catchy slogans
- jargon
- rhetorical questions
- imperatives
- very formal language
- encouragement to buy/do something
- long sentences
- headings and subheadings
- lots of adjectives

3 In the CAE Writing test (Paper 2), you may be asked to write a contribution of approximately 250 words to a leaflet or brochure. Look at the examination questions below and underline the key parts of the writing tasks. Think about who the leaflet/brochure is for, the nature of your contribution and what you are required to include.

A Most tourists who come to your country only visit the same few overcrowded places. Consequently, the Tourist Board is trying to encourage people to spend holidays in the countryside, and it is planning a new brochure called *The Undiscovered Countryside*. You have been asked to write a contribution to the brochure. You should include information about what can be done on a countryside holiday, what kinds of accommodation are available and what the weather conditions are likely to be.
Write your **contribution**.

B You have been asked to write an information leaflet for visitors to your company. You should give a brief history of the company, describe its main activities and plans for the future and mention any other points that you think are important.
Write your **leaflet**.

C In a London museum there is to be an exhibition of some items of great interest from your country, and you have been asked to assist with the publicity. Write a leaflet which outlines the history of the items and explains their importance within and outside your country.
Write your **leaflet**.

4 Now read the question below. With a partner, underline the key parts of the question and decide on content, style and headings.

Your town would like to attract a greater range of visitors, from young people to older people. You have been asked to write a contribution to a new brochure, issued by the Tourist Board. You have been asked to make sure you mention activities or visits for young people and older people. It is also important that there is a balance of fun activities and more intellectual activities for the different age ranges.
Write your **contribution**.

5 Write a first draft of your contribution then give this to another student and ask for comments. Revise your first draft by checking through the Advice box.

Advice

- Make sure you have answered the question.
- Make sure you have covered all the points in the question.
- Use special techniques/features to attract the reader.
- Check that your contribution is clear.
- Use a range of adjectives, adverbs and grammatical structures.
- Check for spelling and grammar mistakes.

Genre	Expressing opinions
Topic	Family life

Speaking 1

1 Work with a partner and match the photographs (a–d) to the speakers (1–4).

1 *At home mum would never let us choose what we had for dinner but now I really miss all that home cooking.*

2 *It's lovely having the children here but it's also nice when they go home to their mum when they've tired me out!*

3 *They're always nagging me to tidy my room and do chores round the house.*

4 *I'm so thankful mum and dad live nearby; they've been a real help since the twins were born.*

2 What kinds of things do you and your family tend to talk about?

3 Among your family and friends, who manages to get their opinion across the most forcefully? How do you think they do this?

Reading

1 You are going to read a newspaper article in which a father gives his opinion about bringing up his three children. What do you think he might say about discipline?

2 Read the article and answer the questions.

1 Jonathan wants to be like his father in that he would like
   A to have the same profession.
   B his children to be proud of him.
   C to teach his children how to get on in life.
   D his children to feel secure.

2 Why is Jonathan strict with his children?
   A He is trying to live up to his father's standards.
   B He is teaching his children where the limits of behaviour are.
   C He is making time to spend with his wife.
   D He is moulding his children according to his beliefs.

3 Jonathan fears society may influence his children so that they
   A cannot come to their own decisions.
   B may be vulnerable to advertising.
   C will grow up far too quickly.
   D resent their parents' authority.

4 Why did Jonathan finally buy Jacob a Nintendo?
   A Jacob felt his father was being unfair.
   B Jacob was behaving well.
   C Jacob had waited a year.
   D Jacob was being made fun of at school.

5 Jacob has been having some difficulties at school because
   A he cannot play football.
   B his top-of-the-form position is hard to keep.
   C he is seen to be a swot.
   D demands on him are becoming unbearable.

3 Work in small groups and put the following things in life in order of importance. Support your opinions with reasons.

love	fun	living up to family expectations
food	health	job status	strong moral sense
money	friends	security	family

4 When you were a child, were your priorities different? How?/Why?

WHAT THESE KIDS NEED IS DISCIPLINE

Jonathan Myers tells Ann McFerran why he has decided to be as strict with his children as his father was with him

I'm a very old-fashioned and strict parent, like my own father. He wanted me to become a barrister, like him, but I used to say to him that he'd made me secure enough not to worry about having a proper job. He was very disappointed when I said I was going to be a writer, but I think that was out of anxiety: he didn't know how I would survive in the world.

As a child I was really proud of my father. I have an image of him, 6ft 5in and broad-shouldered, wearing a smart suit and tie and behaving maturely – an image I feel I should live up to. My father had status in other people's eyes. I worry that I didn't give my children that. They don't see me wearing a suit and going out to work or having status: they see me slobbing around at home in shorts and no shoes.

I think children want to feel proud of their parents because it makes them feel secure in a Darwinian sense. The one time that my children knew how to rate my professional life was when I was nominated for an Oscar for my adaptation of *The Canterbury Tales* – my lucky break. Briefly, I was elevated in their eyes. When I didn't win I felt that I had let them down, which is ridiculous. I had one little cry because I felt I had failed.

I have inherited from my father a strong sense of the importance of doing the right thing. And, like him, I am strict, even though I lack the sort of authority bubble he had around him. In the right context, my children are allowed to be rude to me – they might call me 'fat face' in a jokey way, when I would never have dared.

But I'm also very authoritarian: I believe strongly in proper bedtimes, that chores have to be done and that certain times of the day – when Julie and I have an evening drink – are reserved for adults, which the children are not allowed to interrupt.

Some parents of our children's friends have told Julie that their children are scared of me because I am so strict with my own children. I know I have quite a demonic image in a few families' eyes. But I want to make my children into the sort of children I want them to be.

We live in a terribly liberal age when people feel they should take a back seat in making moral decisions. I don't think that children should make up their own minds – and saying that is about as unfashionable as you can get. But if you don't influence them, they will only be influenced by others.

I don't believe in reasoning with my children. They do what mummy and daddy say. If you say to a child, 'Would you like to go to bed now?' no child in his right mind will agree, and if he does, he needs to be seen by two psychiatrists immediately.

Julie and I don't let our children watch television after 6pm, ever. It's important to think through why a programme is being made. If it's fun, that's fine, but I can't stand all those Saturday morning programmes that are really just to promote the latest pop records and to persuade people to buy accessories. Our children watch it for an hour after school and then it goes off. They never ask to turn it on again.

I think it's a parent's job to preserve childhood as long as possible – which is also terribly unfashionable. We are proud of the fact that Jacob, at 10, still likes cuddly toys.

In our house we never buy toys which are fashionable crazes, such as Furbies. We held out against getting a Nintendo for a year, even though everyone else in Jacob's class had one. But I cracked when he said, 'I don't understand why, if I'm good and I do all my homework and I do everything right, I don't have a Nintendo and all the bad boys do.' I thought that was a very strong argument.

Jacob could not believe it when we got him a Nintendo for his birthday. But we still lay down rules about its limited use, which he has never argued with because that is the atmosphere in the house.

I am strict about homework and achievement. Our children will work hard until they finish university, and I think they will thank me for the rest of their lives. If they do drop out, at least they will have made a conscious choice.

At the moment the older two are doing well at school and sometimes I try to raise the amount of homework they are given. Jacob protests because I make him take it into school, which makes him look clever. He is already at the top of his form – and that in itself is very difficult for him.

I don't watch football, so nor does Jacob. That is also hard for him. Last year he had a tough time at school in terms of low-intensity bullying. Had he been interested in football, he would have had a *lingua franca* with the others in his year. I was not prepared to change, however. I don't like the attitudes in football.

Speaking 2

1 How far do you agree or disagree with Jonathan's opinions? Complete these sentences.

> EXAMPLE: I don't really feel that *Jonathan's ideas on raising children match my own.*

a In my view, ...
b What I think is ....
c As I see it, ...
d If you ask me, ...
e The way I see it is ....

> ### Ⓔxam spot
>
> In Part 3 of the CAE Speaking test (Paper 5) you are given a visual or written prompt for a problem-solving activity. You have to work with your partner and you may be asked to sequence, rank, compare and select, for example. During this task you are expected to invite the opinions of your partner and express your own.

2 It is a good idea to have a selection of phrases ready for starting the tasks in the Speaking test. Look at these phrases and decide which would be appropriate and which would be inappropriate.

1 A Would you like to start or shall I?
  B You start.
2 A I don't know what to say.
  B OK, so we have to talk about each of these goals and say which is closest to our opinion. Well, this …
3 A Shall we go through all the goals first and then decide which is closest to our opinion?
  B OK, a quick look through and then decide; simple!
4 A I think it's obvious that this is the best.
  B What do you think about this idea here?

3 Here are some pictures illustrating parents' goals for their children. With a partner, talk about the different types of goals and decide which two are closest to your own opinion.

> I would like my children to …

4 How did you start the discussion? Which phrases did you use to give your opinion? Did you support your opinions with reasons?

The infinitive

The infinitive in English is the base form of the verb. We call it the full infinitive when *to* is used before it and the bare infinitive when there is no *to*.

EXAMPLE: *I think children **want to feel** proud of their parents because it makes them feel secure in a Darwinian sense.*
*My children **are allowed to be** rude to me.*
*I don't think that children **should make up** their own minds.*

1 Underline the sentences which use the infinitive in the article. Which take the infinitive with *to*? Which take the infinitive without *to*?

2 Correct the sentences below if necessary.

   a I don't want that you think I'm doing this as a punishment.
   b You are not to use the computer after 10 pm.
   c I must to go home before I miss the last bus.
   d In my opinion parents should not let their daughters to wear make-up until they are over 16.
   e No wonder he's proud of his son, he seems to win every school prize there is!
   f I was helped to get on in my career by one of my lecturers from university.
   g I'm writing the address down so that you don't forget it.
   h It was fantastic see so many young children enter the competition.
   i The school made students do their homework on a computer.

3 Do you agree or disagree with the following statements?

   a Having their mother at home all day with them makes children feel more secure.
   b Children should be set high educational goals by their parents.
   c Children from large families seem to do better at school.
   d Children want to be the same as their friends and different from their parents.
   e Parents should let their children begin to make their own decisions from the age of eight.

G ···⟫ page 199

Listening

1 Do you watch more or less television now compared to when you were a child? Do you and your family/friends have the same taste in television programmes?

2 🎧 You will hear five short extracts in which people give their opinions about TV programmes. As you listen, match the speakers (1–5) to the programmes (A–H).

   Speaker 1
   Speaker 2
   Speaker 3
   Speaker 4
   Speaker 5

   A *Naturally Yours*
   B *Elizabeth*
   C *Food and Drink*
   D *Sci-fi Season*
   E *Walking with Dinosaurs*
   F *The Cops*
   G *Wind-down-for-bedtime*
   H *I love the 80s*

3 🎧 Listen again and match the speakers (1–5) to the opinions (A–H).

   Speaker 1
   Speaker 2
   Speaker 3
   Speaker 4
   Speaker 5

   A The programme's normality was what appealed.
   B I'm not sure all the facts are correct.
   C I can't imagine why original pieces weren't used.
   D I think the focus of the programme was all wrong.
   E I don't think the title reflects the programme's content.
   F I admit to being a bit of a nostalgia fan.
   G The jokey undertones and use of special effects made it.
   H The music was inappropriate.

4 Work in small groups and discuss the questions below.

   a Why do you think some people find horror films so exciting while others cannot watch them?
   b What makes a good comedy? Is it the characters the actors play, the story line or the language?
   c Do you think westerns are losing their appeal?
   d What sort of people like action programmes? Do they appeal to the lazy or the dynamic?

Topic review

a Some people say that beauty is in the eye of the beholder. Do you agree?

b Do you think you can judge a book by its cover?

c What was the last really good dream you had?

d Have you ever dreamed in English?

e Do you agree that travelling broadens the mind?

f Chewing is supposed to prevent travel sickness. Do you know any other remedies like this?

g How many different languages can you speak?

h Have you ever had anything stolen? If so, what?

i Do you prefer to spend your holidays with your family or friends?

j What would you like your children to achieve in their lives?

Reading

1 You are going to read an extract from a short story. In it, Mrs Foster hates the idea of being late for anything and her husband deliberately wastes time to make her anxious. At this point in the story, Mrs Foster and her husband are about to take a chauffeur-driven car to the airport. Read the extract and answer the following questions.

a Why does Mr Foster want to go back into the house?

b How does Mrs Foster react?

c What clues about the relationship between the husband and wife does the extract provide?

d How does the use of direct speech add to the atmosphere the author wants to create?

'Hurry, please,' she said to the chauffeur. 'Don't bother about the rug. I'll arrange the rug. Please get going. I'm late.'

The man went back to his seat behind the wheel and started the engine.

'*Just* a moment!' Mr Foster said suddenly. 'Hold it a moment, chauffeur, will you?'

'What is it dear?' She saw him searching the pockets of his overcoat.

'I had a little present I wanted you to take to Ellen,' he said. 'Now, where on earth is it? I'm sure I had it in my hand as I came down.'

'I never saw you carrying anything. What sort of present?'

'A little box wrapped up in white paper. I forgot to give it to you yesterday. I don't want to forget it today.'

'A little box!' Mrs Foster cried. 'I never saw any little box!'

She began searching frantically in the back of the car.

Her husband continued searching through the pockets of his coat. Then he unbuttoned the coat and felt around in his jacket.

'Confound it,' he said, 'I must've left it in my bedroom. I won't be a moment.'

'Oh, *please*!' she cried. 'We haven't got time! *Please* leave it! You can mail it. It's only one of those silly combs anyway. You're always giving her combs.'

'And what's wrong with combs, may I ask?' he said, furious that she should have forgotten herself for once.

'Nothing, dear, I'm sure. But ...'

'Stay here!' he commanded. 'I'm going to get it.'

'Be quick, dear! Oh, *please* be quick!'

She sat still, waiting and waiting.

Grammar

1 You are going to read a newspaper article about Levi jeans. Put the verbs (1–10) in brackets into the correct form.

The $25,000 Levi's

The men who wore them didn't come much tougher and neither did their jeans. This battered pair of Levi's are reckoned (1) .... (be) the oldest in the world – a remarkable survivor of the Wild West. Such is their rarity that, even in their washed out and torn state, they are expected (2) .... (fetch) $25,000 when sold at auction. These Levi's were found (3) .... (lie) in a pile of mud two years ago in an old silver mining town in Nevada. The owner, who wants (4) .... (remain) anonymous, has refused (5) .... (say) exactly where they were found, or how he came by them. Tests have shown, however, that they were made around 1880, when they probably cost the equivalent of 75p, when the miners came (6) .... (flock) to the American frontier in search of their fortune. As they scrabbled (7) .... (find) silver in the harsh conditions of the Nevada desert, the miners needed clothes (8) .... (stand up to) the job – and they found them in the durable, riveted trousers invented by Levi Strauss and partner Jacob Davis. Metal rivets were used (9) .... (secure) the pockets because miners kept (10) .... (complain) their pockets were ripping off as they worked.

Speaking

1 Working in small groups, devise a study questionnaire for other students in the class. Below are some suggested headings for your questionnaire and an example question to help you get started. The aim is to revise past tenses, the present perfect, the passive and the gerund and infinitive so you should try to devise questions using these forms.

Vocabulary: Did you start a separate section of your file for vocabulary when you started this course?

Grammar: How much grammar had you studied before starting this course?

Listening: How much do you think your listening skills have improved?

Speaking: Have you taken full advantage of speaking activities?

Reading: Do you think you have been given too much, too little or just enough reading to do?

Writing: Do you enjoy doing the writing tasks?

Exam preparation: Have you been given enough information about the content of the CAE exam?

2 Using your questionnaire, interview a student from a different group and then let them interview you. When you have finished, discuss your English; how is it progressing and what you are going to do to improve it from now on?

Vocabulary

1 Here is another extract from the short story about Mrs Foster, who hated being late. Use the words in capitals at the end of the lines to form a word that fits the gaps (1–7).

Mr Foster may (1) .... have had a right to be irritated by	**POSSIBLE**
this (2) ....of his wife's, but he could have had no	**FOOL**
excuse for increasing her (3) .... by keeping her waiting	**MISERABLE**
(4) .... Mind you, it is by no means certain that this is	**NECESSARY**
what he did, yet whenever they were to go somewhere, his	
(5) .... was so accurate – just a minute or two late, you	**TIME**
understand – and his manner so bland that it was hard to	
believe he wasn't (6) .... inflicting a nasty private little	**PURPOSE**
torture of his own on the (7) .... lady.	**HAPPY**

UNIT 16 Raving and panning

By George, they've done it!

Unaccustomed as you are to public speaking, this will sort you out

THE BLACK PRINCE ALMOST SCORES

144 levels of fun

Ensnared by love – you'll be caught too

Speaking 1

1 Look at the headlines above which are all from reviews.

  a What do you think they might be reviewing?
  b Can you tell from the headline whether the review is mainly praising or criticising?

2 Work with a partner and answer the questions.

  a What is the significance of the title of this unit?
  b List as many things as possible that may be reviewed in the media.
  c What sorts of things do you read (or listen to) reviews of?
  d Has a rave review or a panning ever affected you?

Reading

1 Read the extracts opposite from the reviews (A–E) and note what kind of thing is being reviewed and whether the critic's opinion is basically favourable or unfavourable.

2 Look at the statements below. Are they true, false or is the information not given in the extracts?

  1 a The writer had planned to stay at The George.
    b The George is near a place called Aviemore.
    c The George is very expensive.
  2 a Howard's story is partially autobiographical.
    b It is a detective story.
    c It tells how a seemingly intelligent middle-aged woman was deliberately deceived by a man.
  3 a Grag and Thog are troll brothers.
    b They are super-intelligent.
    c The game is not too difficult to complete.
  4 a Nick Cave's music has changed style.
    b Nick Cave has a very powerful voice.
    c This new album consists largely of happy love songs.
  5 a The website gives advice about public speaking.
    b It contains a lot of anecdotes suitable for including in speeches.
    c The website was only partially complete when the review was written.

A

I stumbled on The George one holiday when I drove the family mad dragging them everywhere searching for my McPherson roots – there's an area near Aviemore with lots of family connections. It's set on a huge loch with water so deep it looks black and it's framed by charcoal blue mountains and looks like a mock Venetian folly. I had a fabulous night there talking to a genealogist who charges Americans £500 to chart their family tree. I've been back there since on the pretext of doing a documentary about the McPhersons for TV but I never made it out of The George. It's that kind of place.

B

Have you ever wondered how an intelligent woman could fall for a callous con man? Here, with icy inevitability the process is laid bare. Howard examines predator and prey, exposing the workings of both minds as the trap is gently laid and we sit back, transfixed, to watch the kill. This subtle romance of late middle age reads more like a thriller – with the added piquancy of knowing there are parallels with the author's own life. Prepare to be seduced.

C

POOR OLD GRAG AND THOG. The two brothers don't have a care in their pea-sized brains until an earthquake opens the way for hordes of pesky creatures from the surface to invade their troll homelands deep within the bowels of the earth. Due to a little misunderstanding, the brothers manage to volunteer themselves to expel the invaders and so begins their quest to clear all twelve realms of the underworld. Veteran gamers may notice that this game is based on the arcade classic, Mario Bros. It has 144 standard levels divided into 12 themed worlds. Dogs, wasps, spiders and other critters emerge at the top of the levels and proceed across the screen, dropping through holes in the platforms. Grag and Thog won't stretch your new iMac to the limits but they will provide you with hours of light-hearted entertainment.

D

After years playing the darkest, most haunted princeling in all rock's gothic underworld, Nick Cave's finest moment came when he abandoned morose noise-mongering for the quiet piano balladry of 1997's *The Boatman's Call*. With *No More Shall We Part*, Cave takes half a pace backwards towards his anguished past. While songs like *Love Letter* maintain the contemplative style of *Into My Arms*, the record also comes loaded with smoking guns, darkening days and 'black trees bent to the ground'. It's as if, after reflecting on the pain and profundity of love, Cave is rediscovering his anger at the world.

E

Is one of your worst nightmares having to stand up in front of an audience and 'say a few words'? If so, sweat no more. Speechtips.com is a concise guide to speech-writing for every occasion. In easy steps, it teaches you the basics of planning (the occasion, the audience, their expectations), writing (the correct structure) and delivery (notes or memory). Its common-sense advice should be compulsory reading for many would-be orators. Unfortunately, the practical section of Speechtips ('speech guides' e.g. weddings, eulogies, retirement, school, awards ceremonies) was still under construction as we went to press.

3 Now read the reviews in more detail and complete the table below. Identify the words and expressions that tell you about the subject of the review and those which indicate the critic's attitude.

Text	Words identifying the topic	Positive words and expressions	Negative words and expressions
A	*The George – it's set – had a fabulous night there – that kind of place*	*fabulous*	*nothing negative in the piece*
B			
C			
D			
E			

4 To what extent would you like to try out each of the things reviewed?

Speaking 2

E xam spot

In the CAE Speaking test (Paper 5), you need to give your opinions and perhaps suggest how things could be done differently or improved. This is the kind of language that can also be useful when reviewing something.

1 You are going to work on some expressions that a producer of a play uses when trying to decide how to organise a production. Fill the gaps with a suitable word. The first letter of each missing word is provided.

   a Why d..................... we hire costumes?

   b I'd suggest g..................... Jackie Brown the lead – she was the strongest person at the auditions.

   c We might as w..................... have the dress rehearsal on the Sunday before the first performance.

   d So am I r..................... in saying that the theatre will be available for rehearsals every morning?

   e In other w..................... , we should have plenty of opportunity to rehearse on the stage itself.

   f Isn't it mainly a m..................... of careful planning?

   g I'm not entirely c..................... that we should cut that bit you suggest from the second act.

   h I agree with you on the w..................... but there are a couple of things I'd like to t..................... you up on.

2 Look again at the sentences above and underline the expressions that are useful for giving opinions and making suggestions.

3 Work in groups. You are going to plan the reviews section for a class magazine. As you work, try to use some of the language for giving opinions or making suggestions.

   a Discuss what you are going to review, e.g. restaurants, films, books, plays, TV, music, websites, local facilities and so on.

   b Discuss what guidelines the reviewers need to be given, e.g. how many words to write, whether they should aim to give a strong opinion or to be more balanced and what exactly you would like from them.

   c Present your plans to the other students. How are they different?

   d Now write your reveiw (approximately 250 words).

Articles and determiners

1 Look at the reviews in Reading 1 again and underline all the articles and determiners used in them. Answer the following questions about their use.

Review A

   a Why is it *The George*?

   b Why is it *a huge loch* and not *the huge loch*?

   c Why is it *Americans* and not *the Americans* or *some Americans*?

Review B

   a Why is the indefinite article used in the first sentence?

   b Why is it *the process* in the next sentence?

   c Why is it *the author* at the end of this review?

Review C

   a Why is it *their* rather than *the* before *pea-sized brains*?

   b Why is it *the* rather than *an arcade classic*?

Review D

   a Why is it *the* before *quiet piano balladry*?

   b Why is it *the* before *ground* and *world* in the last two sentences?

Review E

   a Why is it *a few words* and not *few words*?

   b Why is *the* used in the first two sets of bracketed notes but not in the third set?

2 These sentences illustrate some of the most common mistakes that advanced learners make with articles in English. Correct the sentences and then explain what the rule is in each case.

   a The life is hard!

   b Life of the poor in a country with no welfare state is very hard.

   c My brother is biochemist in London.

   d Jack broke the leg skiing.

   e He's only 18 but he already has the own business.

   f Maria's on a business trip to People's Republic of China.

   g Do they sell fruit in the USA by kilo or pound?

   h Since they built the tunnel, fewer people are using a ferry.

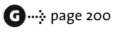 **G** ⋯⟶ page 200

Listening

1 Look at these pictures. What kinds of film or show do you think they come from?

   EXAMPLE: *I think the first picture must be from a cowboy film. You can tell by the costumes and the location!*

2 Which of the types of films or shows in the pictures do you like best and which do you like least?

3 🎧 Listen to two people discussing films they have recently seen and answer the questions below.

   a What is being discussed?
   b List all the facts that you learn about the films.
   c What words and expressions do the speakers use to make their feelings clear?

4 Choose two of the categories in the box. Choose one example from each of these categories that you would recommend to a partner and one that you would not recommend. Explain your choices to your partner.

   | film | website | novel | theatre production |
   | computer game | CD | restaurant | hotel |

Vocabulary

1 Here are some collocations from the reviews you have read and listened to. Match the first half of the collocation (a–l) with the second half (1–12).

a	have	g	arcade
b	breathing	h	light-hearted
c	drive	i	love
d	family	j	smoking
e	lay	k	worst
f	middle	l	compulsory

1	mad	7	entertainment
2	age	8	guns
3	classic	9	tree
4	letter	10	nightmare
5	reading	11	reservations
6	bare	12	space

2 Choose a collocation from Vocabulary 1 to complete the sentences.

   a Is there any .... to do before the history course you're doing this summer?
   b Many people can only do three or four generations of their ....
   c In the attic I found some bundles of old .... tied up in pink ribbon.
   d When do you think .... begins? 45? 50?
   e It's not a profound film in any way – it's just good ....

3 Work with a partner to add to the sets of collocations below.

   a family ......tree...........................
   b to drive someone ......mad..........
   c love ......letter...........................
   d middle ......age...........................
   e to lay ......bare...........................

Exam folder 7

Paper 1 Parts 1 and 4 Multiple matching

In Part 1 and Part 4 of the CAE Reading test (Paper 1), you have to match questions or prompts to bits of text. There are two basic reading skills: scanning and skimming. Scanning means reading for specific information while skimming means reading quickly through a text to get a general impression of the content. You will need to make use of both these skills in these two parts of the reading test.

Advice

- Read the subtitle to get a general idea of what the text is about.
- Read the questions before you scan for the information/opinions needed.
- Read the whole of each question very carefully.
- Skim the whole of the text before you scan for the information/opinions needed.
- Don't rely on matching up individual words or phrases in the question and the text just because they are the same or similar.
- Don't rely on finding all the information you need for a question in just one part of the text.

1 Work with a partner. Read the two film reviews below. Which film appeals to you more and why?

film review

Hannah and Her Sisters

True creativity means that an artist can mine the same seam time after time and still come up with something fresh.

Targeting once again the arty, neurotic residents of New York with his familiar exhilarating combination of melancholy sentiment and witty cynicism, Woody Allen relishes their foibles and celebrates their triumphs, backing up his tale with some touching period tunes.

Michael Caine and Dianne Wiest (both Oscar-winners), not to mention Woody himself, playing a hypochondriac, can do no wrong. This is Allen in complete control of his enormous talent.

It all starts today

Director Bertrand Tavernier will become the hero of teachers everywhere for this no-nonsense portrait of a profession in which surrogate parenting and welfare work are now as important as educating. Winner of the international critics' prize at Berlin, it recalls the fluid starkness of Tavernier's police thriller *L. 627*, as the camera restlessly prowls headmaster Philippe Torreton's school to witness how his staff make light of financial constraints to fascinate and protect their pupils. Torreton's performance is outstanding in its energy and insight and, apart from the disappointingly cosy and optimistic conclusion, this is social drama at its best.

2   Now read the reviews below and answer the following questions.

a   Which of these films does the reviewer like least?
b   Which one is a serious drama?
c   Which is a political comedy?
d   In which two is the reviewer critical of the acting?
e   Which one deals with the less glamorous side of the pop world?
f   In which one does the director not use his full name?
g   Which one relates to a type of film that was popular about forty years ago?
h   Which one is the longest?
i   Which two are the cheapest?
j   Which one has a scene centring round a type of traditional British food?

new on video

★★★★★ **Excellent**   ★★★★ **Very Good**   ★★★ **Good**   ★★ **Poor**   ★ **Give it a miss**

1 Charlie's Angels ★★

Columbia Tristar, 15, 99 mins, 2000; rental, £19.99 (DVD)

As the first scene in-joke has it: "Not another film based on an old TV series?" Well, yes, but one that took £13m at the UK box office and that combines high-tech hyperactivity with arch camp. Plus, it has Drew Barrymore in a shell suit, not to mention the free-dancing, ever-grinning, good-meal-needing Cameron Diaz and foxy brainbox Lucy Liu. Hard to tell whether the name of the director, McG, indicates cool or embarrassment, for this is little more than a stunt-filled extended pop promo.

2 Yes, Minister:
Party Games ★★★★

BBC, PG, 61 mins, 1984; £10.99 (VHS)

Not a bad time given the upcoming election to revisit Antony Jay and Jonathan Lynn's extended episode of *Yes, Minister*, first seen on December 17, 1984, detailing how Jim Hacker rises from ministerial nonentity to national leader via a Churchillian stand on the sanctity of the British sausage. Paul Eddington's minister not only narrowly survives a seasonal drink-driving charge, but uses his position as party chairman effectively to blackmail two more gifted but morally fragile colleagues, played by James Grout and Peter Jeffrey. It's worth noting that, in the old days, senior civil servants like Nigel Hawthorne's Sir Humphrey doubled up as spin doctors, thus saving a figure currently estimated at £80m a year.

3 Perfect Strangers ★★★★

BBC, 15, 237 mins, 2001; £19.99 (VHS)

A quick release by the BBC for Stephen Poliakoff's epic of the family just seen on TV, inspired by his own life and using photography as a way into those hidden parts and secret silences that form part of our individual and collective identity. Superbly cast, it stars Lindsay Duncan and Timothy Spall, who featured in its predecessor, *Shooting the Past*, as well as Michael Gambon and Matthew Macfadyen, in the pivotal role of Daniel. As a director, Poliakoff deliberately avoids the fast-paced cutting of today, which makes for languor and intimacy, but sometimes encourages the actors to strut their stuff at the expense of the whole. That said, it's remarkable.

4 Sugar Town ★★★

FilmFour/VCI, 15, 89 mins, 2000; £12.99 (VHS)

A sly and cynical comedy set amid the rock-music and showbiz world of Los Angeles, made by Allison Anders and Kurt Voss. It may interest fans of soap star Martin Kemp and Duran Duran's John Taylor. The former gets to say all the rude words he's not allowed to say on the soap, as a former 1980s rock icon reduced to dealing drugs. Meanwhile Taylor, of Duran Duran fame, makes his acting debut as another former legend of the mike, now short of a record deal and lumbered with a frustrated wife and a recently arrived angry kid whom he is said to have fathered. Also features Rosanna Arquette, Ally Sheedy and Michael DesBarres.

5 Hammer House of Horror:
Vols 3 and 4 ★★★

Carlton, 15, 150/200 mins, 1980; £10.99 (VHS)

This television nostalgia classic may soothe those who long for a bit of good old-fashioned gothic. They were produced by the immortal Roy Skeggs, who worked on the original Hammer films, which became so renowned in the 1960s and 1970s that the name was franchised out for this series. It was famous for its theme tune, bad scripts, improbable manor-house settings, classic horror plot lines and obsession with car accidents. It also featured the likes of Denholm Elliot, Diana Dors, Pierce Brosnan and Julia Foster in performances that will not be written on their gravestones. Great fun, though.

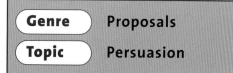

Genre	Proposals
Topic	Persuasion

Exam spot

You may be asked to write a proposal in the CAE Writing test (Paper 2) and you may also have a negotiating or discussion task in the Speaking test (Paper 5). This unit helps you with the language needed for such tasks.

Speaking 1

1 Read the adverts (a–d) below and decide which of the people in the photos might be most likely to apply for each one.

2 With a partner, discuss the travel grant (a). Where exactly would you go and what would you do there? What would you need the money for?

3 Now discuss any other one of the adverts you might like to respond to. What project or course would you want the money for? List all the specific things that you would need to spend the money on.

Reading

1 Imagine that you and your friends are considering applying for the travel grant (a). What would you need to do before you write your proposal to give it a better chance of success?

a

Calling all students who wish to travel to further their studies:

Money is available for:
- travel and living expenses
- computers, books and other relevant study equipment
- fees for appropriate courses.

Phone our office for information about what you may and may not be entitled to and for instructions as to how to submit your proposal.

b

Have you got a good business idea but no funds to put it into practice?

We can offer set-up grants to people with original and viable ideas.

All proposals must be submitted by the end of this month.

c

The local council has money available for projects that would benefit the local community.

Have you got a suggestion for something that would improve the quality of life for local residents?

Call us and we'll arrange an appointment to discuss your proposal.

d

BORED WITH YOUR LIFE? TIME FOR A CHANGE? WHY NOT RETRAIN?

Grants available for deserving applicants who would like to do one of a wide range of retraining courses at a number of local further education colleges. Send us a one page proposal explaining what you would like to do and why.

2 Now read the guidance below. Tick any of the points that are relevant to your travel grant proposal. Mark with a cross any of the points that you do not think would be relevant to your proposal.

Tips on Preparing a Successful Proposal

The following is a list of tips or advice by project reviewers and others familiar with proposal development and review.

● **Be realistic:** what can reasonably be accomplished in the scope (time and resources) of this grant?

● **Be factual and specific:** don't talk in generalities or in emotional terms. Be able to substantiate all statements in your proposal, otherwise don't make them.

● **Use language anyone will understand:** no abbreviations, initials, or jargon. Don't assume the reader will understand your acronyms or abbreviations.

● **Read the guidelines carefully!** Make your proposal fit the funding requirements. Don't ask for things that are outside of the intent of the grant.

● **Choose a format that's clear and easy to read:** readers are overloaded with proposals and appreciate legible, attractive proposals.

● **Stick to the specified number of pages:** extra pages or attachments may either be removed before the proposal is read, or may disqualify your entire proposal from the reading process.

● **Do it yourself:** teach your own staff about proposal writing. But if you hire a development person or a consultant, stay on top of it; proposals exclusively written by development people usually don't make sense because that person isn't familiar with the project.

● **Give details about who will do what:** think of all the details, such as ordering materials, cataloguing and managing them, arranging for staff development, etc. Make sure someone is assigned to manage each step of the project.

● **Be clear** about the type and amount of staff development required, and the amount of time necessary for staff to feel confident about implementing the project. Be realistic!

● **Check** current prices of hardware, software, and materials you plan to purchase for this project. Also include staff development costs: consultant fees, substitute fees and associated materials costs.

● **Give evidence of district or school site support:** if there are matching funds available, or your site or district has a demonstrated commitment to this project, describe the commitment.

● **Call** if you have questions, but realise that many others will be calling as well. Don't wait until the last minute.

- Read the directions.
- Read the directions.
- Read the directions.

Listening

1 With a partner, discuss these questions.

a List any situations when you have had to persuade someone to do something.

b How did you persuade them to do what you wanted? How easy was it to do so?

c When is it particularly difficult to persuade someone to do something?

d What sorts of techniques can be used to try to persuade people to do things that they are reluctant to do?

2 🎧 Listen to eight people trying to persuade others to do different things. As you listen, complete the table.

Speaker	What speaker wants others to do	How speaker tries to persuade them
1		
2		
3		
4		
5		
6		
7		
8		

3 Work with a partner and take it in turns to try to persuade each other to do some of the things below. Use language from Listening 2 where appropriate.

- go on a scary roller coaster ride
- fly to an exotic place for a weekend break with you
- sell you one of their treasured possessions (perhaps a bike, a favourite computer game, CD or piece of jewellery)
- help you move a piano up some stairs
- teach you a skill (e.g. to drive a car or play the violin)
- lend you a large sum of money
- go with you to a social function that they really do not want to go to
- have their hair dyed
- change their job

Language of persuasion

There are often several ways of saying the same thing that are all grammatically correct. One may, however, fit a particular set of circumstances better because it conveys a slightly different nuance of meaning. For instance, it may sometimes be better to be more tentative and polite whereas sometimes it may be better to be more direct.

1 Look at the different ways below of persuading someone to do something. Which would be the better alternative to use in the situations outlined?

1 A new employee thinks his boss has not been as thorough as she should have been in a report.
  a Are you absolutely certain that you've taken everything into account?
  b This is rather careless work.

2 A teenage girl wants her father to change his mind and let her go to an all-night party.
  a Are you quite sure you won't reconsider?
  b Just this once. Please!

3 A husband is trying to persuade his wife that they should take part in a marathon.
  a Please, just do it for my sake.
  b How can I convince you of the sense of what I'm suggesting?

4 The manager of a sales department is trying to persuade his staff to work longer hours.
  a Couldn't you be persuaded to give it a try?
  b Come on, just do it for me.

5 A father is trying to persuade his young son to swim the length of a pool.
  a Oh come on, have a try. It's not as hard as it looks.
  b It's in your own best interests to do what I suggest.

6 A woman is trying to put an end to a small quarrel with a friend.
  a Surely the most sensible thing would be to take some independent advice?
  b Don't be like that. Please!

7 A businessman is trying to persuade fellow workers at a meeting about what the company should do.
  a You're a load of idiots if you can't understand what I'm driving at.
  b The best course of action would be to survey our markets for their reactions.

2 Complete the table in an appropriate way, using formal and informal expressions.

Persuading someone to	Formal	Informal
help you check some written work	Could you possibly find time to check through this report for me, please?	Cast your eye over this for me, will you?
change their mind		Come off it! You're being really stubborn.
lend you some money	I'd be really grateful if you could possibly lend me ten pounds until Monday.	
do something a little dangerous		Come on. Don't be scared. You'll be OK.
change their appearance in some way	Madam would look wonderful if her hair had highlights put in it.	
learn some new computer skills		

3 Work with a partner.

a Write a dialogue in which a teenager tries to persuade a parent to let them do something. There should be at least eight exchanges in your dialogue.

b Write another dialogue in which a manager tries to persuade a member of her staff to do something that they are reluctant to do. Again, there should be at least eight exchanges in the dialogue.

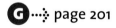 G ⋯ page 201

Vocabulary

Many words in the texts you have been working on in this unit have multiple meanings. For example, in the title *Tips on Preparing a Successful Proposal, tips* means advice, but *tip* can also mean:

- an extra payment for a service
- the pointed end of something like a pencil
- a place for depositing rubbish
- to make something not straight

Proposal here means a formal, written suggestion but it can also mean an offer of marriage.

1 In each of the sets of sentences below, one word from the reading text can be used to complete the three gaps. Which word fits each set?

1 • I even managed to save money from my student ....
   • Sarah's a good writer, I .... you.
   • His request that they .... him asylum was rejected.
2 • University .... tend to be shorter than school ones.
   • Be sure to read all the .... of the agreement before signing anything.
   • Sam always speaks of his boss in glowing ....
3 • She forgot to .... a stamp on the envelope.
   • My grandma's got quite unsteady on her feet and usually uses a ....
   • I wish the speaker would .... to the point.
4 • I've got a terrible .... of direction.
   • Can you make any .... of what he's trying to say?
   • There's no .... in waiting here any longer.
5 • What's her .... address?
   • The strong .... makes it dangerous to swim here.
   • We'd better transfer some money into our .... account.

2 Here are some more words from this unit which have multiple meanings in English. Can you think of at least two senses for each word?

| call | course | direction | fit | order | own | step | sum |

Speaking 2

1 Work in small groups. You are going to go on holiday as a group. Each group should choose a different kind of holiday.

a Discuss ways to persuade the other groups that this would be the best type of holiday for you all to go on. Think also of the objections that the other groups might raise and of how you could counter those objections. You may need to consider these aspects of the holiday:

| activities | accommodation | cost |
| fun | learning experience | weather |

b Regroup and take it in turns to present the holidays you have been thinking about. Try to persuade the others that your idea is the best one. Raise as many objections as you can to other suggestions that are made.

c At the end vote on which holiday you think your group should go on. You are not allowed to vote for your own suggestion.

d Feed back to the class as a whole, saying which holiday your group voted for and why.

Writing folder 7

Reviews

1 What is the purpose of a review?

a to interest and entertain the reader
b to describe the subject of the review to the reader
c to convey the writer's opinion about the subject of the review
d to promote the subject of the review
e something else

2 Read the film review below. As you read, think about whether you would like to see this film (if you have not seen it). If you have seen it, think about whether it seems to be a fair review of the film. Then make notes in the table below.

Facts about the film	Phrases that convey the writer's opinion of the film	Things included to interest and entertain the reader

M:I MISSION: IMPLAUSIBLE

Shortly before Mission: Impossible 2 opened in the United States, the Wall Street Journal ran a front-page story about an editing genius who was called in at the last hour to reorganise the film. Seemingly, the critics were concerned that John Woo's highly anticipated sequel to Brian de Palma's unbelievably complicated but hugely entertaining Mission: Impossible was a bit hard to follow. Now that the finished product has been released, it's possible to report that the sequel, at the very least, has a story line that makes sense. It's klunky, it's goofy, it has holes big enough to drive the entire United States Marine Corps through, but at least it can be followed. Thank heavens for small mercies. And industrious editors.

M:I 2 is the kind of movie that intelligent, self-respecting critics (there are seven of us, globally) hate to review. Because it's a summer blockbuster, because it's already a mammoth hit in the United States, and because, despite its faults, it's quite an engaging film, it seems almost churlish to say anything negative about it. Thus, let me preface my remarks by stating that, while M:I 2 is not nearly as good as the original, it isn't a dud.

This time out Ethan Hunt (Tom Cruise) is forced to abbreviate a rock-climbing vacation in order to save the world in general and Australia in particular from a lethal virus that has fallen into the hands of fiendish villains. Well, in fact, the fiendish villains, though very, very cruel, are such ninnies that they have only secured one half of the virus and need the other half in order to bring the world to its knees. In exchange for returning their half of the virus, or all of the virus, or some combination thereof, the villains are demanding the nice round sum of £37 million.

It is a little unclear why the unspeakable forces of pure, unadulterated evil are asking for a measly £37 million when £3 billion and complete domination of New South Wales seems a more reasonable asking price.

But never mind.

It's a great relief when the tangled threads of the plot finally coalesce. In a way it's almost a shame that Woo had to even bother with a plot since all anyone really wants to see in a John Woo movie is some good-looking guy – or John Travolta – cavorting on a motorcycle, plunging through plate glass windows, just generally raising hell.

3   Is the title of the review an effective one? Why?/Why not?

4   Is there anything else about the language of the review that you think in some way reflects the content of the film?

5   There are a lot of strong collocations in this review. Pick three that you would like to learn. Did you select the same ones as other students in the class?

6   Reviews often use emphatic language. This can be done by using adverb + adjective combinations such as *unbelievably complicated* and *hugely entertaining*.

Find two collocating adjectives for each of these adverbs:

	1 stupid
	2 disappointing
	3 dull
a bitterly	4 cold
b deeply	5 grateful
c intensely	6 irresistible
d highly	7 regarded
e utterly	8 irritating
f perfectly	9 entertaining
	10 suited
	11 formed
	12 personal

7   Now try this exam task.

An international arts magazine is preparing a feature on TV programmes that viewers find particularly original or unusual.

Write a review in which you:

- outline the programme you choose

- explain why you consider it original or unusual

- discuss what you believe the aims of the programme makers were

- comment on whether you felt the programme achieved its aims successfully or not.

Write your **review** in about 250 words.

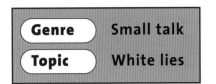

UNIT 18 | May I introduce ... ?

Genre Small talk
Topic White lies

Speaking 1

1 With a partner, discuss these questions.

a Look at the pictures. Which jobs are represented in them?

b Would you expect the people doing the jobs in the pictures to lie? If so, in what circumstances?

c Do you ever lie to people you don't know?

d How often do you think you lie in one day?

e Do you think lying is ever right?

I must not tell lies. I must not tell pointless lies. I must not te *pointless lies at parties. I must not tell pointless lies at partie* *when they are plainly going to be found out in the next te* *minutes. I must not:*

1 Let it be thought that I have caught the name of anyone I am ever introduced t because statistics show that I have never caught anyone's name until I have hea it at least twelve times.

2 Give it to be understood that I have already heard of the owner of the inaudib name, because tests show that, apart from one or two obvious exceptions lik William Shakespeare, I haven't heard of anyone.

3 Say I have read the man's books, or admired his architecture, or used his firm's bra linings, or seen his agency's advertisements, or always been interested in his field research, or know his home town, because I do hereby make a solemn ar unconditional declaration, being before witnesses and in sober realisation of my pa wrong-doing, that I have done none of these things.

4 Say that I know any of the people he is sure I must know, or have heard of any the names that he takes to be common knowledge, because I don't and I haven or if I do and have, I've got them all hopelessly mixed up, and when he says Palm I'm thinking of Palermo, and when he says syncretism, I'm thinking of syndicalisr

5 Try to sustain the fiction that I have heard anything he has said to me over th noise, because I have not and because he has heard nothing I have said either s that by analogy he knows I am lying just as I know he is lying.

6 Bend my lips in an attempt to counterfeit a smile unless I am absolutely assure by the raising of a flag with the word JOKE on it, that the man has made a jo and not announced that his mother has died.

7 In short, get involved in any more conversations that go: 'I've long been a gre admirer of your, er ... stuff, Mr ... er, er ... '
'How kind of you!'
'Oh, all kinds.'
'No, I'm afraid some critics haven't been at all kind.'
'The tall kind? I see. I see. I particularly liked your last boo ... er, pla ... , er, one
'Really? The press panned it.'
'The Press Bandit – of course, it was on the tip of my tongue.'
'Well, the Irish banned it.'
'I mean The Irish Bandit, of course. How stupid of me!'
I smile a cryptic, knowing smile. He smiles a cryptic, knowing smile. We're getti on wonderfully. Just then my wife comes up and wants to be introduced and I ha to ask the man who he is.
Why do I do these things? Do I think the man's going to give me a fiver or a yea free supply of his works for having heard of his name? Is he going to twist my ar and kick me in the kneecap if I don't like his stuff? He doesn't expect me to li it. No one likes it except his wife and the editor of *Spasm*.
I must not waste my valuable talent for deceit on lies which have no conceivab purpose when I could be saving it up for lies which would show a cash return.
I must instead say 'I'm sorry, I didn't quite catch your name.'
I must say 'I'm sorry, I still haven't quite ...'
I must say 'I'm sorry – did you say Green or Queen? Ah, Queen Who? Come aga ... Queen Elizabeth? Elizabeth what?'
I must say 'I expect I should know but I don't – what do you do? I beg your pard – rain? You mean you study it, do you – rainfall statistics and so on? No? You rai You mean you actually rain yourself? I see, I see.'
I must say 'No, I don't see. What do you mean, you rain ...?'
I must ...
I must not, on second thoughts, be pointlessly honest either.

Reading

1 Read the text and think about the writer and the situation he is in.

   a Where is he?
   b What is he doing?
   c Why is he behaving like this?

2 Which of these things does the writer mention lying about?

   a his own name
   b having heard of someone else
   c admiring someone's work
   d the importance of his own work
   e knowing important people
   f knowing someone's home town
   g pretending to like a joke he did not think was amusing
   h pretending to have met the Queen

3 Why does a misunderstanding occur in the imagined conversations between:

   a the writer and 'Mr … er … er'?
   b the writer and the Queen?

4 After listing his seven points, does the writer promise never to lie again?

5 At the end of the article, what conclusion does the writer come to? Why do you think he comes to this conclusion?

6 The writer occasionally uses language that might remind the reader of other types of English. Match the extracts (a–c) with the styles (1–3).

   a … statistics show that … tests show that …
   b because I do hereby make a solemn and unconditional declaration, being before witnesses and in sober realisation of my past wrong-doing, that I have done none of these things.
   c I must not tell lies. I must not tell pointless lies. I must not tell pointless lies at parties. I must not tell pointless lies at parties when they are plainly going to be found out in the next ten minutes.

   1 a schoolchild writing lines as punishment
   2 someone swearing an oath in a law court
   3 the language of advertising

7 Have you ever done any of the seven things listed by the writer in this article?

Vocabulary

As with most texts, this article is full of collocations and longer chunks of language.

EXAMPLE: *pointless lies*
they are plainly going to be found out
in the next ten minutes

1 Read through the text, underlining any chunks or collocations that you think are particularly useful for you. Compare the ones you selected with those chosen by a partner.

2 Form chunks that were used in the text by matching words on the left with words on the right.

a	a cash	1	exceptions
b	field of	2	town
c	a knowing	3	research
d	a year's free	4	thoughts
e	with one or two obvious	5	my arm
f	hopelessly	6	smile
g	no conceivable	7	mixed up
h	on second	8	return
i	to catch	9	your name
j	to make	10	a declaration
k	to twist	11	supply
l	home	12	purpose

3 Choose one of the chunks or collocations from Vocabulary 2 to complete each sentence. Make any grammatical changes as necessary.

   a I'm sorry. It's so noisy here. I'm afraid I didn't ....
   b The twins are identical. I always get them ....
   c I'll send him an email explaining the situation. No, ... , it would probably be better if I phoned him.
   d I'm going to your .... on a business trip next month. Is there anything I should make a point of seeing or doing while I'm there?
   e If I win the competition, I'll get .... of toothpaste!
   f Oh all right then, I'll come to the party with you, as you ....
   g Most of the students in my English class, ... , are pretty good at arriving on time and doing all their homework conscientiously.
   h I can see .... whatsoever for this gadget.
   i Come and meet Jack. He's doing post-graduate work in the same .... as your cousin.

Cleft sentences and other ways of emphasising

Cleft (divided) sentences are a useful way of adding emphasis both when we are speaking and when we are writing. Here are some examples of cleft sentences.

- *Admit that I did not understand is all that I have to learn to do.*
- *What I have to learn to do is admit that I did not understand.*
- *All that I have to do is admit that I did not understand.*
- *Someone who is always totally honest when she doesn't catch a name is my wife.*
- *What I tend to do is pretend to have heard when I haven't.*
- *What happens is that I pretend to have understood when I've hardly caught a single word.*

Vocabulary spot

If possible, look through a magazine or a novel or some other example of written English. See whether you can find any examples of cleft sentences.

Cleft sentences work by putting most of the information into some kind of relative clause – except for the part we want to emphasise.

1 Form as many examples of cleft sentences as you can from these sentences.

   a Paulo loves Maria.
   b Katherine had an accident.
   c Rolf won a million dollars.

Exam spot

If it is appropriate to emphasise something in one of the writing tasks in the CAE Writing test (Paper 2), try to include a cleft sentence. What this will mean is that your chances of getting a good grade will be improved.

2 🎧 Listen to these speakers and decide what technique each one uses to make what he or she says more emphatic.

Speaker	Emphatic technique used
1	Emphasis given to auxiliary verb *do*
2	
3	
4	
5	
6	
7	
8	
9	

3 Make these sentences more emphatic by using a stressed auxiliary verb.

   EXAMPLE: I'm going to get that job.
   I AM going to get that job!

   a Jake admires her work.
   b I love you.
   c Mary did her very best.
   d I used to be able to dive quite well.
   e They've agreed to help us.

4 Put each of the sentences from Exercise 3 into a two-line dialogue in which it would be appropriate to use this kind of emphasis.

   EXAMPLE: They won't consider you for that post as you haven't got any qualifications.
   I don't care what you say. I AM going to get that job.

5 Respond in a natural and emphatic way to these sentences using a stressed auxiliary verb.

   EXAMPLE: I'm sure she never really liked him.
   No, she DID like him.

   a You can't be sure you're right.
   b You didn't give me the right information.
   c Why don't you ever help me with the housework?
   d I think your friend cheated in the exam.
   e I know you won't be able to kick the habit.
   f You've forgotten your purse, haven't you?
   g Jill isn't going to America this year after all, is she?

🅖···⫶ page 201

Listening

1 You are going to listen to an examiner asking two students some questions.

2 🎧 Listen to the examiner's questions in Part One and write them down. Think about how you could answer them.

Now listen to Part Two. Who gives a more appropriate answer to each question, the man or the woman? Complete the table.

Question number	Better answer from	
	man	woman
1		
2		
3		
4		
5		
6		
7		
8		

3 🎧 Listen again and note down the main points made by the speaker who gives the better answer.

4 Work with a partner taking it in turns to ask and answer the questions that you wrote down. Bear in mind the three pieces of advice given in the Exam spot.

5 What sorts of things do you often talk about when you meet someone for the first time?

Exam spot

- In the CAE Speaking test (Paper 5), you must try to answer the question asked, not some other possibly unrelated question.
- You must, if at all possible, avoid giving just two or three word answers. The examiner can't give you a good mark if he or she doesn't hear much English from you.
- You don't have to tell the truth in the exam. You can recount other people's experiences as if they were your own and can express opinions or ideas that you do not really hold yourself. Little white lies may help you to find more to say or may allow you to show off your English in a more effective way.

6 🎧 You are going to listen to a conversation between three people. Answer the questions below.

1 Who are these people?
   a friends
   b work colleagues
   c fellow students
2 What do you think is the main purpose of their conversation?
   a to find out about each other
   b to establish a friendly relationship
   c to check that each person is telling the truth

🎧 Listen again and note down all the facts that you learn about each speaker.

First man	*spent year at graduate school in Philadelphia*
Second man	
Woman	

Speaking 2

1 Work with a partner. Ask each other the following questions. You may answer them either truthfully or with a lie. Be prepared to expand your answers.

   a What did you do last night?
   b What is the best present you've ever been given?
   c What's your favourite kind of music?
   d When did you fall in love for the first time?
   e What did you want to be when you were a child and why?
   f What are you afraid of?
   g What would you do if you won a large amount of money?
   h What is the most exciting thing that you have ever done?

2 Now add two extra questions to ask your partner. Don't show each other your extra questions.

3 Take it in turns to ask each other the extra questions you have prepared. Listen carefully to each other's answers and, for each one, decide whether you think your partner is telling the truth or lying.

4 Tell each other whether you thought each answer was true or invented. Were you right?

Exam folder 8

Advice

- Read the whole of the text first.
- Read through all the paragraphs and notice the difference between them.
- Pay careful attention to linking devices throughout the text and paragraphs, as well as at the beginnings and ends of paragraphs.
- Read the whole of the text again when you have completed the task.
- Don't rely on matching up names, dates or numbers in the text and paragraphs just because they are the same or similar.
- Don't rely on matching up individual words or phrases in the text and the paragraphs just because they are the same or similar.

Paper 1 Parts 2 and 3

In Part 2 and Part 3 of the CAE Reading test (Paper 1), two marks are given for each correct answer, so it is important to do as well as you can.

Part 2 Gapped text

1   Choose which of the paragraphs (A–G) fits into the numbered gaps (1–6) in the article below. There is one extra paragraph which does not fit any of the gaps.

Don't be fooled: *the Queen is not speaking our language*

A deeply fascinating piece of academic research from Australia has managed to ruffle a few feathers. It's really a dispassionate observation of a particular fact, but it can hardly seem anything other than disrespectful to the point of *lèse-majesté*. An expert in linguistics has examined the Queen's Christmas broadcasts, from the earliest to the most recent, and has observed that, in the course of her lifetime, her vowels have shifted from the front of her mouth toward the back.

[1]

If you wanted to track the changes in linguistic usage in a single individual over the course of a long lifetime, you could not possibly find a better subject for your research than the Queen.

[2]

The Queen's vowels, from her first broadcasts, don't strike us as unusually forward in the mouth; they strike us as almost unimaginably posh. "But", "bet" and "bat" all sound very much the same. "House" really does sound like "hice".

[3]

We generally like to assume that the speech of individual classes is a fairly stable thing, but I doubt that is the case. The upper-class dropping of the final "g" is much rarer than it used to be, for instance – something that would aggrieve one famous lady, of whom it was said that she was so grand, she dropped the final "g" from words that didn't have it. In general, the speech of the members of a particular social class tends to sound rather more vulgar than that of its parents.

[4]

And now, the young of the upper classes rarely talk in what we normally think of as an upper-class accent. The upper-class socialite, Tara Palmer-Tomkinson, sounds like Eliza Doolittle before Professor Higgins got his hands on her. A real cut-glass accent, in anyone under 40, is invariably rather an aspirational middle-class thing, acquired by someone who taught himself to stop saying "toilet" and "settee". Middle-class London children, now, always sound appallingly common to their grandparents, but their way of talking is quite distinct from that of real working-class London children.

[5]

In short, pronunciation is in a constant state of change, and individuals' pronunciation is as prone to alteration as anything else. Only people isolated from their linguistic community are unlikely to alter their accent at all; old Indian expats do still talk in the accent of their youth. The rest of us are not going to carry on talking as we did as children, and that includes the Queen.

[6]

What is surprising, however, is that it demonstrates that she has, after all, been listening to other people all these years.

A What is entirely idle is to draw the conclusion that the Queen is now talking in the accents of the lower classes. She is talking exactly as a woman of her class and generation might be expected to in the year 2000, and it is no surprise whatsoever that that does not much resemble the ways of talking of her youth.

B Accents in English have always suggested something about a person's class as much as about their geographical origins and the Queen is no exception. It is very hard to change your original accent unless you have the help of a professional expert like the famous fictional Professor Higgins who taught the Cockney flower-girl Eliza Doolittle (in Bernard Shaw's *Pygmalion,* made into the musical and film *My Fair Lady*) to pass herself off as a lady.

C A very interesting and valuable observation. The Queen is a particularly good subject for such observation, since there are so many recordings of her speech, and they cover such a long period of time. From the famous wartime recording to the children of the Empire – "Come on, Margaret!" – to the present day, there is a record of her speech for practically every year of her life, and there is probably no other speaker of English for whom that is the case.

D All the same, it is difficult to describe such things in a neutral way, and perhaps the researchers might have made a sensible decision to refer to her, in scientific manner, as Elizabeth R. The point about her pronunciation is that the shape of vowels has definite social connotations, and the unarguable shift in her vowels certainly seems like a shift down the social scale.

E Middle-class English of half a century ago, as typified by an announcer on the BBC, tends to sound to us like aristocratic speech. The pre-war novelist Virginia Woolf's accent, which was probably fairly typical of the London upper-middle class, now sounds almost incomprehensibly grand.

F So, the distinctions that the Queen has learnt to make over the years, to the point where she now has more than one vowel to her name, don't seem merely like a neutral linguistic change; they sound as if she has become distinctly more common. Certainly, that was the interpretation widely placed on this fascinating and undoubtedly accurate research, and the Palace greeted the news that the Queen has embraced estuary English – a useful though rather broad linguistic category – with the sort of sniffy response it generally reserves for paparazzo shots of the Duchess of York.

G The accents of the working classes change as much as anything. It's quite rare, now, to hear the old London accent that pronounces "catch" as "ketch"; it has been altered by all sorts of new influences, and particularly by black English, which have turned it into what would probably seem quite a new accent. The Cockney accent of 50 years back, though still familiar from old films, is in reality as dead as that of Sam Weller from *The Pickwick Papers*, which routinely interchanged Vs and Ws.

Now go back and mark the words and phrases which help you to decide what fits where.

Part 3 Multiple-choice questions

1 Following the Advice box below, read the text and answer the questions which follow.

Advice

- Read the whole text very carefully before you begin to answer the questions.
- Read the whole of the question and all the options carefully.
- Read the text for inference as well as fact.
- Remember that the questions follow the order of the text.
- Remember that the final question may ask about the text as a whole.
- Don't rely on matching individual words or phrases in the options and the text just because they are the same or similar.

Where was I?

In nostalgic mood, I alight at Central Station, where, it has to be said, the prospects of catching a train are about the same as an encounter with little green men. That is why it is known to everybody except me by another name.

Despite this, the city has always been at transport's cutting edge. Just around the corner is a canal that, when opened in 1761, was something of a revolution: another, 36 miles long and far more impressive, was only completed in 1894. A little time after that, it was here that a one-time electrical engineer and an aviator first met and so it is home to what, at that time, was one of Britain's first municipal airports. And to bring the story right up to date, it is a place justly admired for a means of getting around that not so long ago was considered well and truly extinct. But I shun them all: shoe leather will get me to the city centre.

1 Which contradiction about the town does the writer bring out?
   A It is right up to date but at the same time historic.
   B It is famous for transport but it is difficult to get a train.
   C It has two different names.
   D It is the home of inventors and development.
2 The purpose of the text is to
   A promote rail travel.
   B provide a competition question.
   C inform the reader about transportation.
   D criticise today's facilities.

UNIT 19 Feeding the mind

Genre   Talks

Topic   Food, pictures and science

Exam spot

Although you do not have to give a talk in the CAE exam you do have to understand a monologue in the Listening test (Paper 4). You also have to organise your ideas in the Writing test (Paper 2) in ways that are similar to organising a well-structured talk.

Speaking 1

1 Look at the pictures above and discuss these questions with a partner.

a How often do you eat out? Where do you like to go? Why do you like it there? Who do you usually go with? What are the advantages and disadvantages of eating out compared to eating at home?

b Would you ever take a photograph of this kind? Would you choose either a photo or a painting of a still life for your wall?

c How many ways can you think of in which science has affected food production?

Reading

1 Look at the pictures with the three texts opposite. Work with a partner. Take it in turns to give a sentence describing one of the pictures. Then do the same thing with the other two pictures.

2 Skim the three texts. One relates to each of the three discussion topics in Speaking 1. Which text goes with which topic?

3 Now read the texts more carefully. Which of the three texts do each of these titles best fit?

a The influence of social background

b Time flies

c Inspired by nature

1

Frequent eating out in commercial premises is associated positively with having high household income, being highly educated, being younger, and being single, and negatively with being a housewife. Significantly, the same factors also operate, and even more strongly, in one sector of the communal mode, eating with friends. People with greater economic and cultural capital are most frequently invited to be a guest in someone else's home, while such characteristics are much less important in respect of kin. Happily, you don't have to be rich for mum to cook for you! Since there is a statistical association between restaurant going and entertaining, it is possible that the expansion of the former has encouraged the latter and even extended the habit of entertaining to a wider population than previously.

2

The first person to examine whether freezing food might delay its deterioration died in the process. In March 1626, Francis Bacon, lawyer, Member of Parliament, wit and philosopher, was passing Highgate in north London. Observing the snow outside his carriage he wondered whether snow might delay the putrefaction of living tissue. He stopped his carriage immediately, bought a hen, and, with his own hands, stuffed it with snow. But he was seized with a sudden chill which turned to bronchitis, and he died at the Earl of Arundel's house nearby on April 9th.

Some three centuries later, Clarence Birdseye, an American businessman, developed Bacon's speculation into a process for freezing food in small packages suitable for retailing. In 1912 and 1916, Birdseye travelled to Labrador in north-east Canada to trade fur. He noticed the natives froze food in winter because of the shortage of fresh food. The combination of ice, wind and temperature almost instantly froze fresh fish straight through. When the fish were cooked and eaten, they were scarcely different in taste and texture than they would have been if fresh. Birdseye, a former government naturalist, realised the fish froze too quickly for ice crystals to form and ruin their cellular structure. In 1924 he founded the General Seafoods Company, having patented a system that packed fish, meat or vegetables into waxed-cardboard cartons, that were flash frozen between two metal plates, under high pressure. His invention significantly changed eating habits.

3

This week's picture, *The Painter's Daughters Chasing a Butterfly*, is a loving depiction of carefree youth and innocence but a faintly troubling picture too, charged with feelings deeper than sentimentality alone. The two girls holding hands are radiant in their silk dresses of silver and yellow, but we find them in a dark wood, under a stormy sky, with dusk approaching.

The day is short and childhood quickly passes: a common enough feeling for any parent to have, but Gainsborough has caught it with absolute precision and authenticity. With an attentive father's keenness of observation, the artist notes the difference made by even the small gap of age that separates the two girls. Mary has already developed a certain air of circumspection and self-consciousness, implicit in her careful gaze, her restrained posture and the nearly adult, upright carriage of her head. Looking across from her to the more impetuous, instinctive figure of her little sister, Margaret, whose arms and legs seem somehow less tense and organised, and whose face still has a certain toddlerish chubbiness about it, one might almost be looking at a single girl at different stages of her life.

Gainsborough has also conveyed his own ambiguous attitude towards his daughters' growing up, paternal pride mingled with the sense that each new stage in life, each new level of maturity attained, also marks a kind of small death, the loss of a little person no less loved. Margaret reaches out towards a butterfly, traditional symbol of life's fragility and brief duration, with an expression of little girl concentration which seems tinged with melancholy.

4 Write a sentence summarising each of the three extracts.

5 Answer these questions about the texts.

Text 1

a What kinds of people are most likely to eat out in restaurants?

b Who is most likely to eat at friends' houses?

c What kinds of people tend to eat in the homes of other family members?

Text 2

d What do Francis Bacon and Clarence Birdseye have in common?

e Why did Birdseye succeed where Bacon had not?

f Why is freezing a successful way of preserving food?

Text 3

g In what ways is Margaret different from her sister?

h What general theme can be drawn from the painting?

i Do you think this painting is basically happy or sad?

6 Which of these three texts do you find most interesting and why?

Vocabulary

1 Look at this extract from the Gainsborough text. What part of speech is required to fill each gap?

2 Write one word in each gap.

This week's picture, *The (1) ....'s Daughters Chasing a Butterfly,* is a loving depiction of carefree youth and innocence	**PAINT**
but a (2) .... troubling picture too, charged with feelings (3) .... than sentimentality alone. The day is short	**FAINT** **DEEP**
and (4) .... quickly passes: a common enough feeling for any parent to have, but Gainsborough has caught it with absolute	**CHILD**
(5) .... and authenticity. With an (6) .... father's keenness of	**PRECISE** **ATTEND**
observation, the artist notes the difference made by even the small gap of age that separates the two girls.	

3 Identify the missing part of speech in these sentences. Then fill the gap with an appropriate word formed from the word in brackets at the end of each sentence.

a Fruit and vegetables have been .... proven to provide some protection against cancer. (science)

b You get a wonderful feeling of the magnificent .... of the artist's vision in this exhibition. (broad)

c Although the investigation was time-consuming and costly, the results were .... and we still cannot be sure whether our basic hypothesis is correct. (conclude)

d Nothing is more pleasant than spending a .... evening at a good restaurant with close friends. (leisure)

e The research wanted to .... the relationship between social background and eating habits. (clear)

f Although his paintings reflect great peace and tranquillity, the artist himself is said to have had a very obstinate and .... character. (argue)

g Would you like another .... of roast potatoes, Charlie? (help)

h It is very important that food should not be prepared in .... conditions. (hygiene)

i This drink is lovely and .... Do try some. (vigour)

j It's a good idea to .... the freezer every few weeks. (frost)

Emphasising

Notice the use of inversion in these sentences.

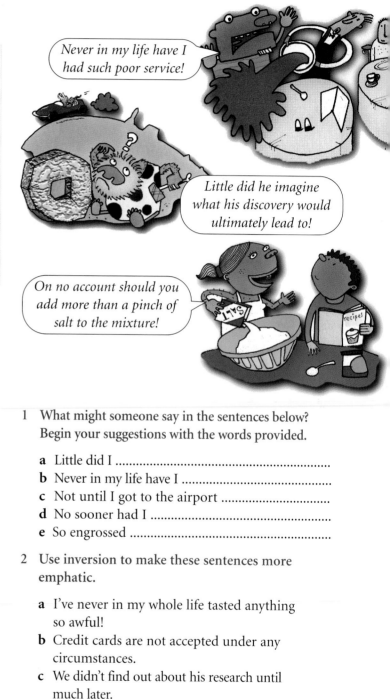

Never in my life have I had such poor service!

Little did he imagine what his discovery would ultimately lead to!

On no account should you add more than a pinch of salt to the mixture!

1 What might someone say in the sentences below? Begin your suggestions with the words provided.

a Little did I ....

b Never in my life have I ....

c Not until I got to the airport ....

d No sooner had I ....

e So engrossed ....

2 Use inversion to make these sentences more emphatic.

a I've never in my whole life tasted anything so awful!

b Credit cards are not accepted under any circumstances.

c We didn't find out about his research until much later.

d We only realised what had happened when we arrived back at the lab.

e We not only lost our passports but also all our money.

f We'd hardly got there when the fire alarm went off.

g He has little idea of what's in store for him.

h I only learned her secret after her death.

3 You are writing about food and restaurants in your country. Complete these sentences in any way that might be appropriate.

EXAMPLE: On no account *should you leave our town without sampling the speciality of the region.*

a Little ....
b Never ....
c Hardly ....
d Only after ....
e Under no circumstances ....
f Not until ....
g Not only ....

Ⓖ⋯⋮ page 202

Listening

1 🎧 Listen to two talks in which people describe their favourite pictures.

2 What are the main points which each speaker is making?

Talk 1
a ....
b ....
c ....
d ....

Talk 2
a ....
b ....
c ....
d ....

3 Would you consider each of these a good talk in terms of content, delivery and use of language? Give reasons for your answers.

4 Prepare a brief talk on one of these subjects:

- eating out
- a favourite painting or photograph
- an influential scientific breakthrough.

5 Give your talk to other students in the class.

Speaking 2

1 Work in groups of four. Two students will act as Examiners and two will be candidates. Note that one of the Examiners simply listens while the other asks the questions and sets the tasks. After fifteen to twenty minutes you will change roles. The Examiners will become candidates and vice versa.

For Parts 1–4, your teacher will give the Examiner some instructions. Candidates should answer the Examiner's questions.

Here are the pictures for Part 2 of the test.

a

b

Here are the words for Part 3 of the test.

| technology | transport | housing |
| education | health care | employment |

Writing folder 8

Articles, reports and memos

1 With a partner, discuss what the differences are between articles, reports and memos.
Complete the following table. Some boxes have already been filled in to help you.

	Article	Report	Memo
Who it is usually written for	*a wide audience who you don't know and who will only read it if it catches their interest*		
What its aims usually are	*to interest, entertain or inform the readers*		
Any special characteristics of its layout			*To, From and Re: are the headings at the top*
Any special characteristics of its register		*unmarked or formal*	
Any other special characteristics of its style		*Must be absolutely clear and unambiguous in what it says. Usually has a clear introduction presenting what it is going to say and usually comes to some distinct conclusion at the end.*	

2 Are the sentences below most likely to come from articles, reports or memos?
What are the clues in the sentences that make you choose your answers?

a Don't forget we need an OHP for tomorrow's meeting.

b In conclusion, I would recommend that we go ahead with our plans for the event but that we take on board the suggestions made by the members of the public whose opinions we surveyed.

c It was a beautiful balmy evening when the little boat chugged into the harbour and our holiday began in earnest.

d Never in a million years would it have occurred to me to do what Janella then suggested.

e All employees are requested to turn off electrical appliances when they are not in use.

f The aim of the investigation was to ascertain local residents' attitudes towards the proposed developments.

g You mustn't use work computers for browsing the Internet unless it is for legitimate company reasons.

h Rowena (secretary, 25, from mid Wales) says that she would be quite 'cool' about the idea of going on a blind date although she admitted that she had never actually done so.

3   Remember that in Part 1 of the CAE Writing test (Paper 2) you may be asked to write more than one task. If you are, you will have to make clear differences in the content, language and register of your answers. Look at this task.

You and ten other students from the institution where you are studying English have just returned from an exchange programme where you spent a month at a school in London. You attended classes with the students and in the evenings did a variety of cultural activities. You lived with the families of the students at the school. You have now been asked to write a **report**, a **memo** and an **article** about this.

You attended a debriefing meeting with the other students who went on the programme and made some notes on the feelings they expressed. List all the bits of information provided below that you will need to use in writing the report, the memo and the article.

> _Journey_ all found it a bit tiring – any easier way to get there another time?
> _School_ great fun (though two or three found some lessons a bit boring and easy)
> _After-school activities_ varied (good theatre trips, e.g. to musical, fantastic end of month dinner in restaurant, interesting exhibition at National Gallery, cinema trips expensive and not very good, not much free time)
> _Accommodation_ some brilliant though two or three complaints – had to travel long way to school, very strict family, not enough food

E xam spot

It is very important in a question like this to read the task extremely carefully and to mark the bits that you need to include in your answers. It is also important to try to put the information from the task into your own words.

Now write your answers to these three tasks.

a   a **report** for your English teacher outlining the good and bad features of the trip and recommending whether any changes should be made if the exchange takes place again next year (200 words)

b   a **memo** to the other students who took part in the programme requesting them to read your report and suggest any changes they think should be made before it is given to your teacher (50 words)

c   an **article** for the magazine of the school in London giving the students there your personal view of the exchange programme (200 words)

Genre	Competition entries
Topic	Mini sagas

Exam spot

You are sometimes asked to write a competition entry in the CAE Writing test (Paper 2). All this means is that you have to try to write in a particularly interesting and effective way (in order to win a prize, i.e. a good grade!).

Speaking

1 With a partner, discuss these questions.

   a Have you ever entered any competitions?
   b What did you have to do?
   c Have you or any of your friends or family ever won anything in a competition? If so, what did you or they win and what for?

2 Here are some common competition prizes. Put them in your order of preference.

3 Here are some popular types of competitions. What are they? Do you ever do this kind of competition?

Reading

One popular competition was organised by a daily newspaper and invited readers to write a complete story in fifty words. These stories were called mini sagas.

1 Read these entries to the mini saga competition. Match the titles (1–5) with the sagas (A–E).

1 **Sophisticated management techniques are not always the panacea for a company's ills**

2 Like Mother, Like Son

3 **Perhaps there's something to be said for the three R's after all**

4 How To Deconstruct Everything You Were Taught in Your Creative Writing Class

5 Priorities

2 Find words and expressions in the mini sagas to match the meanings below.

Text A
a exceptionally good
b using words in a clever and humorous way
c a work of art

Text B
a conspiracy
b infection (colloquial)

Text C
a treat a weaker person in a cruel way
b try to keep cheerful

Text D
a improve
b bankrupt

Text E
a moulding
b thinking about something else

3 Discuss with a partner how you would summarise the point of each saga.

EXAMPLE: *Mini saga A might be It is important to follow instructions.*

4 Discuss in small groups which story you would give the prize to. Give reasons for your choice. Compare your choice of winner with the choices of other groups.

A
At school he had been no good at maths but outstanding at writing and reading. But who needs arithmetic? He entered the competition with enthusiasm and produced a dazzling, witty, profound and paradoxical story. He was inspired. It was an absolute masterpiece. The judges sighed. Another one with 51 words.

B
The King died. A statement. Then the Queen died. A storyline. She died of grief. A plot? Or was it grief? A murder mystery. Then the Prince died, and the Princess, and the Princess's puppydog. All had been poisoned by an E Coli bug in the Royal Beefburgers. A mistake.

C
1955

Dear Mummy,
I hate this boarding school. Food awful, prefects bully me. Please take me home.
Love,
David

Dear David,
Nonsense. Chin up.
Mother

1997

Dear David,
I hate this home. Food awful. Nurses treat me like a child. Fetch me immediately.
Mother

Dear Mother,
Nonsense. Chin up.
David

D
The company was performing badly and morale was low. The board restructured the management and introduced a performance and appraisal system. They established multi-functional system based audit teams, and people and quality initiatives. Structured systems analysis and design methodology was used to enhance information technology projects. The company went bust.

E
Intently, I crafted my fifty words. I carried them with me as I would a ball of plasticine in my pocket, shaping and squeezing them. Distracted, I ignored you when you called me.
Later, I brought them proudly to you, finished.
You'd left a note: 'Three words would have done'.

Vocabulary

In mini saga C we see the idiom *Chin up!*, which means *Try to keep cheerful*! There are many idioms in English based on parts of the body.

1 Complete the sentences (a–h) below, then match the cartoons (1–8) with the sentences.

a Jack is bound to know who we should ask about the matter – he's got a .... in every pie.
b Working with such a bright team of people certainly keeps me on my ....
c He's set his .... on becoming a ballet dancer.
d I'll give you a ....
e Do tell me what happened last night. I'm all ....
f She hasn't a clue what's going on. She's always got her .... in the clouds.
g Put your .... up for an hour or so and then you'll feel refreshed for the evening.
h Try and catch the waiter's ....

2 Here are some more idioms connected with parts of the body. Match each idiom (a–h) to its definition (1–8).

a to bite your tongue
b to be down in the mouth
c to keep your fingers crossed
d to be tearing your hair out
e to rack your brains
f to put someone's mind at rest
g to break someone's heart
h to fall head over heels in love

1 to be very anxious or upset about something
2 to make someone stop worrying
3 to make someone who loves you very sad
4 to hope things will happen the way you want them to
5 to stop yourself from saying something you want to say
6 to start to love someone passionately
7 to feel miserable
8 to think very hard

3 Choose one of the idioms from Vocabulary 1 and 2 to fill each of the gaps in the text below. Make any changes to the verb form that are necessary.

As soon as John met Amanda, he (1) .... with her. They got to know each other when John noticed her loaded down with shopping and offered (2) .... Amanda is a bit of a dreamer and her mother always says she (3) .... Nevertheless, she has a very good position as an MP's Personal Assistant and she (4) .... on getting a job in the Prime Minister's office. She says that having to cope with the demands of life in politics (5) .... Amanda talks a lot about her job and at first John (6) .... But now he has to (7) .... to stop himself from telling her how bored he is with hearing about everything 'her' MP says or does. Today when I bumped into him in town, John (8) .... because Amanda had decided to go to a conference with her MP rather than on the holiday they had planned together. 'Sh (9) .... ,' John said. 'I'm sure she likes her MP more than she likes me.' I (10) .... but I couldn't think of anything that would (11) .... All I could do was promise (12) .... for him.

Hypothesising

Here is some language that is useful for hypothesising.

A
I wonder whether …
Suppose …
What if …
Just imagine …
If only …

B
Let us imagine …
Let us consider …
Let us suppose …
Let us assume …
If we were to …
Were we to …
If we had …
Had we …

C
If I may speculate for a moment, …
Speculating for a moment, …
Let us take a hypothetical case: …
On the assumption that …
Provided (that) …
Allowing for the fact that …
Given (that) …

1 Listen to a dialogue in which two people, who were students together ten years ago, meet up. They are speculating about one of their classmates. Tick any of the expressions from box A that you hear.

2 Rewrite these sentences in which a head teacher is discussing, at a formal meeting, the benefits of employing a new deputy head.

1 If we appointed a new deputy head, that would allow me to spend a lot more time in the classroom.
   a If we were to ....
   b Were we to ....
2 Having more time in the classroom would give me more of a finger on the pulse of school life.
   a If I had ....
   b Had we ....
3 I'd like you to think about how a deputy would use his or her time.
   a Let us imagine ....
   b Let us consider ....
4 It is probably the case that a deputy would take over a lot of the day-to-day running of the school.
   a Let us suppose ....
   b Let us assume ....

3 Listen to a speech in which a politician is arguing for the introduction of a new law. What is he arguing for and what points does he make?

4 Now complete the sentences as if you were a politician discussing the introduction of any different law of your choice.

   a If I may speculate for a moment, …
   b Speculating for a moment, …
   c Let us take a hypothetical case: …
   d On the assumption that …
   e Provided (that) …
   f Allowing for the fact that …
   g Given (that) …

G ⋯⋰ page 202

Listening

1 Here are the titles of three other mini sagas.

How Success Can Go to One's Head

A Moment in Venice

August When the Statue in Her Garden Gives Her Most Pleasure

Work with a partner to speculate about what each of the sagas might be about.

2 Listen to the mini sagas on the tape. Which title and which picture goes with which mini saga?

Topic review

a What is the best film you have ever seen?

b Do you prefer to read reviews in a newspaper or a magazine or to trust your friends' opinions?

c Could you ever be persuaded to do a bungee jump?

d Would you employ someone with purple hair?

e Do you ever pretend to understand English when you really haven't?

f Someone who says they always tell the truth is a liar. Do you agree?

g Which country (apart from your own) has the best food?

h What do you prefer: home cooking or eating in restaurants?

i What would you do if you won a lot of money?

j Imagine you could choose between two prizes: a luxury holiday in the sun or two tickets to the World Cup football final. Which would you choose?

Vocabulary

1 Insert all the necessary punctuation and capital letters into this paragraph.

Little lies, big mistake

1   now be honest most of us in the course of our working day tell the odd little fib we
2   may pretend weve nearly finished something when weve barely started it or say
3   someone is in a meeting when they dont want to take the call but its very easy for
4   white lies to turn into something more serious and the assumption that little
5   porkies are a necessary part of a secretarys role is a dangerous one most
6   secretaries and pas are used to telling white lies for the boss says ros taylor
7   business psychologist and author of the key to the boardroom if he asks you to
8   do something that is slightly more dishonest the easy thing is to assume that its
9   ok that he wouldnt ask you to do something illegal unfortunately that isnt always
10 the case last month a pa to a chief executive who was being tried for fraud
11 admitted in court that she had faked documents to smooth the passage of a huge
12 deal she argued that lying was standard practice in the city and that she was
13 simply trying to protect her boss but must secretaries sign up to a culture of
14 dishonesty what happens if you want to tell the truth ive done things that i know
15 are dishonest says kate matheson pa to the director of a large property company
16 its easy to feign ignorance ive shredded things that deep down i know should be
17 kept and been asked to change figures on documents that if i really thought
18 about it id know shouldnt be changed but my boss is top dog in a huge
19 organisation and im not about to say no to him ive always assumed that since im
20 doing what im asked it couldnt get me into trouble
21 this is a common misconception the fact is that any untruth even a seemingly
22 harmless white lie can lead to trouble and the best policy is to try to avoid
23 dishonesty from the start because ive done the odd thing that is a bit
24 questionable in the past its even more difficult to say no now says kate matheson
25 my boss can say oh well you did it last time what can I say to that

Grammar

1 Fill in each of the gaps in the text with one word. The first one has been done for you as an example.

Art's old masters draw the queue

It is enough (0) ....to......... make a pickled shark weep. In the new millennium, with contemporary art universally touted as the new rock'n'roll, a huge international survey shows that people may (1) .... know much about art, but they know (2) .... they like: old pictures.

The National Gallery director, Neil MacGregor, who emerged from the survey as organiser of (3) .... of the world's most popular exhibitions, saw no contradiction. "Old master paintings speak powerfully (4) .... a contemporary audience," he said yesterday.

In a survey by *The Art Newspaper*, in city after city, from Melbourne to Athens, from London to New York, the pattern was (5) .... same: the exhibitions people queued (6) .... the block to see were of old masters or of long dead craftsmen. The nearest to a contemporary artist in the international top 10 is Picasso.

Seeing Salvation is the most startling statistic from the survey. This exhibition at the National Gallery, was not (7) .... by far the most popular exhibition in Britain, with more than 5,000 visitors a day, it was the fourth (8) .... popular in the world.

It was sponsored by a charity and admission (9) .... free. Within a day staff knew they had a phenomenon. People were queuing for hours to get in, moving (10) .... a snail's pace because visitors spent so (11) .... studying the works.

Mr MacGregor said "*Seeing Salvation* investigated (12) .... theme that has shaped western art through the centuries. This historical approach to familiar material clearly captured the public's imagination."

Reading

1 Choose which of the paragraphs (A–G) fill the numbered gaps (1–6) in the newspaper article below. There is one extra paragraph which you do not need to use.

Is honesty the best policy?

Lying is bad for your health, according to an American psychotherapist. But telling the truth is tricky, says Thea Jourdan.

'Does my bum look big in this?' said my friend. It had to happen. The question I had been dreading for the past few hours needed an answer. As she looked at me inquiringly, turning this way and that in an aquamarine micro-mini at least one size too small for her, I mentally steeled myself before replying in a whisper. 'Yes, I'm afraid it does.' Hopes for a jolly afternoon's shopping fell, along with her face. So much for telling the truth.

1

'We all lie like hell. It wears us out. It is the major source of all human stress,' says Brad Blanton, psychotherapist and founder of the Centre for Radical Honesty. The best-selling author of *Practising Radical Honesty: How to Complete the Past, Live in the Present and Build the Future with a Little Help from Your Friends* has become a household name in the States, where he spreads his message via day-time television talk shows.

2

Well, fibbing may be murderous, but honesty started becoming inconvenient for me just after breakfast, when I needed change for a parking meter. The cashier in the corner shop looked at my £10 note with a jaundiced eye. Did I really want the gobstopper or was I after change for the parking, he wondered? If so, the shop always had a policy of refusal. On a normal day, I would have lied. Traffic wardens in these parts show no mercy. Instead, I admitted everything and was shown the door, change-less.

3

The alternative, he believes, is the stress of living 'in the prison of the mind', which results in depression and ill health. 'Your body stays tied up in knots and is susceptible to illness,' he says. Allergies, high blood pressure and insomnia are all exacerbated by lying. Good relationship skills, parenting skills and management skills are also dependent on telling the truth.

4

'I have always believed that honesty is the best policy. Obviously, there are moral and ethical values in business. If you want to make deals, you have to have trust.'

5

Richard Wiseman, a psychologist at the University of Hertfordshire, says that lies can protect people as well as harm them. He is also certain that people will continue to tell them because human beings follow the law of survival of the fittest. 'I suspect Dr Blanton has devised an unstable strategy. If we all told the truth all the time, it would be fine, but the advantage would then go to the few who were prepared to lie.'

6

A Dr Blanton, who lives in Virginia with his wife and two children, is adamant that minor inconveniences are nothing compared with the huge benefits of truth telling. 'Telling the truth, after hiding it for a long time, reopens old wounds that didn't heal properly. It hurts a lot. It takes guts. It isn't easy. But it is better than the alternative.'

B Radical honesty therapy, as it is known in America, is the latest thing to be held up as the key to happiness and success. It involves telling the truth all the time, with no exceptions for hurt feelings. But, as I found out, this is not as easy as it might sound. Altruistic lies, rather than the conniving, self-aggrandising variety, are an essential part of polite society.

C People who tell lies get so confused about what they have said to whom that they can sometimes get to the point where they no longer know what the truth is. This is very bad for their physical as well as their mental health and is one reason for the stomach complaints and headaches frequently reported by frequent liars.

D By the end of my day of telling nothing but the truth, I definitely regretted my honest approach. Forget personal gain. My big-bottomed ex-friend decided to tell some home truths of her own. I still haven't quite recovered.

E Honesty, according to Dr Blanton, brings many rewards, not least in business – and perhaps he is right. Gifi Fields, chief executive of Coppernob Communications, who has made tens of millions of pounds in a long career, insists that his own integrity has helped him succeed.

F On the other hand, Anne McKevitt, an interior designer and television presenter, is happy to admit to frequent fibbing. She points out that the truth can sometimes be too painful. 'I think white lies are good,' she says. 'I tell them all the time.'

G He certainly has his work cut out for him. In a recent survey of Americans, 93 per cent admitted to lying 'regularly and habitually' in the workplace. Dr Blanton is typically blunt about the consequences of being deceitful. 'Lying kills people,' he says.

| Genre | Travel writing |
| Topic | Trips and travel |

Speaking

1 With a partner, discuss these questions.

a Have you ever been on a holiday like the ones in the photographs? Did you enjoy it? Why?/Why not?

b What sorts of people might prefer a package holiday?

c What are the advantages and disadvantages of having a backpacking holiday?

d Would you agree that a holiday in a mobile home satisfies people's desire for freedom? Why?/Why not?

e Which is the most exciting part of travelling for you: the preparation before you go, the excitement of first arriving in a place or getting to know somewhere new?

f What is the strangest, funniest, best or worst thing that has happened to you while travelling?

Listening

1 You are going to hear three people talking about their travel experiences. Before you listen, look at the three pictures (a–c). What do you think each story is going to be about? Think of five words you are likely to hear for each picture.

2 🎧 Listen to the speakers, Alan, Simone and Mick and number the words in the order they occur in the story. The first one has been done for you as an example.

Picture a: Alan

France	[1]
an attendant	[ ]
there's a strike	[ ]
free vouchers	[ ]
the train stopped	[ ]
about twenty passengers	[ ]
stuck at this platform	[ ]

Picture b: Simone

north of Queensland	[1]
big billboard	[ ]
the beach was fantastic	[ ]
start running	[ ]
a river that cut off our side of the beach	[ ]
a short cut	[ ]
go for a walk	[ ]

Picture c: Mick

in Greece for three years	[1]
they got the wrong pages	[ ]
someone who spoke English	[ ]
a phrase book	[ ]
completely mad	[ ]
start laughing	[ ]
really cheap	[ ]

3 🎧 Listen again and complete the tapescript opposite.

4 Look at the words and phrases you used to complete the tapescript. Are they fillers, words that show feeling or examples of direct speech?

5 Why do people use fillers when they speak? Which fillers do you use when you speak in English? Which fillers do you use in your own language?

6 Write down five nouns relating to your last holiday or the last time you travelled. Now add an interesting adjective to each noun.

7 What other techniques do people use when telling stories to make them more interesting or dramatic?

8 Tell your partner about the last time you travelled. Make your story interesting.

So we start walking through this river and you know, I'm thinking, it's only going to go up to my knees so it'll be OK. We get to the middle and it's up to our waist. And (1) ...., I'm thinking this was (2) ...., you know. (3) .... we'll walk nice and slowly, we'll get to the other side and we'll just have to sit in wet, wet clothes for about twelve hours while we're travelling south on the bus. (4) ...., what happened was, (5) ...., we got about half way through and suddenly my husband goes, 'Quick! Run!' And I said, (6) .... And he said, 'Just run, just run'. So we start running and the water is literally in waves over our head and you know, we get to the other side, and I'm standing there with water dripping off my hair and everything is drenched at this point, and I'm going, er, and (7) .... And he goes, 'Well , I just had a really bad feeling'.

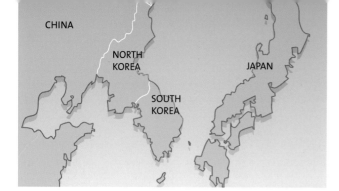

Reading

1 Read these extracts from an account of a trip
around the Pacific Rim. Extract 1 describes arriving
in South Korea by ship from Japan and Extract 2
describes arriving at a hotel. Choose the best
answer, A, B, C or D for the questions which follow.

Hakata to Pusan

Extract 1

Day 46 Pitch darkness. Rudely awoken by a thunderous rumbling roar
which sounds as though the ship is being disembowelled beneath me.
It's the anchor going down which means we must already have covered
the 140 miles of the Korea Strait to Pusan.

Dawn: Our ferry, the *Camelia*, stands off the rocky undulating coast
of South Korea, one of the queue of vessels waiting to pierce the hazy
brown veil of pollution that all but obscures the country's second
largest city. Several passengers are up on the deck exercising. I'm going
through my travel documents in an anxious pre-Customs and
Immigration way, ticking boxes to aver that I am not carrying 'guns,
knives, gunpowder, drugs, psychotropic substances or any items
harmful to the national constitution, public security or morals'.
(I always wonder what sort of person answers 'yes' to a question
like that.)

With a mournful blast of the horn, our ship moves slowly towards
the dockside. It's only 7.30 am. But South Korea is already at work,
making itself bigger. Cranes are swinging and concrete is pouring into a
vast land-reclamation project. Shoreline highways are choked with
morning traffic and a powerful array of multi-storey blocks bear
familiar names – Daewoo, Samsung, Hyundai.

Extract 2

The bus deposits us at the town of Kyongju, 55 miles north of Pusan.
At my hotel personal cleanliness is tackled with a vengeance. An
enormous communal bathing area offers just about everything you
might want to do with water. There are showers enough for a small
army; a hot tub and a semi-hot tub, a cold tub with high-pressure
waterfall simulator, several jacuzzis, a ginseng-flavoured steam room
and two capacious saunas. This palace of hydrophilia is filled with the
soft, the soothing sound of sloshing and scrubbing, spraying and
gurgling, swilling, slapping and lathering.

1 How does the writer feel as he prepares to get off
the ship?
A terrified by strange noises
B irritated by the delays
C nervous about formalities
D suspicious of other passengers

2 What does the writer think about Pusan?
A It is difficult to understand why it was built in
a rocky area.
B It has all the signs of a rapidly developing city.
C He cannot identify with any aspect of the city.
D He is surprised at the old-fashioned methods of
working.

3 The writer's overwhelming impression of the hotel
is one of
A obsessive hygiene.
B overcrowded facilities.
C confusing traditions.
D relaxing luxury.

Vocabulary

1 The words in italics in the sentences below come from
Extract 2. They are all connected with water in some way.
Match the words (in 1–7) with their definitions (a–g).

1 When you go round a corner, you can hear the
petrol *sloshing* about in the tank.
2 He *scrubbed* the old saucepan clean and it looked
as good as new.
3 Can you feel the *spray* from the garden hose?
4 The water went down the plughole with a loud *gurgle*.
5 The dentist handed me a glass of water to *swill* my
mouth out with.
6 We could hear the *slap* of the waves against the side
of the boat.
7 Most soaps won't *lather* in sea water.

a a liquid forced out of a special container under
pressure so that it becomes a cloud-like mass of
small liquid drops
b produce a pale mass of small bubbles when soap
is mixed with water
c moving around noisily in the bottom of a container
or causing a liquid to move around in this way by
making rough movements
d flow around or over something, often in order to clean it
e flow with a low, uneven noise
f rubbed something hard in order to clean it, especially
using a stiff brush, soap and water
g a noise made by quickly hitting something with a flat
object

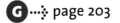

Vocabulary spot

Look carefully at the endings of words. Try to recognise patterns which tell you if a word could be an adjective, an adverb, a verb or a noun. For example, a word ending in -ic is usually an adjective, -ly an adverb, -ise a verb, -age a noun.

2 You are going to complete the text using the words provided in the box below. There is one extra word which is not needed. First read the text and decide which type of word goes in each gap.

My holiday

I was brought up in a little fishing (0) ....village....... so we didn't really have holidays as kids. The place was so (1) .... that the whole summer was like a holiday. We had a lot of (2) .... and we even had our own (3) .... boat. We used to go out in it for hours. I used to just sit in it and read books.

I find now that for my holidays I always (4) .... towards the sea, and I've realised that unless I can see the sea, I don't feel that I'm on holiday. Of all the places I've been to, I think India is the most (5) .... stimulating. Every little town we went through there was this (6) .... of colour – even the clothes hanging on the washing lines had an extraordinary (7) .... quality to them. I'd never been anywhere like it before. At the end of my holiday in India, we splurged out on an amazing hotel; it was like a (8) .... I love staying in interesting places when I travel.

3 Now look at the endings of these words and decide which are the adjectives, the adverbs, the nouns and the verbs.

aesthetic	fairy tale	freedom
gorgeous	gravitate	ocean
riot	rowing	visually

4 Now fill the gaps with the correct word.

Range of grammatical structures

Exam spot

In the CAE exam, you are expected to produce a range of structures when writing and speaking. This does not only mean a range of tenses but also the use of the passive form, modal verbs, gerund and infinitive and complex sentences.

1 Look again at the text in Vocabulary 2 and underline the different tenses and grammatical structures.

2 Complete this extract by putting the verbs (1–15) in an appropriate form.

> Looking back on it now, it seems like a dream – my year off after university travelling the world. The best bit (0) ......was...... (be) definitely Indonesia. Intuition (1) .... (tell) me even before I left rainy England that Indonesia was where something special (2) .... (to happen). A friend of mine (3) .... (cycle) through China with paintbrushes and a sketch pad and we (4) .... (arrange) to meet in Bali. We (5) .... (lie) on the beach for a day and then decided that what we (6) .... (need) was more of a cross-Indonesia adventure. So we (7) .... (set) off for the idyllic island of Lombok. And it was there that I (8) .... (see) him. He (9) .... (sit) with his back to me under the shade of a palm tree, (10) .... (look) out to sea. He (11) .... (turn) and (12) .... (smile), which at once (13) .... (render) me incapable of even (14) .... (think) of moving on to another island. And that is how I (15) .... (come) to stay for six months in the one place!

3 Incorporating one of the sentences below, write a paragraph which demonstrates a range of structures and a range of descriptive vocabulary.

- *But for the mosquitoes, it would have been pleasant to be perched on a wobbly wooden platform in an oak forest in …*
- *This is my first summit – but it seems I have made one glaring error. I have forgotten to bring the champagne.*
- *Our guide assures me we are lucky with the weather as at this time of the year we could just as easily be swirled in fog or soaked by rain.*
- *The following morning we were anxious to immerse ourselves as quickly as possible in the wonderful atmosphere of the city.*
- *Across the other side of the lake, an unmade, stony road runs along a gorgeous stretch of unspoilt coastline that reminds me of …*

4 Work with a partner and exchange your paragraphs. Read your partner's paragraph and highlight the interesting structures and vocabulary.

5 With your partner, discuss any improvements that could be made to the paragraphs you have written.

G ···❖ page 203

Exam folder 9

Paper 2 Parts 1 and 2

1 How much do you know about the CAE Writing test (Paper 2)? Answer these questions.

> a How many parts are there in the Writing test?
> b Which question is compulsory?
> c How many questions do you have to answer in total?
> d How long is the Writing test?
> e How many words do you have to write in total?
> f Do the questions carry equal marks?
> g What types of writing might you be asked to write (e.g. formal letters)?
> h What is the assessment focus in Part 1?
> i What is the assessment focus in Part 2?
> j How many markers mark your writing?

Advice

- Remember that in Part 1, you may need to select points to be mentioned; there may be some information in the 'input' that you do not need to use. You have to choose the information which is appropriate to the question.
- Spend plenty of time reading the question carefully and highlighting the points which you need to include in your answer.
- Spend time planning your work.
- Think about who you are writing for and why you are writing.
- Think carefully about how to paragraph your work in an appropriate way. Too many paragraphs may be just as unsatisfactory as too few.
- Allow time to check what you have written – and check not only the language of your answer but also that you have dealt with all the necessary parts of the question.
- Write legibly and make corrections as tidily as possible.
- Put a line through any work that you do not want the examiner to read.
- Don't repeat yourself if there are two parts in Part 1 – each part will require something different in terms of content and register.
- Don't waste time writing out your answers and then rewriting them.
- Don't copy language directly from the question paper – try to reword it in your own way, if possible.
- Don't attempt the work-oriented question unless you have the knowledge and the experience, as well as the language, to deal with it effectively.

2 Read the exam writing task below.

While studying English, you are helping to organise an after-class 'English Club'. You have just received a letter from your English teacher enclosing an article from an International Magazine about young people's attitudes to learning English.

Read the magazine article, the extract from the letter, and the English Club programme with the notes you have made on it. Then, using the information provided, prepare to write the **article** and the **letter** of invitation.

Learning English
Why can't it be fun?

Sadly, most people learn English by attending rather traditional courses where the English taught does not meet the requirements of modern living. In a recent survey we discovered that most young people would like to learn English in a communicative way. They want to be involved with the language through watching films in the original language, listening to music, reading authentic articles from newspapers and magazines and having lively debates on 'real' international issues. So why is no one offering English language learners this motivating way of studying?

... so I knew you'd be interested in read this. I think it would be interesting for the magazine and its readers to hear about our English Club. I think an articl from you, a student, would be much bett than an article from me, a teacher. You could make it clear that not all English language learning is traditional and borin You could make this point by mentioning just some of the activities on our Englis Club programme and how successful the cl is. I also think it would be a good idea invite the editor of the magazine, Jane Stuart, to come and present the awards our 'Film Festival' in April. Could you de with that as well?

ENGLISH CLUB
PROGRAMME FOR JANUARY – APRIL

January: Film Evening

Post-Christmas and New Year blues? What you need is a thrilling evening watching *What lies beneath*, the latest, scariest movie. Discussion review with refreshments afterwards.

Great fun to see about 20 people jumping out of their seats with fright! A great success!

February: Top of the Pops

A music evening where you listen (with video) to the latest pop music and then vote for the top ten tracks. Dance to the number 1 hit at the end of the evening.

Music, dancing, singing along. Lots of people brought friends. People really let their hair down. We got 12 new members!

March: Regional Food of Britain

Yes, you might be amazed by this gourmet evening. Regional dishes prepared by Club members. And recipes to take home!

This was truly amazing. People often say English food is awful; that was until they tasted these regional dishes. We really got to know more about the regions and culture and hopefully laid a few prejudices to rest.

April: Film Festival

As you know, many groups have been working on their 3-minute films to present at this award winning evening. You will vote for the winner. The winner will receive five videos of the latest English language films.

This next event looks incredible. I've seen previews of some of the films and all I can say is Hollywood look out! (invite Jane Stuart to this)

Now write an article for the International Magazine (approximately 200 words) and a brief letter of invitation to Jane Stuart (approximately 50 words).

---

3 Choose **one** of the following writing tasks. Your answer should follow the instructions given exactly. Write approximately 250 words.

A A guidebook called *Off the Beaten Track* is being produced. It gives information about interesting parts of towns or cities which are rarely discovered by tourists. You have been asked to write a contribution recommending a weekend break in your town or city for visitors who want to do something other than see the usual tourist sights. Your contribution should include information about:

- the area in general and why it is interesting for visitors
- the route visitors should take and the new things they will be able to see and do
- the best time of year to go.

Write your **contribution to the guidebook**.

B You see the following advertisement in your local paper.

International Summer Camp

For the 10th year running we are organising our very successful Summer Camp for young people aged between 8 and 16. We are looking for energetic, creative people to help our kids have fun. Do you have:
- an outgoing personality?
- an ability to get on with youngsters from all over the world?
- a knowledge of foreign languages, including English?
- a knowledge of sports or games suitable for youngsters?

Write your **letter of application** for this job. You do not need to include addresses.

C An international magazine has asked its readers to send in a review of two different English dictionaries. Write a review for the magazine in which you compare and contrast **two** different English dictionaries, commenting on the following points:

- the layout and organisation
- the grammatical detail and examples of words in sentences
- value for money.

Write your **review**.

D You work for a branch of a multinational company. You have been asked by the Managing Director to prepare a report on the need for more language training in your branch. Write a report outlining the reasons why more language training is necessary and make recommendations as to which staff would benefit from this training.

Write your **report**.

UNIT 22 | Under the weather

| Genre | Interpreting facts and figures |
| Topic | Climate change |

Speaking 1

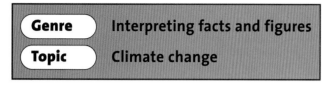

TOMORROW

Blizzards

Windy

Seasonal Affective Disorder –
connection with cosmic storms established
The mood of Alaskans may be related to cosmic storms and the Northern lights, according to an expert in the study of brainwaves. Depression in the far north …

1 With a partner, discuss these questions.

   a What climatic area of the world do you live in? What are the features of this climate?

   b Do you think climate affects people's personalities? Give examples.

   c How is the local weather forecast presented on TV? Is the weather presenter glamorous/ handsome or academic-looking?

   d What would be your idea of a perfect climate?

Reading

1 Have you ever experienced weather conditions similar to the ones in the photos?

2 Look at the diagram below. What does it tell us?

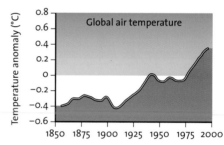

3 Read the magazine article opposite and discuss the questions below.

   a What tone does the writer establish at the beginning of the article with the phrases *Hold on to your hat* and *we're heading for a rough ride*?

   b Do you think this tone is suitable for the topic of this article? Why?/Why not?

E xam spot

In addition to being able to interpret charts and graphs, you also need to be able to sort out fact from opinion. This reading skill is tested in the CAE Reading test (Paper 1).

4 Read through the article again and make notes about what each person says under the headings below. Put O after the notes if it is the person's opinion and F after the notes if it is a fact.

Gabrielle Walker	David Easterling	Phil Jones

Wild weather

Hold on to your hat. Gabrielle Walker consults the long-range forecast and finds that we're heading for a rough ride.

What's with the weather? An unruly beast at the best of times, it now seems to be lurching out of control. Wildfires raged across the western US. Then there was a blistering heatwave in Greece, a bizarre contrast with a spectacular hailstorm in the UK, which left the streets of Hull looking for all the world as if it had snowed in August.

Open any newspaper or flick on the television and you'll find the same questions. What have we done? Is global warming upon us? Are we finally seeing the effects of our rash experiment with the world's climate?

They're hard questions to answer, not least because extreme weather has always been with us. "You can't say we had a flood in Mozambique and another in India and that must be down to global warming," says David Easterling, principal scientist at the National Climate Data Centre (NCDC) in Ashville, North Carolina. "Even if CO_2 levels hadn't changed in the 20th century, we would still see these events happen. You're going to have extremes of climate somewhere every year. The real question is: are we going to see a lot more of these in the future?"

To find out, researchers around the world are scouring records of temperature, wind and rain, trying to spot the patterns that will tell them whether things really are changing. Though they're still figuring out the details, one thing's for sure: even if the recent weather tantrums turn out to be nothing particularly new, the signs are that there's much worse to come.

Of all the changes researchers are watching for, warming is the easiest to spot. Reliable temperature records stretch back to the mid-19th century.

Before that, the data are more sparse, but there is evidence from ice cores, corals, old documents and tree rings of temperatures going back a thousand years or more.

Thanks to these records, there's no longer any serious argument about whether the Earth is heating up. The past century has seen average global temperatures increase by more than half a degree, with the majority of that warming piled up in the latter half. The seven warmest years on record occurred in the 1990s, and 1998 was the hottest of all. "It was the warmest year in the warmest decade in the warmest century in the millennium," says Phil Jones, joint director of the University of East Anglia's Climatic Research Unit in Norwich.

Vocabulary

1 Here are some more words related to the weather. Match a word from the list (a–i) with a word which collocates (1–9).

a	torrential	1	defences
b	high	2	freezing
c	ice	3	forecast
d	sea	4	gale
e	below	5	gusts
f	long-range	6	cap
g	squally	7	rain
h	ozone	8	tide
i	force nine	9	layer

2 Complete this weather report with some of the collocations from Vocabulary 1.

It may be Easter in the UK but no one seems to have told the weather! The west coast is receiving a constant battering from a (1) .... which has ripped roofs from houses in Devon and Cornwall. What's more, this is bringing with it (2) .... which has caused flood alerts to be issued for some areas. This makes you really believe what they say about the (3) .... melting; floods seem to have been a much more common occurrence in the UK over the last year or so. Coastal areas are prone to flooding too as this spring sees (4) .... at record levels in the Severn estuary. In this area too (5) .... have been breached and waves rolled into town centres in some cases. As if all this wasn't enough, night temperatures have been (6) .... all week leaving gardeners bewildered as to what they should do with their spring plants.

Linking devices

Country	Argentina	Brazil	Greece	Japan	Sweden
A snapshot of the world's weather on 16th April					
City	Buenos Aires	Rio de Janeiro	Athens	Tokyo	Stockholm
Temperature	18°C	26°C	18°C	17°C	8°C
Humidity	84%	26%	53%	58%	38%
Wind speed	9 (NE)	4 (NE)	4 (NW)	4 (SW)	6 (SW)
Visibility	good	moderate	very good	n/a	n/a

When we interpret information in charts, graphs or statistics, we usually:

- make a general statement about the information
  This chart shows the main weather features of a number of cities on a particular day.

- comment on significant features of the information provided (often by comparing and contrasting data)
  It can be seen from this table that the warmest place was Rio de Janeiro whereas the coldest place was Stockholm.

- discuss the important features (often by providing examples or giving reasons)
  According to the information, visibility was very good in Athens; this is particularly important as there is often concern about the levels of pollution in large cities, and as we can see this was not the case in Athens.

- draw a conclusion.
  In conclusion, depending on your preferences, Rio de Janeiro or Athens might have been very pleasant places to spend that day.

> **E** xam spot
>
> You can adopt this strategy for the CAE Speaking test (Paper 5), where you have to compare and contrast pictures.

1   Complete the text about how the weather can affect your mood with linking devices from the box below.

because   contrary to   however   on the other hand   whereas   indeed

On the one hand, some people say they feel dull and gloomy when the weather is grey. (1) .... others say they feel cosy and secure when they are inside on grey days, reading in front of the fire. (2) .... , it is true to say that higher levels of light do raise the spirits. You know yourself when you wake up and it's sunny, you feel brighter, (3) .... when you wake up and it's dull, you feel sluggish. Interestingly, recent research has shown that, (4) .... popular belief, people are more creative in colder climates. For example, more inventions have been made by people living in colder climates than in hotter ones. (5) .... , it could be that they stay at work longer (6) .... the weather is so awful outside!

2 Complete the words in the third column. They are all nouns which describe changes in quantity. The number of dashes tells you how many letters there are in the words. Indicate with an arrow if the change is upwards or downwards.

There was/ has been a(n)				
	minimal			
	slight			
	small	i _ _ _ _ _ _ _		temperature.
	gradual	r _ _ _		humidity.
	steady	f _ _ _ _ _ _ _ _ _		rainfall.
	marked	d _ _ _ _ _ _ _	in	hours of sunshine.
	significant	d _ _ _ _ _ _		wind speed.
	steep	r _ _ _ _ _ _ _ _		the number of storms.
	sharp	f _ _ _		the amount of damage.
	rapid	d _ _ _		night-time temperatures.
	sudden			

3 These sentences all contain phrases for drawing conclusions. The words are jumbled up. Rewrite the sentences with the words in the correct order.

a conclusion the temperature over the couple in we world's has risen last of can say decades that significantly.

b whole weather experiencing the may are extreme conditions on be we more it said that.

c scientists following with interest increased are therefore concluded it that all changes climate be can.

d reduce the threat given that unless emissions is this be countries under climate carbon may deduced it.

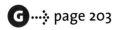 **G** ·····⋮> page 203

Listening

1 🎧 You will hear two friends, Tim and Wendy, giving their views on climate change. Listen and tick which aspects of climate change each speaker mentions.

Aspect of climate change	Tim	Wendy
El Niño		
Floods and droughts		
Global warming		
Greenhouse gas emissions		
Sea level		
Storms		

2 🎧 Listen again and make notes about each speaker's views.

3 Work with a partner and compare and contrast Tim and Wendy's views using linking devices where appropriate. Say whether you agree with them or not.

Speaking 2

1 Your teacher will give you some charts comparing daily life now and in the future. Your chart has some missing information.

Find out the missing information to complete your chart by asking your partner. As you do, discuss the information using linking devices. Make sure that you:

- make a general statement about the information
- comment on significant features of the information provided (by comparing and contrasting data)
- discuss the important features (by providing examples or giving reasons)
- draw a conclusion.

2 How do you think things will change in the future? Do you agree with the predictions in the chart?

Writing folder 9

Descriptive writing

1 Read the following CAE writing tasks and discuss whether there would be an element of description in your answer.

A You see the following announcement in an educational magazine.

> ## Competition
>
> The ideal school of the future
> - What will the ideal school be like in 50 years' time?
> - How will it be different from schools today?
> - What subjects, technology and facilities will schools of the future have?

Write your **competition entry**.

B You have recently been to two music events and have been asked to write a review of these events for a music website. Your review should compare and contrast:
- the instruments and singers at each event
- the ability of the performers at each event
- the audiences' reactions.

You should also say which event you enjoyed more and why.

Write your **review**.

C You see the following announcement in an international students' magazine.

> ## How to survive examination preparation
>
> We would like our readers around the world to share their ideas and experiences.
> Write an article suggesting how best to prepare for exams, and say what you should and should not do the night before the exam.

Write your **article**.

D Your department has recently asked for your offices to be refurbished. You have received the following memo from the Managing Director.

> Re: your request for office refurbishment
> I need more information before I can make a decision. Could you write me a report stating the problems with the present furniture, decoration and layout of the offices? Indicate how this refurbishment will improve working conditions and performance.

Write your **report**.

2 Here are some steps to go through when planning your answer to a writing task. Put them into a logical order. Write number 1 next to the first step and so on.

a think about sentence structure
b reorganise your brainstorming notes into a logical order
c think about the vocabulary
d write and edit the text
e think about your introduction
f think about your conclusion
g think about the reader
h read the question
i brainstorm the topic
j think about the layout, including the number of paragraphs

3 You are going to prepare a review in answer to question 1B.

a Look back at question 1B and underline the key words.

b Tell your partner about a music event you have been to (or seen on TV or in a film). What were your impressions of it?

c Who is the intended reader of your description?
- a friend
- a music teacher
- people interested in music

d What style of writing is appropriate?
- formal and factual
- lively and entertaining
- chatty

e Brainstorm your topic again but this time complete the word webs as you go along.

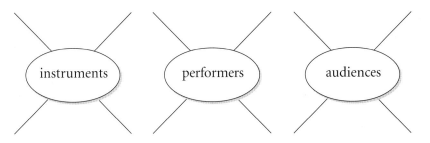

f What are you going to include in each paragraph?

Introduction:

Conclusion:

g Think about sentence structure. Which structures do you think you will be able to use in your description? Put ✓ next to the ones you are quite sure you will use, ? next to the ones you are not sure if you will use, and ✗ next to the ones you really don't think you will use.

- past simple
- past continuous
- past perfect
- past perfect continuous
- present perfect
- present perfect continuous
- present simple
- present continuous
- conditional forms
- passive forms
- gerunds
- infinitives
- relative clauses

h Write your first draft. It is often useful to leave a generous margin and/or write on alternate lines so that you can make changes and corrections clearly.

i Exchange your first draft with another pair of students and edit their first draft using this code:

SP	spelling
X	unnecessary word
GR	grammar
WW	wrong word
P	punctuation
RW	repeated word
WO	word order

j Write the final version of the task and check it again.

UNIT 23 I'm afraid I really must insist

Genre	Formal letters
Topic	How to complain

Speaking 1

1 Read these situations and discuss them with a partner. Choose A, B or C, whichever is closest to your opinion.

1 You are in a restaurant with a group of friends. The waiter is taking ages to come and take your order and now you've been waiting for 45 minutes. You are going to the cinema after your meal so you don't want to spend a long time waiting. The restaurant is very busy so you know it is not the waiter's fault. Do you

A walk out of the restaurant glaring at the waiter but saying nothing?

B go up to the head waiter and demand to see the manager?

C attract the waiter with your best smile, explain the situation and try to get what you want by being nice?

2 You paid a lot of money for a designer label T-shirt. The first time you washed it you followed the washing instructions carefully but still the colour ran and ruined some other clothes you washed it with. When it dried it was obvious it had shrunk. You think the material is of poor quality and does not represent the amount you paid for it. Do you

A throw it in the bin and vow never to go to that shop again?

B phone the shop and tell them that they are frauds and you're going to sue them?

C go back to the shop with your receipt and ask for your money back?

3 You went on a day trip to a beach with a tour company. The trip was advertised as using comfortable buses with experienced drivers. The trip took much longer than expected so you did not have much time at the beach. The coach was awful and the driver was reckless. Do you

A get a taxi back to your hotel and pay for it yourself?

B get a taxi back to your hotel and insist that the tour company pays for it and gives you £300 as compensation?

C mention to the driver that you are a nervous passenger and explain to the tour company why you are dissatisfied when you get back?

2 With a partner, discuss these questions about complaining.

a What sort of complainer are you? Do you just moan to your friends or do you complain calmly to the shop or company concerned?

b Do you get angry when you have to complain about something?

c If you had to complain about something in English, what do you think might be the best way to do it: face-to-face, by phone or by letter? Why?

Reading

1 Imagine a visitor to your country wants to complain about something. What is the best way to do this?

2 You are going to read an article called *How to complain*. With a partner, make a list of the pieces of advice you expect to read.

EXAMPLE: *Do not complain when you are feeling angry.*

3 Read the article and match the headings (A–H) to the paragraphs (1–6). There are two headings which do not fit.

A Who will I complain to?

B How can I get my money back?

C How do I feel?

D What are the facts?

E What do I do if I don't get satisfaction?

F What are my rights?

G How will I complain most effectively?

H What do I want?

4 Choose three pieces of advice in the article which you consider the most important.

How to complain

Most people love to complain, but while moaning to friends is a national pastime, when it comes to protesting to a retailer, for example, we often prefer to suffer in silence about faulty goods or services.

When we do decide to make our point, we can become aggressive, gearing up for battle and turning what should be a rational negotiation into a conflict.

To complain effectively, you need to be clear in your communication, specific about your problem and how you want it solved, and objective in the words you choose to make your point. Good negotiators tend to be calm and logical. You should first ask yourself:

1 ▢

Was the product faulty or are you complaining about rude service or a delay? Sift out feelings from hard fact. This will help you to be concise and to the point.

2 ▢

What will it take to put the problem right? Most complaints become negotiation and it's important to know what you'll accept. Do you want your money back, or the product replaced? Or will an apology be sufficient?

3 ▢

If the complaint is a serious one, you need to go armed with your legal rights.

4 ▢

Have you ever begun to complain with the words: "I know this isn't your fault, but ..."? Spouting hot air to the wrong person is a waste of time and energy. Start off by finding out exactly who you should be speaking to, and who has the authority to handle your problem. Take the name of the person who deals with your complaint.

5 ▢

In person, by letter, or over the phone? If face-to-face isn't possible or you feel you lack confidence, a phone call may be easier. Start by explaining the situation and stating your requirement clearly, without threat. If you are not satisfied with the response, remind the other person about the agreement that's been broken.

6 ▢

Most complaints prompt an emotional response, but being reasonable is more likely to get the positive result you want. If you feel angry or upset about what has happened, go ahead and tell the company, but do it calmly. Demonstrate that you understand the situation from the other person's point of view. "I appreciate that it might be difficult to arrange a special delivery, but I really need the order by tomorrow." Do state clearly the consequences of your request being ignored. ("I'm going to place the order elsewhere and cancel my account with you"), but never make a threat that you can't carry out.

G ⋯⟫ page 204

Phrasal verbs

1 Look at these examples of two-part phrasal verbs from the article. What do they mean?

- *When we do decide to make our point, we can become aggressive, **gearing up** for battle and turning what should be a rational negotiation into a conflict.*
- ***Sift out** feelings from hard fact.*
- *Start off by **finding out** exactly who you should be speaking to, and who has the authority to handle your problem.*
- *If you feel angry or upset about what has happened, **go ahead** and tell the company, but do it calmly.*
- *… never make a threat that you can't **carry out**.*

2 Correct the sentences below if necessary.

EXAMPLE: *They refused to enter any discussion into about the matter.* ✗
They refused to enter into any discussion about the matter. ✓
(*to enter into* = to start to become involved in something, especially a discussion)

a Before you go to the shop to complain, jot down the points you want to make.

b I looked the guarantee through but I couldn't find out how long it was valid for anywhere.

c The engineer's explanations as to why it doesn't work just don't add up.

d I didn't expect a problem to crop up so soon after buying a new computer.

e We don't hold much hope out, but we are still trying to get compensation.

f Trying to get a satisfactory answer to my queries took the whole morning up.

g If you had taken out an extended guarantee, the cost of the repairs would have been covered.

h I didn't really want to spend so much on a TV but Frank talked me it into buying.

3 Read the note below all the way through first to get a general understanding of what it says. Then fill the gaps (1–8) using phrasal verbs from the box.

get on with	make out	pluck up	put across
sink in	stick up for	take to	turn out

Hi Sandy
You know I'd been having problems with my noisy neighbours? Well, last week I couldn't (0) ...put up with... the din any longer so I (1) .... courage and went and knocked on their door. They live in the flat above me and I hear their music day and night. During the day it's awful because I can't (2) .... my studies, I can't concentrate, and in the evenings when I want to relax, I can hardly (3) .... a word from my own TV, theirs is on so loud. Anyway, I thought I've got to (4) .... myself and go and face them. This woman came to the door and I tried to (5) .... what I wanted to say as calmly as I could. She listened and then said how glad she was that I'd come to her and explained that it's her teenage son who has his music on so loud. She said she'd told him it would disturb the neighbours and he'd said it obviously didn't as no one had complained. She explained that once I'd complained, she'd have ammunition to confront him with and it might (6) .... that he can't behave as though he lived on a desert island. Funnily enough I really (7) .... her and she asked me in for a coffee. So after being afraid of going to see my neighbour, it (8) .... that I've made a new friend.

Listening

1 You are going to listen to someone giving advice about how to ask their boss for a pay rise. Before you listen, discuss these questions with a partner.

a What sort of person would your ideal boss be and why?

b What do you think is the strongest reason for asking for a pay rise?

c If your boss was rather 'difficult', how would you go about asking for a pay rise? Which of these suggestions might be useful?

- Make sure you make a formal appointment with him/her to discuss the matter.
- Wear more formal clothes to work for some time before you ask for a pay rise.
- Go into his/her office frequently and drop hints about how much work you are doing and how good it is.
- Make a list of all the reasons why you should have a pay rise.
- Tell your boss how much better you are than other employees.

E xam spot

In the CAE Listening test (Paper 4), you may be asked to complete a multiple-choice task like the one opposite. Read all the questions before you start listening so that you are prepared to choose the right answer. You hear the recording twice.

2 🎧 Listen to the recording and choose the best answer A, B, C or D according to what you hear.

1 The key factor when asking for a pay rise is
   A voicing your demands in a convincing way.
   B making it clear you feel undervalued.
   C proving you are an asset in the business.
   D comparing yourself to the rest of the staff.

2 If you have any failings, you should
   A check that no one knows about them.
   B put them right gradually so that it is not too obvious.
   C accentuate your strengths, such as punctuality.
   D make sure your boss likes you as a person.

3 When preparing what to say in your salary negotiation,
   A put yourself in your superior's shoes.
   B do not forget that you really need that extra money.
   C make a list of all the points in your favour.
   D focus on what you can do for the company in the future.

4 What should you do if your boss raises objections to your pay rise?
   A pre-empt them by raising them yourself and giving a counter argument
   B make sure you can quote company rules to him or her
   C appreciate that your boss is only doing his or her job
   D accept any offer as it is better than nothing

5 During salary negotiations, it is important to
   A mention that the company is very successful.
   B ensure your boss is aware that you are taking these negotiations seriously.
   C arrange to see your boss early in the day when he or she is fresh.
   D try not to put your boss in an awkward position.

6 What should you do if you do not get a pay rise or as much as you wanted?
   A be prepared for a long drawn-out conflict
   B know that you might have to resign as a matter of principle
   C either have an alternative or ask for constructive criticism
   D either get a colleague to back you up or talk to your boss again soon

Writing

xam spot

In the CAE Writing test (Paper 2), you may be asked to write a letter of complaint or an article complaining about something. Read the situation carefully and make the purpose of your writing clear.

1 Read the writing task below and then discuss the questions which follow with a partner.

> You recently bought a piece of electronic equipment from a shop. After a very short time it began to go wrong so you took it back to the shop where they said they would have it repaired. You waited four weeks to get it back and when you did, you discovered that it had not been repaired at all. If anything, it was worse. You took it back to the shop again and they took it again for repair, you waited three weeks and when you got it back it still did not work properly. You are annoyed because you have not been able to use your purchase for about two months and the shop has done nothing to repair it. You decide the only solution is either to have a new one or get your money back. You decide to write a letter to the manager of the shop.

a Which pieces of advice in the article *How to complain* might be appropriate to this situation?

b Plan your letter. Think about:

- the number of paragraphs you need
- the main content of each paragraph
- some formal phrases suitable for your letter
- some grammatical structures suitable for your letter
- the overall organisation of your letter.

2 Write your letter in approximately 250 words.

Speaking 2

xam spot

In the CAE Speaking test (Paper 5), one of the things the examiner is listening for is your interactive communication.

1 Getting your views across is all part of being a good communicator. Below is a list of suggestions as to what makes a good communicator. Tick the suggestions which you think are important.

A good communicator is someone who:

- listens actively and responds logically
- always starts speaking first
- can paraphrase and reformulate what they want to say
- can explain precisely what they want to say
- only says what is necessary
- uses body language to emphasise what they want to say
- doesn't interrupt others when they are speaking
- helps other people to finish their sentences
- summarises periodically what they have said so far
- has a large vocabulary
- makes few grammatical errors.

xam spot

In the CAE Speaking test (Paper 5), you are given an activity which you discuss with your partner. Then the examiner will ask you some more general questions which relate to the topic of the activity. You will need to show that you can get your views across.

2 Look at these items that a company might offer as compensation for faulty goods or unsatisfactory service. Discuss with a partner which ones you would be prepared to accept.

Exam folder 10

Paper 4 Parts 1 and 2

1 How much do you know about the CAE Listening test (Paper 4)? Answer the questions below.

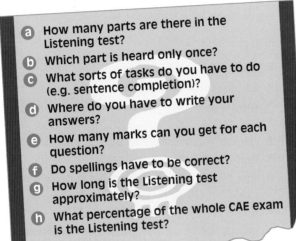

- **a** How many parts are there in the Listening test?
- **b** Which part is heard only once?
- **c** What sorts of tasks do you have to do (e.g. sentence completion)?
- **d** Where do you have to write your answers?
- **e** How many marks can you get for each question?
- **f** Do spellings have to be correct?
- **g** How long is the Listening test approximately?
- **h** What percentage of the whole CAE exam is the Listening test?

2 You are going to hear part of a radio programme about blue jeans. Before you listen, discuss the questions below with a partner.

- **a** Do you know when jeans were invented and by whom?
- **b** What sort of clothes were they intended to be? When do you think they became popular among young people?
- **c** Do you think jeans should be blue or do you like wearing other colours?
- **d** Who wears them these days?

3  You are going to hear part of a radio programme about blue jeans. For questions 1–4, fill in the missing information.

Young people in the 1950s started wearing jeans as a symbol of (**1**) .... As parents thought of jeans as (**2**) .... , they disapproved of them being worn as 'going out' clothes. Jeans became internationally popular because they are, according to the speaker, (**3**) .... and make everyone equal. The (**4**) .... of jeans and youth culture are in the United States.

4 Check your answers with a partner. Do your answers make full, grammatically correct sentences? Check your spelling.

5  Listen again to check your answers.

6 🎧 You are going to hear some more of the same interview. Remember that in Part 2 you have to listen very carefully as you hear the recording **once** only. As you listen, complete the notes.

Most jeans in Europe imported from: (1) ....
Jeans fall into two categories: the classics and (2) ....
Jeans are worn by members of the establishment now, e.g.:
(3) ....
The place to 'rebel' by wearing torn jeans would be:
(4) ....

7 Check your answers with a partner.

Advice

- Read the questions carefully before you start listening.
- Write down the actual words you hear.
- The answers are short; one to three words.
- Check your spelling.
- In Part 1 make sure you have made a grammatically correct sentence.
- Always try to write something even if you are not sure it is the correct answer.

UNIT 24 News and views

| Genre | Investigative journalism |
| Topic | Stories in the news |

Speaking

1 With a partner, discuss these questions.

  a How do you usually find out about the news?
  b What are the main purposes of broadcasting?
  c What do you think TV viewing will be like in the future?

2 What sorts of programmes do you think make ideal Saturday TV viewing? Work in small groups and match the types of programmes to the best times in the schedule.

Types of programmes
Sport   Chat show   Children's TV
Chart music show   Hospital drama
News and weather   Documentary
Lottery   Quiz show   Wildlife programme
Comedy impressionist   Film   Learning zone

TIMES OF SATURDAY'S PROGRAMMES

7.00 am
12.10 pm
12.15 pm
5.55 pm
6.50 pm
7.45 pm
8.55 pm
9.55 pm
10.15 pm
10.30 pm
11.40 pm

3 Form new groups and present your choice of schedule. Be prepared to support your choices with reasons.

Exam spot

In the CAE Listening test (Paper 4) you may be asked to listen to extracts from documentaries, news bulletins, sports reports or arts reviews. Watching television or listening to the radio will familiarise you with the style and language of these programmes.

Listening

1 🎧 You are going to hear the headlines from a world news broadcast. Listen and note down which news item in particular you would like to listen to.

2 🎧 Now listen to two short news items and complete the table.

	Where	Who	Topic
Item 1			
Item 2			

3 You will hear a broadcast called *Those who break the labour laws*. What do you think this story will be about?

4 🎧 Listen to the broadcast and answer the questions below.

   a Is the problem of illegal employment confined to one country?
   b What are the two types of illegal employment the journalist mentions?
   c Give one reason why the employees do not complain.
   d What sort of work is Janine doing?
   e What happened when she said she might leave the job?
   f Does the reporter think it is likely that she will go back to school?

5 Do you think that investigative journalism can actually improve conditions by exposing exploitation? Why?/Why not?

Vocabulary

A homophone is a word which has exactly the same pronunciation as another word but has a different spelling or meaning. For example, in Listening 3 you heard the word *steak*. *Stake* (which means *a thick strong stick or metal bar with a pointed end* or *a share or financial investment in something*) has the same pronunciation as *steak* but a different meaning and spelling. *Steak* (/steɪk/) and *stake* (/steɪk/) are therefore homophones.

Homophones are often used in newspaper headlines to catch the reader's attention.

1 What is the homophone for the underlined word in these headlines?

a **RED THE NEWS LATELY?**
A new newspaper has decided to print not only pictures in colour but also text. *The Daily …*

b **No way!**
A health farm with a difference has recently opened. Guests are forbidden to jump on the scales and …

c **WHO WOULD HAVE GUESSED?**
Fellow visitors to a small seaside Bed and Breakfast were astonished to discover that Brad Pitt was booked in …

d **MALE DELAYED**
A woman who thought she was getting married to the man of her dreams had to wait …

e **THE HOLE STORY!**
A golfer who thought he had missed …

f **A minor! But you're 55!**
When Bert Smith filled out a form for the local government, his spelling got him into trouble …

g **If bingeing on chocolate makes your trousers too tight, blame the genes**
Chocoholics no longer need to feel guilty about their craving …

2 Think of a homophone for the following words.

   a won   e stairs   h where
   b meet   f blue   i waste
   c sell   g sail   j through
   d so

Reading

1 Newspaper headlines often proclaim a new scientific breakthrough or discovery. You are going to read an article about the 'sweet tooth gene'. Before reading, discuss these questions with a partner.

a Where do you get most of your information about new scientific discoveries from – newspapers, documentaries or your studies?

b Have you got a sweet tooth? Does this trait run in your family?

c If scientists could discover a sweet tooth gene, what could they do with this information?

2 Read the article and then decide if the following statements are true or false.

a Having a sweet tooth is an inherited trait.

b A drug has been developed which can put you off sweet food.

c The two teams of researchers used different types of mice.

d The sweet tooth gene produces a protein.

e Aubrey Sheiham believes dieting is futile if you have the sweet tooth gene.

f It is natural for humans to be attracted to sweet foods.

g This discovery may lead to the production of a new type of chocolate.

3 What do you think about newspaper articles which herald new 'wonder discoveries'? Are you sceptical of them? Why?/Why not?

4 What scientific developments do you think we will see in the near future as a result of work on DNA?

IF BINGEING ON CHOCOLATE MAKES YOUR TROUSERS TOO TIGHT, BLAME THE GENES

CHOCOHOLICS no longer need to feel guilty about their craving. They are simply the victim of their genes, scientists have found.

The so-called 'sweet tooth gene' has been identified by separate teams of researchers and helps explain why some find it harder to resist chocolate bars and cream cakes.

It also raises the possibility of designing a drug which could 'switch off' the gene and help people resist sugary foods. Children, in particular, risk their health by eating too many sweets and chocolates.

To identify the gene, the research teams - based at Harvard Medical School in Boston and Mount Sinai School of Medicine in New York - conducted almost identical experiments using mice which have differences in their ability to taste sweet foods. They compared the DNA of the two types of mice and noticed differences in the gene called T1R3.

Dr. Gopi Shanker, of the Mount Sinai team, said: 'It contains information which produces a protein called the sweet taste receptor.

This recognises the sweet content of food and initiates a cascade of events which signal to the brain that a sweet food has been eaten.' Dr. Shanker added: 'Exactly the same gene exists in humans, so it means that if your parents have a sweet tooth then you probably will as well.'

Research by the Harvard team has come to the same conclusion.

But Aubrey Sheiham, professor of dental public health at University College, London, said the results did not provide chocoholics with an excuse to give up dieting.

He said: 'We have always known that some people have a sweeter tooth than others. But it has also been proved that if you gradually expose people to less sugar, then the body becomes accustomed to less. They will be satisfied with a lower level of sweetness.'

Mr. Sheiham warned against any form of gene therapy which sought to deactivate the sweet tooth gene.

'We have produced this gene through evolution because sweet foods in nature are not poisonous and also give us energy. We all need to have some sugar in our diet.'

The U.S. researchers are using their discovery to develop artificial sweeteners without an aftertaste.

Linking devices

1 Fill the gaps (1–10) in the article below with the linking devices from the box. There are two linking devices which do not fit.

and what's more	as
but because	by then
even despite	
provided resulted in	
so to cap it all then	

30,000 runners take London in their stride

(0) ....No sooner.... had the gun sounded than we were all off, including me and my running flatmate, Fran, jostling for position **(1)** .... we crossed the starting line, which was awash with plastic bags, unwanted clothing, bottles and banana skins.

The real running began as Greenwich came into view and the crowds, which were already big, increased even further. People shouted at friends. Anyone with their name on their vest became public property **(2)** .... everyone wanted to be part of this event. Screams of encouragement mixed with brass bands and Beatles tribute bands.

The 12-mile point. I must have lived this part at least a dozen times from my armchair. I could hear a commentator murmuring about how plucky we all were.

(3) .... the halfway mark was within reach and it was getting tiring. Tower Bridge loomed, magnificent, with thousands of people screeching encouragement.

I knew what was coming. At 13 miles out I saw a small flag fluttering and annoying someone's ear and then the words: "There he is." My parents had spotted me. I stopped for a chat, and went on my way. **(4)** .... someone was watching after all.

(5) .... regularly ingesting isotonic fluid and strawberry and banana flavoured gels (350 calories a sachet) we were getting only fleeting benefits. Children were pressed to the barriers offering support and sometimes sweets.

Through a haze of discomfort Canary Wharf appeared. It went on forever. Things were flagging. Knees were sore, ankles pinching, **(6)** .... my arms were tingling. Twenty miles gone and it was agony. I guessed this was my wall coming. Tall and slippery with broken glass on the top. How I got past that point without hiring a cab I have yet to unravel.

Things worsened. The closer to home, the harder it became. My feet

were sticking to the floor. Fran was looking worried. We did not stop and walk **(7)** .... just ran at a walking pace.

The last mile felt like the first 13. Nothing was much fun. I was gone. **(8)** .... , I was hungry.

(9) .... , turning past Big Ben I saw a man holding an advert for McDonald's bacon double cheese burger. Unbelievable cruelty. **(10)** .... I would have eaten my hand if it was encased in a bun and covered in mayo with a couple of those gherkin-type things for relish. And I am a vegetarian.

The finish was in sight. Past Buckingham Palace and a couple of screeching friends and to the end. The fullstop finish, no more, never again. Around me people staggered, their faces covered in dry salt deposits from sweat, lips trembling, a few crying.

Strangers offered congratulations, touched our backs, smiled the brightest smiles, spoke the most beautiful words. I loved the world and it loved me.

2 Would you ever consider taking part in a marathon or similar event?

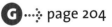 page 204

Writing folder 10

Formal writing

1 The sentences below mean approximately the same thing. What is the difference between them?

   a Give us a ring soon.
   b We look forward to hearing from you at your earliest convenience.

   Written English tends to be more formal than spoken English. You may have to write both formal and informal English in the CAE Writing test.

2 Here are some of the types of writing that you may need to do. Put them on a scale with the most formal at the top and the most informal at the bottom.

   • article for a student magazine
   • competition entry for an international magazine
   • contribution to a tourist guidebook
   • leaflet for a local sports club
   • letter of complaint to a newspaper
   • letter to a pen friend
   • proposal to a benefactor on how you would spend the money he might give you
   • report for your boss
   • review for an English Club newsletter

3 With a partner, discuss these pieces of advice relating to formal writing. If necessary, modify the pieces of advice to make them more appropriate.

   • Avoid verb contractions in formal writing.
   • Avoid phrasal verbs in formal writing.
   • Never use slang or colloquial expressions in formal writing.
   • Keep to formal layout conventions.
   • It is particularly important in formal writing to make the structure of what you are saying totally clear.
   • Use linking words and phrases to help clarify the structure of your writing.

4 These sentences all come from a report which should have been written in a formal style. Improve each one in any way that seems appropriate to you.

   a It was kind of difficult to collect as much data as we'd originally hoped.
   b The guys tended to express views that were a bit more conservative than those of the girls.
   c A number of our respondents brought up some very important things in response to our questions.
   d Interviewees' responses depended on how old they were and whether they were male or female, not to mention their occupation and educational background.
   e I'd like to go on a bit more about some important parts of the survey.

5 Replace the adjectives in italics in the sentences below with more interesting and appropriate adjectives.

   a Thank you for your very *nice* letter. You have been doing a lot of *good* things!
   b The job you are advertising sounds very *good*, working with *nice* people.
   c In our restaurant you can enjoy a *nice* meal while admiring the *beautiful* view.
   d Club members have enjoyed a very *nice* programme this year.
   e The first interviewee for the position was a *beautiful* woman with very *good* qualifications for the post.

6 Add the linking devices in the boxes to each paragraph.

Secondly	Moreover	Finally	Firstly

a

The people present raised a number of objections to the plan for the club's yearly programme proposed by the committee. (1) .... they felt that the proposed programme did not contain enough to attract new members. (2) .... they considered that there were not enough meetings geared towards younger members. (3) .... several people made the point that the events suggested were not varied enough. (4) .... it was suggested that some new young members be co-opted onto the committee and a new programme be proposed as soon as possible.

So	However	Consequently	Although

b

Employed for five years in a small company in the remote town where she lived, my cousin knew that she ought to find herself a better job but she found it very hard to make the decision to leave. (1) .... she liked the job and she had enjoyed the company of her colleagues, the work itself was not very challenging. (2) .... she knew that it would make sense, from a career point of view, to look for something else before too many more years elapsed. (3) ...., the fact that her mother was in failing health made the decision a more serious issue for her. (4) ...., she realised she could not consider taking on a job in another town.

After that	Finally	because	especially
then	Firstly	when	Gradually

c

If you have only a couple of hours to spend in the countryside near our town, (1) .... this is the most valuable way to spend them. (2) ...., starting from the city centre, walk out of town along the river. Pay attention to the very interesting old industrial buildings that look quite different (3) .... viewed from the river. (4) .... you will move into residential areas where there are large expensive homes with long gardens stretching down to the river. You will see some very nice boats moored there. (5) .... you will be away from the town and will be able to enjoy magnificent views over the broad expanses of the local countryside. Keep an eye open (6) .... for bird life and for flowers (7) .... both are particularly rich in this area. (8) ...., you will come to an attractive pub on the river where you can enjoy lunch or a drink before catching the bus back to the city centre.

7 A benefactor is prepared to give a large sum of money to your college if a good case is put for how it will benefit the students there. Write your proposal, bearing in mind all the work on formal writing which you have done.

UNIT 25 Powers of observation

| Genre | Academic texts |
| Topic | Research methods |

Speaking

1 Discuss these questions with a partner.

   a Do you prefer to study alone or with friends?

   b Do you use a variety of resources when you study such as the Internet, CDs, reference books or TV programmes?

   c Can you study better at night or in the morning?

   d Do you ever use English to study other subjects?

Reading

1 You are going to read an extract about using observation as a research method. Read this sentence from the extract and discuss what you think the text might be about.

Hans answered questions by tapping with his forefoot or by pointing with his nose at different alternatives shown to him.

Now read the first part of the text opposite.

Research methods in psychology

OBSERVATION

We can learn a great deal about behaviour by simply observing the actions of others. However, everyday observations are not always made carefully or systematically. Most people do not attempt to control or eliminate factors that might influence the events they are observing. As a consequence, erroneous conclusions are often drawn.

Consider, for example, the classic case of Clever Hans. Hans was a horse that was said by his owner, a German mathematics teacher, to have amazing talents. Hans could count, do simple addition and subtraction (even involving fractions), read German, answer simple questions ('What is the lady holding in her hands?'), give the date, and tell the time. Hans answered questions by tapping with his forefoot or by pointing with his nose at different alternatives shown to him. His owner considered Hans to be truly intelligent and denied using any tricks to guide his horse's behaviour. And, in fact, Clever Hans was clever even when the questioner was someone other than his owner.

2 How do you think Hans was able to answer the questions? Read on.

Newspapers carried accounts of Hans's performance, and hundreds of people came to view this amazing horse. In 1904, a scientific commission was established with the goal of discovering the basis for Hans's abilities. The scientists found that Hans was no longer clever if either of two circumstances existed. First, Hans did not know the answers to questions if the questioner also did not know the answers. Second, Hans was not very clever if he could not see his questioner. A slight bending forward by the questioner would start Hans tapping, and any movement upward or backward would cause Hans to stop tapping. The commission demonstrated that questioners were unintentionally cueing Hans in this way.

This famous account of Clever Hans illustrates the fact that scientific observation (unlike casual observation) is systematic and controlled. Indeed, it has been suggested that control is the essential ingredient of science, distinguishing it from non-scientific procedures (Boring, 1954; Marx, 1963). In the case of Clever Hans, investigators exercised control by manipulating, one at a time, conditions such as whether the questioner knew the answer to the question asked and whether Hans could see the questioner. By exercising control, taking care to investigate the effect of various factors one by one, a scientist seeks to gain a clearer picture of the factors that actually produce a phenomenon.

3 To what extent do you think animals can communicate with humans?

4 Look at these examples of formal language from the first paragraph of the text.

*We can learn **a great deal** about behaviour by **simply observing the actions of others**. However, everyday observations are not always made carefully or systematically. Most people do not **attempt** to control or **eliminate factors** that might influence the **events they are observing**. As a consequence, erroneous conclusions are often drawn.*

Now go back to the texts and underline some more examples of formal language.

5 Rephrase the words and phrases which you have underlined into informal language.

6 Read the formal letter below. Use the information in it to fill the numbered gaps (1–7) in the informal letter which follows.

Dear Mr Barrat

I am writing to you on behalf of my colleagues in the English Group to inform you about the compulsory weekend for students starting the MA course in English in September. The weekend provides a valuable opportunity for you to meet both the teaching staff and your fellow MA students. It is held here at the University.

Please find enclosed a programme for the two days, and a plan of the University. All sessions will be held in Room 639 on Level 6. Some very interesting speakers with research backgrounds in Language Learning have been invited. Materials for the first module will be distributed.

The weekend affords an opportunity to introduce you to the MA in English and to discuss any questions you may have about the course. We are looking forward to meeting you.

Yours sincerely

Caroline Tanner
Lecturer in English

Hi George
You know I start my MA course soon? Well, I got a letter (1) .... all about the first weekend which we (2) .... as it's part of the course. I'm really looking forward to it because it'll (3) .... to meet the lecturers and (4) .... students. The weekend course (5) .... at the university.
They've (6) .... the programme for the weekend which looks really interesting and they'll (7) .... all the materials we're going to need in the first module.
Looks like I'm going to be working hard from now on. See you soon.

Cheers
Mark

Complex sentences and adverbial clauses

Complex sentences have at least two clauses: a main clause and at least one subordinate clause. Adverbial clauses are subordinate clauses which give more information about the main clause, such as time, place, manner, reason, condition and so on.

Here are some examples of adverbial clauses:

Main clause	Adverbial clause
The horse could answer the questions	every time his owner asked a question.
Hans's fame began in the village	where his owner lived and worked.
The horse answered questions	by tapping his forefoot.
The horse became famous	because he could answer any question asked of him.
The scientists found that Hans was no longer clever	if either of two circumstances existed.

E xam spot

Using complex sentences both in your writing and speaking is a sign that you are working at an advanced level, and so is appropriate in CAE.

1 Complete these sentences as appropriate.

a Hans's owner believed him to be truly intelligent because ....

b Hans could answer questions even if ....

c Hans could not answer questions when ....

d A scientific commission unravelled the mystery by ....

e Although Hans was never denounced as a fraud, ...

f The person asking Hans the questions had to stand in a place where ....

2 Do you think that people these days are less likely to believe stories like the one about Hans? Why?/Why not?

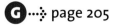 page 205

Listening

1 You are going to listen to a talk on how to devise a good questionnaire. Before you listen, look at this very amateurish questionnaire about study habits and say what is wrong with it.

STUDY HABITS

a You are a good student, aren't you? **Yes/No**

b How many hours do you study?

c Are you a high school student / university student / evening-class student?

d Where can you study most effectively?

e What advice would you give to a high school student?

f At what age are most people the best students?

g What physical conditions are good for studying?

        warm/cool enough?
        not too hungry/full?
        time of day?
        place?

h Could you study more than you do at present?

2 🎧 Listen to the talk and complete the notes below.

First step: Decide (1) ....

Problems of many questionnaires: (2) ....
and (3) ....

Second step: (4) ....

Who will ask the questions? (5) .... or
trained interviewers?

Check whether you can use (6) ....

Third step: (7) ....

Consider (8) ...., ordering of questions
and (9) ....

Fourth step: (10) ....

Get help from people who know about surveys and
(11) ....

Aim of fourth step: (12) ....

Fifth step: (13) ....

People in sample must be (14) ....

Check with respondents if any questions were
(15) .... or
(16) ....

Also supervise (17) ....

Sixth step: (18) .... and write down
how the questionnaire is to be conducted.

3 You want to carry out a class questionnaire to discover what people would be prepared to do to get something they really wanted. For example, are they prepared to cheat in an exam to go to the university of their choice? Start your questionnaire with situations in which many people might be tempted to cheat and make the questions progressively more risky. Prepare your questionnaire in small groups and then carry out your survey.

4 Report back your findings anonymously.

UNITS 21–25 | Revision

Topic review

a If you could go anywhere in the world, where would you go?

b Would you like to be a travel journalist? Why?/Why not?

c Has the climate in your country changed since you were a child?

d Do you agree that people are to blame for the world's climate change?

e Have you ever taken anything back to a shop? If so, what happened?

f What characteristics do you find difficult to put up with in your neighbours?

g How much chocolate do you eat every week?

h Who should decide what children should watch on TV and when?

i How far can humans train animals to do different things?

j Have you ever taken part in a survey? If so, what for and what did the results show?

Grammar

1 Linking devices can be divided into the following categories: listing, concession and contrast, cause, result and summing up. Add more examples of the categories to the table below and mark formal words with F, neutral words with N and informal words with I.

Listing	Concession and contrast	Cause	Result	Summing up
first and foremost F	despite / in spite of N/F	because N	therefore F	in conclusion F

2 Look at this extract from a book. The linking devices are in italics. Which category does each linking device belong to?

Individual development

Effective teamwork seeks to pool the skills of individuals and to produce better results by so doing. *Whilst* the effectiveness of the team can be greater than the sum of the parts, it *also* follows that effective teams need to pay attention to the development of individual skills. Just as different societies have different views of the developed group, *so* throughout the history of man different societies and cultures have had different views as to what constitutes the developed and effective individual. *As* one obvious fact about teams is that they are a collection of individuals, *then* their effectiveness must in part be a function of individual ability.

Reading

1 In the following extract, the author suggests that different people take on different roles in group activities. Look at the list of different types of roles. What type of team member do you think you are?

> the innovator   the challenger   the judge
> the diplomat   the expert

The challenger

Often seen as the 'Maverick' of the team as s/he often adopts an unconventional approach. This is an individual who will look afresh at what the team is doing and why, and who will challenge the accepted order. Because of this, such an individual is often unpopular with those who prefer to conform and can be accused of 'rocking the boat'. The challenger provides the unexpected and whilst many ideas may prove to be worthless, some may become 'the idea of the year'. Without a challenger the team can become complacent, for it lacks the stimulus to review radically what the team is doing and how it is doing it.

The expert

We live in an age of ever increasing specialisation and the team may require several specialists whose primary role is to provide expertise which is not otherwise available to the team. Outside their area of specialisation, these people make little contribution; in meetings they assume the role of 'expert witness' giving a professional viewpoint which the rest of the team may need to evaluate in the light of other constraints and opportunities. The expert may be an accountant, engineer, marketing adviser, trainer, personnel specialist, corporate planner or any other specialist, whose primary role is to provide the team with the expertise required.

The judge

Like the judge in the courtroom this team member listens, questions and ponders before making a decision. This character tends to keep out of the arguments and does not see himself or herself as an advocate for any particular view or cause, but is concerned to see that ideas are properly evaluated and that the right decisions are made.

A judge will not be rushed, preferring to pay the price of slow progress to make sure that the team follows the right path. Down-to-earth and logical, regarded by some as slow and ponderous, this person provides a balance and check on those who may be carried away by their own enthusiasm; like the courtroom judge seeking out the truth and seeing justice done.

2 Read the text quickly to get a general impression of the different roles people play.

3 For questions 1–9, match the statements with the types of team members. There may be more than one possible answer for some of the statements.

1 This member realises the importance of support from further afield.
2 If a team does not have this member, it may be satisfied with present results and not try harder.
3 This team member can see a creative way through difficulties.
4 Some team members find this person a destabilising influence.
5 This person smoothes the process towards the result.
6 This person makes sure the team is not swayed by someone's flights of fancy.
7 Although this team member makes an invaluable contribution, their influence is limited.
8 The whole team has to consider this member's advice in relation to the bigger picture.
9 The overriding concern of this team member is to guide the team in a favourable direction.

4 With a partner, discuss these questions.

a What type of team member do you think you are? Have you changed your opinion since reading the descriptions of the roles? Does your partner agree?
b Which types of team members are indispensable and dispensable?
c What do you think causes the most conflict in teamwork?

he innovator

Here is one who uses imagination to the full: an ideas person who is always proposing new ways of doing things. The innovator ensures that new ideas are evaluated, nurtured and developed and builds on the original ideas of others, visualising opportunities and transforming ideas into practical strategies. A fearless capacity to grapple with complex problems which demand new approaches provides the team with a rich source of vision, ingenuity, imagination and logic and can usually help the team to understand the unconventional and the new.

he diplomat

The diplomat is the team member who knows the diplomatic solution. This character generally has high influence within the team and is a good negotiator, and because of these skills plays a large part in the orientating of the team towards successful outcomes. Building alliances within and outside the team and trying to ensure that solutions are acceptable to all, the diplomat can sometimes be seen as 'papering over the cracks' in an effort to compromise, but is often dealing with the 'art of the impossible' rather than the ideal solution. Ways are found through difficult problems and in difficult times this is often the person who leads the team through dangerous ground.

Vocabulary

1 Complete all three sentences in each question with the same word.

a • It would be silly to let things that have happened in the past .... a wedge between us now.
• Of course, banning boxing will simply .... the sport underground.
• You want £200 for that old car? You certainly .... a hard bargain.

b • The .... to success is fraught with difficulties.
• The Weather Service issued a warning to people in the .... of the hurricane.
• They followed the .... until they came to a gate.

c • The cart was pulled by a .... of oxen.
• It was a real .... effort – everyone contributed something to the success of the project.
• All the players perform well individually but they seem to lack a little .... spirit.

d • We put an advertisement about a nursery school in the newspaper to .... the water.
• That lecturer really does .... your powers of endurance, he is so boring.
• This machine is designed to .... people's hearing.

e • After a .... of five years, Jennifer decided to go back to work full-time.
• There is a .... in the magazine market which needs to be filled.
• The children squeezed through a .... in the wall.

f • The doctor promised that these pills would .... the pain.
• If it will .... your mind, I'll speak to the boss for you.
• At last the rain began to .... off.

UNIT 26 Natural wonders

| Genre | Travel articles |
| Topic | Beauty spots |

Exam spot

You are quite often asked to write on the topic of travel in the CAE Writing test (Paper 2). Practise by using the language in this unit about your own country or another place that you know well.

Speaking

1 Work with a partner and answer the questions below.

 a Do the pictures on the right remind you of the place where you live or anywhere that you have visited?
 b How could you use the phrases in the box to describe the scenes in the pictures or a place that you know well?

> internationally recognised   outdoor restaurant
> complete range of   spectacular   the ultimate adventure
> perfect for   luxurious facilities   sumptuous lunch
> guided tours   luxury   diverse marine life
> once-in-a-lifetime experience

Listening

1 You are going to listen to a text that refers to one of the seven natural wonders of the world. Do you know what these are? Suggest what you think might be on the list and why they would deserve to be there.

2 🎧 Listen and explain how the pictures on the left relate to what you heard.

3 🎧 Listen again. Are the following statements true or false? If they are false, correct them.

 a Cairns is in south west Australia.
 b Cairns is on the Great Barrier Reef.
 c Cairns has the fifth busiest airport in the southern hemisphere.
 d Great Adventures is the name of a travel company.
 e Green Island is 100 years old.
 f It takes 45 minutes to fly to Green Island from Cairns.
 g The pontoon is a kind of underwater capsule.
 h You are only allowed to go to the pontoon once.

4 Work with a partner and list all the things that the destination described offers. Which three aspects of the destination appeal to you most?

Reading

1 You are going to read an extract from a book called *Running a Hotel on the Roof of the World*. What kind of place do you think the text is going to be about?

2 Read the first part of the text about two men, Dorje and Tashi, then complete the notes below.

Dorje had an interesting driving technique which involved keeping the car off the ground for as much time as possible. 'Terrible' Tashi called out whenever we were airborne, grinning from ear to ear and bracing himself for the inevitable impact whenever the Landcruiser would hit the tarmac again. It was hardly surprising that our car had practically no suspension.

Dorje had an advantage which would have made his taxi comrades in the city I had just flown from green with envy: visibility. In the pure rarefied air of Tibet, the view is not hindered by smog or pollution. Mountains which are tens of miles away appear crisp against the horizon. Apart from a few army trucks, the roads are free of traffic and the only limiting factor on Dorje's driving was how hard could he keep his foot pressed down on the accelerator pedal weighed up against the likelihood that at any moment one of the rattles could lead to the total disintegration of the vehicle.

Just visible through the vibrating windows were rectangular coracles setting out across the river. Tashi saw me trying to look at them. 'Yak-skin boats' he shouted over the roar of the Landcruiser engine. It seems that every part of the yak has a use. To make water-tight boats, the skins are stretched over a wooden frame, sewn together with wool made from yak hair and the joins are then sealed with yak butter.

\ \ \ \ \ \ \ \ \ \ \ \ \ \ \ \ | | | | |
● ●

Travelled by: ....

Driver's aim: ....

How Tashi felt about the journey: ....

Difficult aspects of the journey: ....

Good aspects of the journey: ....

Scenery: ....

What could be seen on the river: ....

Boats made of: ....

3 Now read the second part of the text. Imagine you wanted to paint a picture of the villages being described. Underline all the things the writer mentions which would help you with your picture.

Every now and then we would speed through a village lined with waving Tibetan children. Their villages looked wonderful and so inviting but Dorje was not showing any signs of slowing down. Small clusters of single and double storey buildings with walled-in courtyards jostled together in the foothills to gain maximum exposure to the sun. The houses looked solid, built to withstand the harsh environment. Walls were made of stone up to waist height and finished off with mud bricks to the roof.

Tin cans lined the window ledges, with the bright orange of marigolds in full bloom livening up the stark black and white of the houses. Branches of trees adorned with colourful prayer flags stood high into the wind from the top of the flat roofs. The auspicious blue, white, red, green and yellow colours of the fabrics stood out against the rich blue of the Tibetan sky. Each prayer flag carries a picture of *lungta*, the jewelled dragon-horse, who carries the owners' prayers up to the divinities every time the flag flaps in the wind.

The larger villages had a healthy copse of trees, usually willows or poplars which looked quite out of place in the generally treeless landscape. Wood is a precious commodity in the highland areas of Tibet and is never wasted. The few shrubs which grow wild on the hill-sides are harvested for use as brushwood and each courtyard wall is piled high with kindling gathered from the mountains.

4 Look at the picture of a Tibetan village. Which of the things you underlined are shown in the picture?

5 Now read the third and final part of the text and answer the following questions.

1 What problem is being discussed here?
  A getting rid of yak dung   B finding building materials
  C getting materials to burn   D looking after the yaks

2 Who does not seem to play a part in solving the problem?
  A young children   B older children
  C women   D men

3 Why is the dung mixed with water and barley straw?
  A to help make it into biscuits   B to make it look nicer
  C for the children to play with   D to make it more useful

4 Why is the dung put on walls?
  A to dry in the sun   B for decoration
  C to make the walls higher   D to help keep the homes warm

The lack of solid fuel in the shape of wood is of little consequence to the Tibetans who have an ingenious wood substitute: yak dung. The dung is collected during the day by young children who are out on the hills tending to flocks of sheep or yaks. What better way to spend the time when out on the hills than by collecting every piece of dung which can be found? It certainly sounds more attractive than being locked up in a school room.

When the children return in the evenings with their panniers of dung, it is usually the mother of the household, or an older sister, who has the task of mixing the raw material with a little water and, if available, some barley straw. This concoction is then made into attractive chocolate chip cookie shapes and slapped against the whitewashed walls to bake in the sun. Once dry, the cookies are stacked in rows on top of the walls to be used as fuel throughout the year.

Vocabulary

1 Tibet is described as being *on the roof of the world*. This simply means that Tibet is very high up. Below are some more idiomatic expressions which can be used to describe places, and explanations of the meanings of the idioms. Match each idiom (a–j) with its explanation (1–10).

a a black spot
b a tourist trap
c home from home
d no room to swing a cat
e picture-postcard
f a stone's throw from
g as the crow flies
h hit the road
i off the beaten track
j put a place on the map

1 attractive in a slightly artificial way
2 crowded place selling souvenirs, entertainment, etc. at high prices
3 make a place important or famous
4 place where you feel very comfortable
5 very small
6 a bit of road that has seen a lot of accidents
7 distance when measured in a straight line
8 leave a place, begin a journey
9 very close to
10 where not many people go

2 Choose one of the idioms above to complete each of the sentences below.

a I prefer to spend my holidays .... , far away from any other tourists.
b It's getting late and we've got a long drive home. It's really time we ....
c We stayed in a lovely .... village nestling in the valley.
d Take care on the drive across the mountains. There's a notorious .... just as you leave the main road to start the climb up to the pass.
e There was .... in our hotel room but the view we had was superb, so we didn't mind too much.

3 Which of the expressions in Vocabulary 1 would you be most likely and most unlikely to find in a tourist brochure? Why?

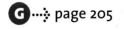 page 205

Like, alike, as, so and *such*

1 Look at these sentences. What is the grammatical difference between *like* and *alike*?

The Scottish Highlands are very like the Southern Alps in New Zealand.
The Scottish Highlands and the Southern Alps are very alike.

2 Now look at these sentences. What is the grammatical difference between *so* and *such*?

Our holiday was so wonderful despite the fact that we had such terrible weather!
This is such a beautiful hotel. It is so beautiful here.
I had never been to so remote a place before.
I had never been to such a remote place before.

3 Now look at these sentences with *as* and *like*. What is the grammatical difference between *as* and *like*?

The mountain is rather like a cathedral spire in shape with a pointed top and steeply sloping sides.
The water in the mountain streams is as clear as crystal.
On this mountain, as on any mountain, you have to be careful.
Its peak was first reached, as were most of the peaks in the range, in the nineteenth century.
It looks like a mountain whose surface was smoothed by glaciation.
It looks as if its surface was smoothed by glaciation.

4 Now look at these sentences. What do they show you about the meaning of *as* and *like*?

As the highest mountain in the range, it is popular with both tourists and mountaineers.
Like the highest mountain in the range, it is popular with both tourists and mountaineers.

5 Change each sentence to use the word in brackets at the end. Your new sentence should mean approximately the same as the original.

a Oxford and Cambridge in some ways are like each other. (alike)
b The scenery we saw in the Himalayas was so amazing. (such)
c It was such a long way to the campsite. (so)
d Our holiday cottage and the one allocated to our friends looked alike. (like)
e She looks like someone who has just returned from a tropical holiday. (as)

Writing

1 Read the text below about a hotel. Some of the sentences are from an informal letter and others are from a holiday brochure. They have been mixed up to make one text. Can you separate them out to make the original two texts? There are three sentences from each.

The hotel has a magnificent location overlooking the broad spread of the gulf and most of the bedrooms enjoy sea views. It's a great hotel with loads of character. The bedrooms get a bit chilly at night and the uncarpeted corridors can be noisy but it's worth putting up with a few minor inconveniences as it has so much atmosphere in other ways. Each room has its own luxuriously-appointed en suite bathroom and is individually decorated with many original finishing touches. The superb restaurant offers a wide range of delicious dishes to suit all tastes. The food is fantastic and you can stuff yourself at breakfast so you don't need to eat again till the evening.

2 Read the following texts from a luxury holiday brochure. Which of the two places would you prefer to stay in?

a

The exuberance of the Canary Islands appears in all its splendour at the Hotel Botanico. Here, amidst an atmosphere of quiet elegance, every creature comfort is catered for by its 24-hour room service. The lavishly-appointed Ambassador rooms and magnificent top-floor penthouse suites combine private luxury with spectacular views and, for those in search of the ultimate in luxurious living, the Royal Suite exudes regal opulence with its antiques, original paintings and unique private terrace.

b

Cashel House offers its guests a charming confusion of cosy nooks and crannies, comfortable sofas, polished antiques and warm, welcoming fires. 32 guest rooms and 13 garden suites all enjoy that home-from-home feeling with pretty floral fabrics and views over the hotel's magnificent 10 acres of gardens. Gourmet dinners, with an emphasis on locally caught seafood, are served each evening in the delightful restaurant, whilst snack lunches are available in the bar. The hotel boasts its own equestrian centre with guided treks and other daytime pursuits, including tennis, shore-walks, sea fishing and golf.

Cashel House

3 Imagine you are spending a holiday in the Hotel Botanico. The hotel is just as good as **advertised**. Write a postcard to a friend describing it.

4 Imagine you are writing an entry for a guide book which simply presents the facts about hotels for its readers without making any subjective comments. Look at this description of a Brussels hostel from such a guide book.

Jacques Brel, Rue de la Sablonniere, Brussels 30, (tel. 218 01 87).

An official HI hostel – modern, with a hotel-like atmosphere. Facilities include showers in every room, bar, restaurant, meeting room. Beds in 6-12-bed dorms F395, triples or quads F450, doubles F660, singles F560. No access to rooms between 10 am and 3 pm. No curfew. Prices include breakfast. Sheets can be hired for F125. Métro stops – Madou, Botanique.

Write an entry in a similar style for Cashel House.

5 Imagine that you spent a very expensive week in one of the hotels and that two or three of the claims made in the advertisement for it proved to be false. Write a letter of complaint to the manager of the hotel, explaining what you are unhappy about and saying what action you would like to be taken.

Exam folder 11

Paper 4 Parts 3 and 4

Part 3 of the CAE Listening test (Paper 4) can be either a sentence completion task or a multiple-choice task with four options; A, B, C or D. You hear a conversation between two or three speakers twice. You must listen for specific information, general meaning and attitude.

1 You are going to listen to part of an interview about women in business. Before you listen, discuss these questions with a partner.

   a Can you find women in top business jobs in your country?
   b Are there any jobs which you consider to be exclusively male or exclusively female jobs?
   c When a company is run by women, do you think there are any differences in the way the company is run? What might those differences be?

2 Read through the sentences below before you listen and think about what the answers might be.

3 🎧 Listen to part of an interview about women in business and, for questions a–d, complete the missing information.

   a When Julia started her own company, her philosophy was to work .... with other people.
   b Jennifer Alderton's business principle was to have .... for everyone in the company.
   c Julia's criticism of 'command and control' is that it wastes ....
   d Julia believes that a female-run company would allow the possibility for ....

4 🎧 Compare your answers with a partner's and then listen again.

5 Check that the sentences are grammatically correct and that the spelling is correct.

Part 4 of the CAE Listening test (Paper 4) can be either a multiple-matching task or a multiple-choice task with three options, A, B or C. In the multiple-matching task you hear five short extracts twice. Within the multiple-matching task there are two tasks. You may be asked to identify the speaker, topics, opinions, to interpret what was said or to say what the speaker is doing when he or she speaks (e.g. apologising).

6 🎧 You will hear five short extracts in which different people at a party are explaining how they know the host, Sarah. Match the Speakers 1–5 as you hear them with their relationship to Sarah listed A–H.

   Speaker 1
   Speaker 2
   Speaker 3
   Speaker 4
   Speaker 5

   A dentist
   B colleague
   C daughter's teacher
   D hairdresser
   E former employee
   F neighbour
   G old school friend
   H member of same gym

7 🎧 Now listen again. Match the Speakers 1–5 as you hear them with their opinions of Sarah listed A–H.

   Speaker 1
   Speaker 2
   Speaker 3
   Speaker 4
   Speaker 5

   A She's competitive.
   B She gets on well with everyone.
   C She's efficient.
   D She's sympathetic.
   E She's eager to help.
   F She arranges things quickly.
   G She's changed from when she was a child.
   H She's keen to become successful.

🎧 Check your answers with a partner and then listen to the tape again for a final check.

The skills for multiple-choice tasks in both Parts 3 and 4 are essentially the same. You have to read the first part of the sentence and all the options carefully. Then choose the answer which best completes the sentence or answers the question.

8 🎧 You will hear three short extracts in which different people are talking about performances they have been to. For questions 1–6, choose the correct option A, B or C.

1 The theatre was unusual in that
   A it only held 50 people.
   B it was round in shape.
   C the stage was level with the audience.
2 How did the speaker react to the performance?
   A She felt involved in the drama.
   B She appreciated the skill of the actors.
   C She was impressed by the creative set design.
3 At the start of the concert, the speaker was surprised by
   A how elegantly dressed the audience was.
   B the number of musicians in the orchestra.
   C the concentration of the audience.
4 Which section of the orchestra did the speaker find disappointing?
   A the violins
   B the pianist
   C the brass section
5 What does the speaker say about the film?
   A It was better than the book.
   B The main actor's accent was convincing.
   C The story was true to life.
6 The speaker found the ending of the film
   A surprising.
   B disappointing.
   C predictable.

9 With a partner, discuss your answers, giving reasons for your choice.

Advice

- Use the listening preparation time to think about the kind of information you can expect to hear and the likely language structure you will need to complete a question.
- Check that your spelling is correct throughout.
- Check that what you have written is grammatically correct, that singular and/or plural forms are used correctly and that you have included articles and prepositions where appropriate.
- Make sure that you read what is written after the question box as this may affect the grammatical structure of your answer.
- Write clearly and boldly.
- Don't write overlong answers. Try to use language which you are familiar with and know how to use accurately.
- Don't repeat information in your answer which is already included in the question.
- Don't worry about missing a question in Part 2 (which you hear only once). At the end, you will have time to think about a question you may have missed and then be able to attempt an answer.
- Don't waste time rubbing out your answers on the question paper.

UNIT 27 A friend in need

Genre	Fiction
Topic	Personality traits

Speaking

1 What sorts of people do you think the ones in the photos are? Describe their characters and how they live.

2 Do you think it is possible to determine people's characters from their appearance?

3 What character traits (if any) do people sometimes associate with the following physical characteristics?

> large, wide eyes small, close-together eyes
> a thin mouth a full mouth a high forehead

Reading and Listening

1   You are going to read the start of a short story about a man called Burton. Which of these pictures do you think matches the written description of Burton best?

b

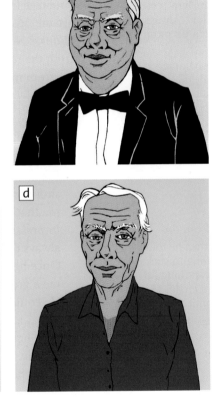

d

2   Discuss these questions with a partner.

   a   Does the narrator believe that people's appearance reveals their characters?
   b   Does he believe in the importance of first impressions? Why?/Why not?
   c   What does he say about his oldest friends and why is this paradoxical?
   d   What do we learn about Burton's appearance?
   e   What do we learn about his life?
   f   What do we learn about his personality?

A FRIEND IN NEED

For thirty years now I have been studying my fellow men. I do not know very much about them. I should certainly hesitate to engage a servant on his face, and yet I suppose it is on the face for the most part that we judge the persons we meet. We draw our conclusions from the shape of the jaw, the look in the eye, the contour of the mouth. I wonder if we are more often right than wrong. Why novels and plays are so often untrue to life is because their authors, perhaps of necessity, make their characters all of a piece. They cannot afford to make them self-contradictory, because then they become incomprehensible, and yet self-contradictory is what most of us are. We are a haphazard bundle of inconsistent qualities. I shrug my shoulders when people tell me that their first impressions of a person are always right. I think they must have small insight or great vanity. For my own part I find that the longer I know people, the more they puzzle me: my oldest friends are those of whom I can say that I don't know the first thing about them.

These reflections have occurred to me because I read in this morning's paper that Edward Hyde Burton had died in Kobe. He was a merchant and he had been in business in Japan for many years. I knew him very little but he interested me because once he gave me a great surprise. Unless I had heard the story from his own lips I should never have believed him capable of such an action. It was all the more startling because both in appearance and manner he suggested a very definite type. Here, if ever, was a man all of a piece. He was a tiny little fellow, not much more than five feet four in height, and very slender, with white hair, a red face, much wrinkled, and blue eyes. I suppose he was about sixty when I knew him. He was always neatly and quietly dressed in accordance with his age and station.

Though his offices were in Kobe, Burton often came down to Yokohama. I happened on one occasion to be spending a few days there waiting for a ship, and I was introduced to him at the British Club. We played bridge together. He played a good game and a generous one. He did not talk very much, either then or later when we were having drinks, but what he said was sensible. He had a quiet dry humour. He seemed to be popular at the club and afterwards, when he had gone, they described him as one of the best. It happened that we were both staying at the Grand Hotel and the next day he asked me to dine with him. I met his wife, fat, elderly and smiling, and his two daughters. It was evidently a united and affectionate family. I think the chief thing that struck me about Burton was his kindliness. There was something very pleasing in his mild blue eyes. His voice was gentle, you could not imagine that he could possibly raise it in anger, his smile was benign. Here was a man who attracted you because you felt in him a real love for his fellows. He had charm. But there was nothing mawkish in him; he liked his game of cards and his cocktail, he could tell with point a good and spicy story, and in his youth he had been something of an athlete. He was a rich man and he had made every penny himself. I suppose that one thing that made you like him was that he was so small and frail, he aroused your instincts of protection. You felt that he could not bear to hurt a fly.

3   With a partner, discuss how you think the story might continue.

4   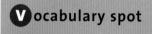 Now listen to the next part of the story. As you listen, decide whether these statements are true or false.

    a The narrator is sitting in his flat.
    b The view from the window is of the harbour with lots of vessels in it.
    c The narrator finds the view a little frightening.
    d The narrator has a drink with Burton.
    e Burton starts telling the narrator about a man called Turner.
    f The man in Burton's story shared Burton's first name.
    g The man in Burton's story was very good at playing cards.

5   Now read the next part of the story. What was the same and what was different about the two men called Burton?

Burton sipped his gin fizz.

'It's rather a funny story,' he said. 'He wasn't a bad chap. I liked him. He was always well-dressed and smart-looking. He was handsome in a way with curly hair and pink-and-white cheeks. Women thought a lot of him. There was no harm in him, you know, he was only wild. Of course he drank too much. Those sort of fellows always do. A bit of money used to come in for him once a quarter and he made a bit more by card-playing. He won a good deal of mine, I know that.'

Burton gave a kindly chuckle. I knew from experience that he could lose money at bridge with good grace. He stroked his shaven chin with his thin hand, the veins stood out on it and it was almost transparent.

'I suppose that is why he came to me when he went broke, that and the fact that he was a namesake of mine. He came to see me in my office one day and asked me for a job. I was rather surprised. He told me that there was no more money coming from home and that he wanted to work. I asked him how old he was.

"Thirty-five," he said.

"And what have you been doing hitherto?" I asked him.

"Well, nothing very much," he said.

I couldn't help laughing.

"Come back and see me in another thirty-five years and I'll see what I can do."

'He didn't move. He went rather pale. He hesitated for a moment and then he told me that he had had bad luck at cards for some time. He hadn't been willing to stick to bridge, he'd been playing poker, and he'd got rammed. He'd pawned everything he had. He couldn't pay his hotel bill and they wouldn't give him any more credit. He was down and out. If he couldn't get something to do, he'd have to commit suicide.

'I looked at him for a bit. I could see now that he was all to pieces. The girls wouldn't have thought so much of him, if they'd seen him then.

"Well, isn't there anything you can do except play cards?" I asked him.

"I can swim," he said.

"Swim!"

'I could hardly believe my ears, it seemed such an insane answer to give.

"I swam for my university."

'I got some glimmering of what he was driving at. I've known too many men who were little tin gods at their university to be impressed by it.

"I was a pretty good swimmer myself, when I was a young man," I said.

'Suddenly I had an idea.

Pausing in his story, Burton turned to me.

'Do you know Kobe?' he asked.

'No,' I said, 'I passed through it once, but I only spent a night there.'

'Then you don't know the Shioya Club. When I was a young man I swam from there round the beacon and landed at the creek of Tarumi. It's over three miles and it's rather difficult to do on account of the currents round the beacon. Well, I told my young namesake about it and I said to him that if he'd do it I'd give him a job.

6   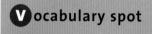 What do you think will happen next? Listen to the end of the story. To what extent were your predictions correct? Why do you think Burton behaved as he did?

Vocabulary

Vocabulary spot

Try to be aware of chunks of language when you are reading. You will be able to find some good examples of language chunks in any text that you look at.

1   Here are some chunks of language from the story. What are the missing words in the chunks? Note that a–f come from the reading extracts and g–j from the second listening extract.

    a We .... our conclusions from the shape of the jaw.
    b I .... my shoulders when people tell me that their first impressions of a person are always right.
    c Once he .... me a great surprise.
    d He could not bear to .... a fly.
    e He'd have to .... suicide.
    f It's rather difficult to do on .... of the currents.
    g I could see he was rather taken ....
    h I'm not in very good ....
    i I only just .... to get to the creek.
    j He .... a little mild chuckle.

2 Here are some more chunks of language from the story. The words in italics could each be replaced by three of the words from the box. Which words can fit? Note that changing the word may result in a big change in meaning.

annoyed	asked	intending	scratched
come	just	strangely	puzzled
curiously	merely	stroked	doing
only	wiped	hoping for	predictably
worried	apologised		

a … the chief thing that *struck* me about Burton was his kindliness …

b … you had *but* to stretch out your hand to touch it …

c … *oddly* enough a namesake of mine …

d … I got some glimmering of what he was *driving at* …

e … I needn't have *hurried* …

f … he *rubbed* his chin with his hand …

Emphasising

Look at this sentence.

The harbour at Yokohama looks romantic.

Here are some ways of making this statement more emphatic.

The harbour at Yokohama is extraordinarily romantic.
Nowhere on earth looks more romantic than the harbour at Yokohama.
The most romantic place on earth for me is the harbour at Yokohama.
What strikes me about the harbour at Yokohama is its romantic appearance.
What a romantic place the harbour at Yokohama is!
The harbour at Yokohama is such a romantic place!
Never have I seen such a romantic place as the harbour at Yokohama.

1 What has happened in each of the variations above to make the statement more emphatic?

2 Now write each of these statements in a more emphatic way.

a You can't draw reliable conclusions about people's characters from their appearances.

b Burton's behaviour surprised me.

c He shocked me with his next words.

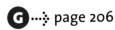 **G** ⋯▸ page 206

Writing

1 Which of these techniques does the writer use to hold the reader's attention? Where appropriate, find one example of each technique in the reading texts.

- direct speech
- describing the scene in an interesting way
- describing people in an interesting way
- a striking opening
- an effective ending
- combining general statements with specific examples
- using language of emphasis
- dropping hints about what may happen later

2 All of the techniques below are used in the story. One example is provided for you. Can you find another example of each technique from the reading texts?

a involving the listener by asking him questions:
'Do you know Kobe?' he asked.

b using vivid adjectives or other descriptive expressions:
'He was handsome in a way with curly hair and pink-and-white cheeks.'

c making use of an element of surprise:
'When you made him that offer of a job, did you know he'd be drowned?'

d linking the story to the listener's own experience:
'Then you don't know the Shioya Club.'

e adding comments on how he (Burton) reacted to the incident being described:
'I've known too many men who were little tin gods at their university to be impressed by it.'

f using language of emphasis: 'I could hardly believe my ears, it seemed such an insane answer to give.'

3 Think of an incident where someone you know (or thought you knew) did something unexpected. Describe the situation to your partner. If possible use some of the techniques listed above.

4 Write an article in response to the announcement below. Try to use as many as possible of the techniques worked on in this section.

TRUE STORIES MAGAZINE

We are looking for articles in which readers describe how they were once surprised by a friend or relative's unexpected behaviour. The best articles will be published and will win a gift voucher.

Writing folder 11

Informal writing

If you are not sure whether it is appropriate to write in an informal register or not, it is better to write in a neutral style. Below is part of a letter of reference for a friend who had applied for a holiday job on a cruise liner. A letter of reference should be written in a neutral to formal style, but the extract below is too informal.

1   Underline all the parts of the reference that are too informal.

2   Rewrite the reference, replacing everything you have underlined with more appropriate equivalents.

> I've known Ted for donkey's years – in fact, ever since we were kids at school together – and he's a really nice guy, one of the best. I'd give him the job like a shot if I were in your boat (excuse the pun!). Don't be put off by the fact that he can sometimes seem a bit bossy – that's just because he's such a well-organised bloke himself, he can't stand it when other people are slow to get their act together. He's got loads of experience of working with other people and he can be relied on to get things going. Go for it and give him the job – you won't regret it.

3   Sometimes students lose marks in the CAE Writing test because they do not use register in a consistent way. They use both formal and informal words in the same sentence in an inappropriate way. In the sentences below, mark the words which are inappropriately formal or inappropriately informal.

   a   It's daft to alight from a bus while it is moving.
   b   Jack lives in a flat adjacent to the local chippie.
   c   Julia always wears very snazzy apparel.
   d   John's life was torn asunder by the death of his missus.
   e   When talking to the fuzz, it behoves you to be polite.
   f   Jenny's birthday bash ceased at midnight.
   g   The deceased man left all his clobber to his nephew.
   h   You must give the office a bell if you intend to change your domicile.
   i   Lawrence dwelt in a remote village in Tibet for yonks.
   j   Richard is an erstwhile mate of my husband's.

   Now rewrite each sentence twice. One sentence should be consistently formal and the other consistently informal.

Exam spot

In the CAE Writing test (Paper 2) you will probably only need to write in an informal style when you are writing a letter or note to a friend. You might also choose to use a slightly informal style if you are writing an article for a more informal type of publication, e.g. for a student newspaper.

4 One of the most noticeable characteristics of informal writing is its use of colloquial or slang words. Match the words (a–s) below with their neutral equivalent (1–19).

a	argy-bargy	1	friend
b	brat	2	insane
c	chuck	3	lively
d	broke	4	insect
e	crabby	5	badly-behaved child
f	mega	6	large amount
g	bubbly	7	disagreement
h	crony	8	hard work
i	barmy	9	information
j	higgledy-piggledy	10	mixed up
k	jumpy	11	bad-tempered
l	beastie	12	nervous
m	chomp	13	customer
n	info	14	steal
o	oodles	15	throw
p	pinch	16	chew noisily
q	punter	17	very good or very big
r	slog	18	without money
s	grand	19	thousand pounds or dollars

5 Choose one of the words (a–s) above to complete each of the sentences (a–i) below.

a There's no need to hurry – we've got .... of time.

b Sally's a lovely .... girl – I'm sure you'll have a great time with her.

c Last Saturday I decided to .... out all my old school books – I've made a lot of extra space in my cupboard.

d I wish she wouldn't .... like that when she eats.

e The party was ....! Everyone was there!

f Her bedroom is always untidy with clothes lying .... all over the place.

g The problem with picnics is all the .... that crawl over you and the food.

h I can't possibly go away for the weekend – I'm ....!

i It was quite a .... but I managed to get my assignment finished on time.

6 You receive this email from a friend. Underline all the informal words and expressions in the email, then write a reply to your friend. Your reply should be in informal English.

You'll never guess what's happened! My boss is going to send me on a business trip to your town! So get ready for me to drop by some time next week. Hope we can hit the town together one evening. What'd you suggest we do? I'm really into folk music at the moment – is there anywhere we could go and have a bite or a drink and listen to music at the same time? But I'm open to other suggestions if you don't fancy that. Also, could you just let me know about a few other things:

What's the weather like at the mo, i.e. what sort of clothes should I bring with me?

I've got to take a prezzie for some friends of my boss (he's arranged for me to crash with them). What d'you think might be good for a middle-aged couple? Here we'd usually take chocs or a bottle but maybe things are different with you?

What's public transport like in your town? I'm trying to decide whether it's worth hiring a car or not. Have to be travelling quite a bit during the week – am not wild about the idea of driving on the right but may have to brave it.

Looking forward to hearing from you and to seeing you soon,

Sammy

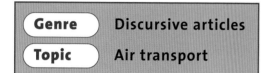

Speaking 1

1 Match the words and phrases in the box to the appropriate pictures.

the check-in	carry-on luggage
the carousel	overhead bin
to board	the hold

2 Divide into three groups, A, B and C.

A You work for an airline. You have to be polite but firm to all passengers.

B You want to take all your bags on board a flight as hand luggage because you have an important meeting to get to soon after the flight lands. Your hand luggage is only a little bigger and heavier than the airline permits.

C You have just arrived after a very long flight. There is no sign of your luggage. You are very upset as you had all your clothes and some important papers in the missing suitcase.

In your groups, discuss how you might feel and behave.

3 Now work in groups of three with one A, one B and one C. Role play a scene at the airport.

4 After doing the role play, discuss with your group how you think each of your characters felt.

5 Have you ever had an experience like those above? If so, describe what happened.

Exam spot

Discussing a topic and giving your opinion is often part of the CAE Writing test (Paper 2). In the Reading and Listening tests (Paper 1 and Paper 4), you also have to understand texts that present opinions.

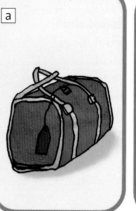

a

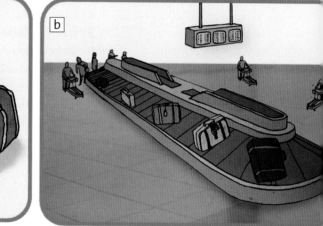

b

c

d

e Airlines

f

Reading

1 Read the following article. As you read, answer the following questions.

    a What problems are referred to in the article?

    b What suggestions are made for solving those problems?

    c What do you think about the suggested solutions?

Oh, what a carry on!

'I feel about airplanes the way I feel about diets.'

'They are wonderful things for other people to go on,' Jean Kerr, an American dramatist once quipped. Flying has become safer, faster and cheaper but it seems ever more stressful. One frequent cause is the noise that children, especially bored ones, inflict on other travellers. A year ago one magazine proposed that all planes should have child-free zones, just like no-smoking zones; children (and parents) should be confined to the back of the plane. As yet, sadly, no airline seems to agree that children should be screened and not heard.

Undeterred, we would like to raise another case of what economists call a *negative externality.* i.e. something which is nice for you but imposes costs on others. This is excessive carry-on luggage. In America six out of ten passengers now take a suitcase on to a flight rather than check it in, three times as many as in 1990. The result is delay, because flights take longer to board. Passengers trying to squeeze 3-foot suitcases into 2-foot bins hold up people trying to board behind them. Some travellers have tried to take refrigerators, television sets and even a stuffed moose-head on board.

The problems of both children and luggage could be solved in one stroke by putting the children in the hold, to make more space for carry-on luggage. But that, we concede, might be unacceptable. Instead, to reduce delays, most airlines are rightly imposing stricter limits on the size or weight of bags that can be carried on to planes. This has provoked outrage as passengers are forcibly separated from their belongings at check-in. Understandably: if you put luggage in the hold, you have to wait ages for it at the other end – if it shows up at all.

Once you have experienced the nightmare of waiting at the luggage carousel until it stops, with no sign of the suitcase you checked in, it is clear why people prefer to *lug* their cases on board. You took a flight from London to Tokyo; your luggage and your smart clothes decided to hop on to one to Los Angeles. Not an externality but certainly negative.

In America only 0.5% of bags go missing, but if you are a frequent traveller, that risk is too high. A survey of 150 frequent fliers found that two-thirds had experienced some sort of delay or loss to their luggage in the previous 12 months. And, if luggage remains lost, your likely compensation is *paltry* – a maximum of $1,250 regardless of whether your clothes were bought at Wal-Mart or Armani.

If airlines are to restrict carry-ons, therefore, they also need to offer better compensation for delayed or lost luggage. At the least they should extend frequent-flier miles to luggage as well as its owner: if your luggage travels to Tokyo via Los Angeles, you should get triple frequent-flier miles. In addition, passengers could be made to pay if they want to take extra luggage on board. Better still, given the frequent correlation between the size of the traveller and the weight of his (*yes, his*) carry-on, why not take a tip from Papua New Guinea? When flying within the country, a passenger used to be weighed along with his luggage before boarding the plane. Fight the flab and you can bring your bag on board. Aeroplanes and diets would then indeed be closely connected.

2 Answer the following questions.

    a Articles or essays quite often begin with a quotation. Why do you think this can be an effective way to start a piece of writing?

    b Explain what *negative externality* means and how taking a fridge on a plane as hand luggage is an example of it.

    c What word in the third paragraph tells you how passengers react to having restrictions put on the amount of luggage they can take on board?

    d In the next paragraph, why do you think the writer wrote *lug* rather than *take*?

    e *Luggage* is personified in one sentence of the fourth paragraph. In which sentence does this happen?

    f What do you think the word *paltry* means? Use the context to help you.

    g What contrast is being made between Wal-Mart and Armani?

    h Why do you think *yes, his* is inserted in the last paragraph?

    i Explain what the last two sentences in the article mean and why they make a particularly effective way to end the article.

Vocabulary

1 The table below contains some more words from the article. Fill in the meanings and three phrases for each word in the third column.

Words from the text	Meaning	Other words from same root (in typical phrase)
stressful	causing worry and anxiety	a stress-free environment; to feel stressed; stresses and strains
agree		
undeterred		
excessive		
concede		
forcibly		
frequent		
compensation		
correlation		

2 Complete each sentence with a word derived from the word in brackets at the end.

a Air traffic control is said to be one of the most .... jobs of all. (stress)

b I found him very unpleasant and .... and I hope that I never have to spend another evening in his company again. (agree)

c Some people claim that nuclear bombs actually prevent wars as they act as a .... (deter)

d There are severe penalties for .... the speed limit. (excessive)

e The government has slightly relaxed the tax regulations as a .... to small businesses. (concede)

f It is very hard to .... speed restrictions on the roads here. (force)

g After administering the questionnaire, the sociology student had to classify the answers according to their .... (frequent)

h There is a direct .... between being depressed and being in debt. (correlate)

i If your train is delayed by more than one hour, you may be able to claim .... (compensate)

Adverbials expressing opinion

1 Look at these sentences from the text.

a *As yet, **sadly**, no airline seems to agree that children should be screened and not heard.*

b *Instead, to reduce delays, most airlines are **rightly** imposing stricter limits on the size or weight of bags that can be carried on to planes.*

c ***Understandably:** if you put luggage in the hold, you have to wait ages for it at the other end – if it shows up at all.*

What do the words in bold tell you about the opinion of the writer?

2 Here are some more adverbials which can be used to express opinion.

apparently	evidently	fortunately
indisputably	inevitably	ironically
predictably	surprisingly	
unbelievably	undoubtedly	

Think of each of these adverbials in the sentence *Mark and Susanna have got married* and then answer the questions below.

Which of the adverbials tells you that the speaker …

a is pleased about their marriage?

b is not totally sure that they did actually get married? (2 possibilities)

c is absolutely sure that they did get married? (2 possibilities)

d would have expected them to marry? (2 possibilities)

e would not have expected them to marry? (2 possibilities)

f finds something slightly amusing or curious about the fact that they got married?

3 Choose the most likely adverbial from the options provided to complete each of the sentences below.

a *Fortunately/Undoubtedly/Ironically*, no one was hurt in the accident.

b After having eaten so much, I *surprisingly/inevitably/evidently* began to feel rather sleepy.

c *Predictably/Unbelievably/Undoubtedly* Jack passed his exam with flying colours – he always does do well in exams.

d I didn't see it happen myself but *ironically/apparently/indisputably* she fainted in the heat.

G ⋯⟶ page 206

Listening

1 You are going to listen to some people talking about three different forms of transport: plane, train and bicycle. What do you think they might say about the advantages and disadvantages of each of these means of transport?

2 🎧 Now listen and list the advantages and disadvantages they mention of flying, rail travel and cycling.

3 🎧 Listen again and note the discourse markers that you hear. What functions do they serve?

> **V**ocabulary spot
>
> Using discourse markers when you speak and write helps to clarify the structure of what you want to say – as long as you use them appropriately. When you read or listen to English, pay attention to the discourse markers that are used and try to use them in similar ways in your own speaking and writing.

Speaking 2

1 Complete the dialogue with expressions from the box.

> as I was saying   certainly   I know   I suppose
> just my luck   so   stupidly   then   you mean

Brian: Well, anyway, (1) .... , I left home at the normal time but the traffic jams were terrible.

Jill: Mm, (2) .... , it's got a lot worse recently.

Brian: Yes, (3) .... I was a bit late when I got to the station and (4) .... you should have seen the queues there. There was no chance that I'd be able to buy a ticket before the train left, so I (5) .... decided to take a risk and just get on the train without one.

Jill: What, (6) .... a ticket inspector actually got on the train?

Brian: Yes, (7) .... The first time in months that I've seen one.

Jill: You had to pay a fine, (8) .... ?

Brian: Yes, twice the price of the fare. I (9) .... won't do that again!

2 Work with a partner. Write a brief dialogue using some of the discourse markers you heard in the listening text.

3 Perform your dialogue to the other students. If possible, do it from memory rather than reading it. While listening to each dialogue, the other students in the class should note down the discourse markers which they hear.

Exam folder 12

Paper 5 Speaking

The CAE Speaking test (Paper 5) is quite short and so it is important not to waste time with unnecessary silences. Don't worry too much about making mistakes – the important thing is to show that you can communicate in English both with the examiner and with your partner.

Advice

- Smile at the examiners as you greet them – it will relax you and create a pleasant first impression.
- Try to relax – imagine you are talking to a new friend.
- Answer the examiner's questions fully, not just with one-word answers.
- Listen carefully to the instructions and do what you are asked.
- If you did not understand or do not remember all the instructions, it is fine to ask the examiner to clarify or repeat something.
- Speak clearly and loudly enough for both examiners to hear you.
- Give your partner a chance to speak too.
- Talk to your partner – you get marks for interacting, so ask each other questions, and react to what your partner says (as in a normal conversation) but try to do so without interrupting.
- When you ask questions, try not to use an intonation which rises too much as this can sound aggressive.
- Try not to repeat what you or your partner has already said – add something new.
- Don't worry about making mistakes – you will get marks for communicating your ideas and not just for accuracy.
- In Part 1, give reasonably full answers to the examiner's questions.
- In Part 2, you should simply listen to each other and not speak until the examiner asks you to.
- In Part 3, you will have more to say if you do not simply agree with your partner but react either by taking their ideas a step further or by disagreeing – remember you don't have to tell the truth in the exam, so you may find more to say if you deliberately disagree a bit.
- In Part 4, as with all the other parts, it is above all important to listen carefully to what the examiner asks you to do.

1 Imagine you are talking to someone you have never met before. Introduce yourself and talk about your own experience of learning languages. What do you enjoy and what do you find most difficult?

2 Look at these cartoons. Describe them and comment on what points they are making.

3　Work with a partner. You are going to set up a self-access centre for people who want to learn English and other languages in the place where you live. Discuss which of the resources in the pictures it would be most important to include in your self-access centre and why. In what ways (if at all) do each of these things help people to learn languages? Is there anything else that you would want to include in your self-access centre?

4　If, for reasons of cost, you could only have three of these resources in your self-access centre, which three would it be and why?

UNIT 29 A testing question

Speaking 1

1 Work in groups and answer the following questions.

   a Which (if any) of the pictures remind you of your own schooldays?

   b Describe two or three pictures that would sum up your memories of your schooldays.

   c People sometimes say that your schooldays are the best days of your life. Would you agree?

   d What do you think is the main educational issue in your country at the moment and how do you feel about this?

Listening

1 You are going to hear three people presenting the case for these points of view:

   a schoolchildren are disciplined too much

   b children do not spend enough time at school

   c all education should be free

   What arguments do you think they might make in favour of these points of view? What objections might they raise to them?

2 🎧 Listen to the three speakers. For each speaker, note down the main arguments. Note also the points against these arguments made by other speakers.

3 Would you vote for or against each of the three points of view? Give reasons for your answers.

Reading

1 Look at the title of the text. What do you think it is going to be about and what points do you think it might make?

DON'T CRITICISE EXAMS:
They're a lesson in life

George Marsh, head of posh Dulwich College Preparatory School in London, probably thought he was doing kids and parents a favour with his rousing speech at the annual prep school conference this week.

He spoke of the pressures facing young people, who need to be nurtured during difficult pre-teen and teenage years. Above all, he said, we had reached a stage where the obsession with passing exams was 'killing the fun' of school.

We've all read this before. We've heard of the burnout kids, pushed by ambitious parents until they're at the end of their tethers, and gasped at the stories of the hothouse flower children who wilt in the real world. We've seen the headlines. 'Pressures of work too much for our teenagers', they scream. Now we have Mr Marsh's contribution about too many horrid exams spoiling the school's broth.

In our child-obsessed society, the worst sin of all is to stop a child having 'fun'. It is right up there with smacking in the new millennium book of bad parenting. Children must be endlessly indulged, treated with kid gloves, escorted to amusement parks, given computer games and showered with pocket money.

They must never have a minute when they're neither protected nor enjoying themselves. Heaven forbid that they should be told to study, strive and compete – words which seem to have taken on the quality of blasphemy.

But whoever said school was meant to be fun? Yes, school is a place where a child develops and a rounded curriculum is vital. Our children should play sport, do drama, join choirs, hang out at playtimes. The rest of the time, however, they are there to learn and to achieve some basic qualifications that will, whether they want to accept it or not, cushion them when life gets really hard. Yet, in the current climate, saying that exams matter is tantamount to saying that our children should spend their teenage years at an Army boot camp.

This is the same mentality that dictates there should be no winners at sports day in case other children get upset by coming second. It's the same misguided attitude that drives parents to spray their kids with antiseptic to protect them from all known germs when actually they only end up sickly because their immune system never develops. Cosseting children in cotton wool does them few favours in the long run.

Mr Marsh is right when he says that we should shelter our children from the pressures of growing up too soon but there is a difference between sheltering and smothering.

If he really wanted to do us all a favour in his speech, he should have told parents to get real. School can be tough and exams always are but then so is life – and it's best that children learn that particular lesson as early as possible.

2 Answer these questions about the text.

a Who is George Marsh?
b What are the main points he is making?
c To what extent do you think that other people agree with his views?

3 These words and expressions from the article all have strong positive or negative associations. Divide them into two groups, positive and negative, and explain what each word suggests.

rousing	nurtured	burnout	hothouse flower children
wilt	scream	sin	showered
blasphemy	rounded	cushion	boot camp
misguided	cosseting	sheltering	smothering

4 To what extent do you agree with the views that George Marsh is putting forward? How far do you think his opinions would be generally accepted in your country?

Vocabulary

1 Match the two parts of these collocations used in the reading text.

a	to do someone	1	a stage
b	a rousing	2	curriculum
c	to reach	3	a qualification
d	at the end of	4	run
e	the real	5	climate
f	to treat someone with	6	your tether
g	pocket	7	speech
h	a rounded	8	world
i	the current	9	money
j	to achieve	10	a favour
k	in the long	11	kid gloves

2 Now match the completed phrases from Vocabulary 1 to their meanings.

a a well-balanced programme of studies

b to be very polite and careful in your behaviour towards someone

c the way things are at the moment

d to get a certificate showing you have taken courses or passed some exams

e how things are rather than how we might like them to be

f very upset or anxious

g looking to the distant rather than the immediate future

h a talk that stirs the audience

i cash or notes given to someone on a regular basis to help them pay for their everyday needs

j to do something nice for someone

k to get to a particular point of development

3 Now choose which of these collocations best fit each of the sentences below.

a It's a lot of hard work now but I'm sure you'll feel it's worth it ....

b I wonder if you could .... and get me a newspaper when you're in town.

c When she rang me last night she was .... and so I thought I'd better go round at once and see if I could do anything to help.

d It's taking a bit of a risk to give up a steady job in ....

e There's no need .... ; I won't bite your head off.

f Now she's left university she's going to have to get used to life in ....

g The building work has now .... where we can begin to imagine how things will eventually look.

h How much .... did your parents use to give you?

Gerunds and infinitives

1 Look at these sentences from the text and underline all the uses of the gerund and the infinitive in them. Why is the gerund or the infinitive used in each of the cases you underline?

a The rest of the time, however, they are there to learn and to achieve some basic qualifications that will, whether they want to accept it or not, cushion them when life gets really hard.

b It's the same misguided attitude that drives parents to spray their kids with antiseptic to protect them from all known germs when actually they only end up sickly because their immune system never develops.

c Mr Marsh is right when he says that we should shelter our children from the pressures of growing up too soon but there is a difference between sheltering and smothering.

d If he really wanted to do us all a favour in his speech, he should have told parents to get real.

2 Complete these sentences about the rules for the use of gerunds and infinitives. Fill in the gaps with either gerund or infinitive.

a You always use the .... (or a noun) after a preposition.

b When the word *to* is used as a preposition as in *be used to, look forward to, object to*, it is followed by a(n) ....

c The .... can be used to express purpose. For example, you might use one to give an answer to the question *Why are you studying English?*

d Phrases like *It is impossible/easy/nice for Mary/me/the children* are usually followed by the ....

e *It's not worth/There's no point/It's no use* are usually followed by the ....

3 Put the verbs in the box into one of the two columns below.

mind	feel like	promise	deny	enjoy
refuse	arrange	risk	suggest	tend	give up
offer	expect	decide	agree	manage

Verbs followed by a gerund	Verbs followed by an infinitive
enjoy	*decide*

4 Now put the verbs from the box below into one of the following groups:

A can be followed by either (with a change of meaning) e.g. *remember*

B can be followed by either (with no change in meaning) e.g. *begin*

C can be followed by either (depending on the grammar of the sentence) e.g. *allow*

forget	start	intend	permit	advise
regret	allow	go on	begin	remember
forbid	continue	try	can't bear

5 Rewrite each sentence using the words in brackets in an appropriate form.

a Jack said it would be a good idea to go to the new Chinese restaurant. (suggest)
b No eating is allowed in the classrooms. (permit)
c The police officer wouldn't let anyone into the building. (forbid)
d Could you possibly open the window? (mind)
e Melinda said she would paint my son's portrait. (offer)
f I hope you remembered to buy some apples. (forget)
g I'm really sorry that I wasted so much of my time at school. (regret)
h Despite his injury he continued to play his violin. (go on)
i Everyone is sure that he will do well in his exams. (expect)
j Passengers are not permitted to smoke on any of that airline's flights. (allow)

G ⋯⁚ page 206

Speaking 2

When you are presenting an argument in a more formal way, it is usually most effective to be brief and to the point. This is particularly important when you are summarising something.

1 🎧 Listen to this speaker talking to children about how to pass exams. Complete the notes below.

Aim of exams:

Types of examinees:

1

What to do if you are one of these:

a

b

2

What to do if you are one of these:

a

b

What other things did the speaker mention that you did not include in your notes?

2 Think about how you might summarise what the speaker said for someone who missed her talk. What can you leave out from the original? How can you modify the rest of the language used? Summarise the main points made by the speaker.

3 With a partner, discuss how to get the best possible marks in the CAE exam. Think about the following points:

- before the exam
- during the exam
- general advice for all the Papers
- Reading test (Paper 1)
- Writing test (Paper 2)
- English in Use test (Paper 3)
- Listening test (Paper 4)
- Speaking test (Paper 5).

When you have discussed this fully, talk about how you would summarise the discussion.

Present the summary of your discussion to the rest of the class.

Writing folder 12

Descriptive, narrative and discursive articles

1 Look at these exam-type writing tasks and answer the questions below.

   a In each case, what do you have to describe, what (if anything) do you have to narrate and what do you have to discuss?

   b In one of the tasks, a narrative element would not be appropriate. Which one is this and why is it inappropriate?

A Many students in the college where you are studying complain that they have to live in conditions which make it difficult for them to study. Write an article for the local students' magazine in which you outline the conditions that many students have to put up with, including examples from your friends' experiences. You should also suggest ways in which students can make the best of the situations they are in.

Write your **article**.

B You see this announcement in an international magazine.

COMPETITION

Modern methods of communication have transformed our world. What means of communication do you personally find most useful? Email? Mobile phone? Fax? Teletext? Something else? Choose ONE means of communication and explain exactly how you use it. Then comment on how it has changed your life, pointing out ways in which it has had negative as well as positive effects.

Write your **competition entry**.

C As a college student, you recently took part in a week's work experience in a company. You learned a great deal from the programme and found it an enjoyable experience on the whole. However, there are a number of ways in which you feel it could be improved, so that next year's participants would benefit even more from the experience. Write a report for the college committee that organises work experience placements, in which you summarise your personal experience and make suggestions for improvements.

Write your **report**.

D A large international sports company is considering donating money for sports facilities in a number of different areas of the world. To apply for money, it is necessary to send the company a proposal in which you outline what facilities are already available and then propose one specific facility which your area needs, explaining why it is necessary and what benefits it would bring your community.

Write your **proposal**.

E This is part of a letter which you receive from a pen friend in the United States. Write a reply to the letter.

We are doing a project on punishments and rewards used in schools in different countries. Can you write and tell me what sorts of punishments and rewards are used in schools in your country? What experiences have you personally had of punishments and rewards at school? What do you think is good about this system and what is bad? What changes would you like to introduce if you were a head teacher or a Minister of Education and why?

Write your **letter**.

2 Think about the descriptive parts of writing tasks A–E. With a partner, discuss how you could make each of the descriptive parts more interesting. Consider the questions below and make notes on how you could proceed with each of the tasks.

a In Task A, what specific living conditions are you going to describe? Note down some good expressions that you could use in order to convey these living conditions vividly.

b In Task B, what general points are you going to make about how you use the means of communication you choose? Think of one or two specific examples.

c In Task C, you will need to invent a specific situation if you have never had any real experience of a situation like this. Could you base what you describe on your parents' workplace, or something you have seen on TV? Remember that it is more important to write in an accurate and relevant way than to write about an experience you have actually had.

d In Task D, think about what the sports company needs to know. Is it relevant here to give personal anecdotes? What sort of situation is likely to inspire the company to give money? How could you slant your description to strengthen your case?

e In Task E, make a list of all the punishments and rewards you can think of that are used in schools in your country. Beside each one, note down a typical kind of behaviour that would result in that punishment or reward. An anecdote might be relevant here. Note down some good words and expressions you could use in this letter.

3 Think about the narrative parts of these tasks. Note down some ideas that you could include for the narrative parts of questions A, B, C and E.

4 Think about the discursive parts of each of the tasks. For each one, prepare a mind map using the information below to help you.

a For Task A, your mind map should be based on the aspects of living conditions which you have described. At least one solution should relate to each of the problems identified.

b For Task B, your mind map should centre on the means of communication chosen, indicating the changes it has enabled and noting its good and bad effects – the map might possibly culminate in some kind of overall conclusion.

c For Task C, your mind map should indicate both the good and bad points in the experience with at least one solution relating to each of the bad points indicated.

d For Task D, your mind map should focus on the proposed facility with a set of supporting ideas which will help to argue the case for that facility.

e For Task E, your mind map should have areas devoted to good and bad points and your suggested changes.

5 In some tasks containing descriptive and discursive elements, it will be appropriate to deal with all the description first and then to move on to the more discursive parts of the task. In other tasks, the descriptive and discursive tasks are likely to be interwoven. With a partner, discuss which approach would probably work best for each of the five tasks, A–E.

6 Write an answer to two of the five tasks worked on in this Writing folder.

UNIT 30 Why should we employ you?

Genre	Interviews
Topic	Job interviews

Speaking 1

1 Discuss these questions in groups.

a Can you identify all the jobs in the pictures?

b Have you ever had a job interview? If so, describe to the other students in the group what happened and how you felt before, during and after the interview. Describe the experience in as much detail as you can.

c What advice would you give to an interviewee about dress and body language?

d What else can an interviewee do in order to create the best possible impression at the interview?

Reading

1 Below are some typical interview questions.

a Do you like routine tasks / regular hours?

b Why do you think you would like this type of work?

c What is your general impression of your last company?

d How interested are you in sport?

e Do you make your opinions known when you disagree with the views of your supervisor?

f What kinds of decisions are most difficult for you?

g What is your greatest strength?

h Do you prefer working with others or alone?

With a partner, discuss how you think it would be appropriate to answer these questions if you were at an interview for a job:

- in middle management in a supermarket chain
- as a driving instructor
- as a chef
- of the kind that you would like to apply for.

2 Look at the possible answers opposite. Match the answers (1–8) to their questions (a–h).

3 Do you think the advice provided is appropriate for the kind of job that you might consider applying for?

❶ Always answer positively. Keep your real feelings to yourself whatever they might be. Your answer is 'Very good' or 'Excellent'. Then smile and wait for the next question.

❷ Your answer in part might be: 'I believe in planning and proper management of my time and yet I can still work well under pressure.'

❸ A trick question. The interviewer knows from experience that most recent graduates are hopeless employees until they come to terms with such facts of life. You could say: 'No, there's no problem there. A company expects to make a profit, so the doors have to be open for business on a regular basis.'

❹ If you can, state that you come from an environment where input is encouraged when it helps the team's ability to get the job done efficiently.

❺ A recent survey of management personnel found that the executives who listed group sports among their extracurricular activities made an average of £3,000 a year more than their sedentary colleagues. Don't you just love football suddenly?

❻ This question is usually asked to determine whether you are a team player. Before answering, however, be sure that you know whether the job requires you to work alone.

❼ You are human, admit it, but be careful what you admit. If you have ever had to fire someone you are in luck, because no one likes to do that.

❽ This is a deceptively simple question because there is no pat answer. It is usually asked to see whether you really understand what the specific job and profession entail on a day-to-day basis.

Listening

1 🎧 Now listen to two different job applicants answering the same interview questions. Complete the table with notes on each applicant's response.

Question	Mr Higgins	Miss Smith
Why should we employ you?		
Are you willing to take calculated risks?		
Which of the jobs you have held have you liked least?		
In what areas do you feel that your last boss could have done a better job?		

Which applicant do you think gives the better answer to each question and why?

2 🎧 Here are some phrases used by one or other of the job applicants. Which applicant uses each phrase and in what context? Listen again and complete the table.

Phrase	Used by	Context
better suited		You won't find anyone better suited to this job than I am.
badly need		
take the instructions		
I wonder if		
good and bad points		
which is why		
it's hard to know		

3 Overall, which of the two candidates would you offer the job to?

Using a range of structures

1 Here are some situations in which you might find yourself having to write something in English. How could you use each of the verb forms listed under the topic in such a situation? Add one other verb form to each of the four sets.

a giving advice to someone, e.g. about ways of economising

conditionals
modals
inversion
present simple

b reminiscing, e.g. about your early years at school

used to
would
past simple
present perfect

c telling a story, e.g. about a difficult situation you had to face

past simple
past continuous
past perfect
inversion

d hypothesising, e.g. about how your life would have been different if you had been born the other sex

conditionals
wish
indirect questions
inversion

2 Fill the gaps in the situations below. You need one word for each gap.

a giving advice

> You could save quite a bit of money if you (**1**) .... to work instead of taking the bus. I think you (**2**) .... also try to spend less on food. In your position, I would try to eat out less often. Growing your own vegetables also, of course, (**3**) .... many people a lot of money.

b reminiscing

> I think the first years at school were the best in many ways. I (**1**) .... to stay for school dinners. As most of the kids (**2**) .... home for lunch, we school dinner kids had a lot of time to play and we (**3**) .... invent all sorts of games. I've always (**4**) .... good at making up games and I'm sure it's because of all the practice I (**5**) .... at primary school.

c telling a story

> It was a very difficult decision to take. I could either stay in a dull but secure job or I could take the chance I was being offered to travel the world. I (**1**) .... worked in the same job for ten years and had many good friends there so it was not an easy decision. However, one day as I (**2**) .... sitting at the computer writing yet another tedious report, I (**3**) .... that I had to get out or it (**4**) .... be too late. No sooner (**5**) .... I made up my mind than I (**6**) .... on my way to hand in my letter of resignation.

d hypothesising

> I sometimes wonder (**1**) .... my life would have been different if I (**2**) .... been born as a boy. First of all, I (**3**) .... not have (**4**) .... the opportunity to wear such interesting clothes. (**5**) .... I (**6**) .... male, I think I'd also (**7**) .... felt more pressure to get a secure job. My brother sometimes says that he wishes he (**8**) .... a girl, as we (**9**) .... things easier and I must say that I think I (**10**) .... inclined to agree.

3 Look at A and B below, both of which are grammatically correct. Improve them as much as you can.

A
> I am very much against the proposed new factory. Firstly, building it will involve cutting down a lovely wood. Secondly, it will cause additional traffic problems in the area. Last but not least, it will lead to increased air and water pollution in our area.

B
> It was an excellent film. I liked the way in which the main actress presented her character. I also liked the way in which the plot was developed. I loved the camerawork and the music too.

E xam spot

If you want to get more practice in spoken English, you should take every opportunity to speak to other people in English and to watch films and TV in English whenever you have the chance. You might even try talking to yourself in English!

G ⋯⟶ page 207

Vocabulary

V ocabulary spot

It is important to try to use a range of vocabulary when you are answering a question in the CAE Writing test (Paper 2).

1 Replace the words in italics below with as many alternatives as you can think of. How do the different words you suggest affect the meaning of the sentences?

a I was *surprised* by the writer's account of his adventures in Peru.

b I spent my first evening in the town where I would spend the next five years of my life *walking* round the city streets.

c My brother *said* that he would always support me if I needed help.

d My first day in my new job turned out to be very *interesting*.

e There was a *man* sitting opposite me reading a newspaper.

f You can *get* a variety of souvenirs at the market.

2 Look at the two sets of verbs below. For each set, match the verbs (a–d) with the person (1–4) most likely to behave in this way.

A

a	tiptoe	1	a drunk person
b	lurch	2	an arrogant person
c	strut	3	someone who has no special aim
d	wander	4	someone who is anxious not to wake others up

B

a	yell	1	someone who feels very strongly that something should be done
b	murmur	2	a nervous person
c	stammer	3	an angry person
d	insist	4	someone who wants only one person to hear

3 What words can you add to the two sets of verbs (A and B) and what shades of meaning do these words provide?

4 Think of two different adjectives to describe the following:

- everything that you can see from the window of the room you are in at the moment
- everything that you have in your pockets or handbag.

Speaking 2

1 Are the following good or bad pieces of advice for the CAE Speaking test (Paper 5)?

a Look down at the ground when you are speaking.

b When you are talking to your partner, it is more important that your partner should hear you than that the examiner should hear you.

c You will sound more natural if you talk very quickly.

d It is a good idea to shout at the examiner in case he or she is hard of hearing.

e Speak very slowly and clearly and pronounce each word as distinctly as you can.

f English intonation patterns go up and down quite a lot and so using a very flat intonation will sound unnatural.

g Keep eye contact with the examiner at all times.

h Speak a little bit indistinctly so that the examiner will not realise if you make pronunciation mistakes.

2 Now turn any of the bad pieces of advice from Speaking 1 into a positive recommendation.

EXAMPLE: ~~Look down at the ground when you are speaking~~ – *Keep your head up and speak directly to the examiner and/or your partner as fits the part of the test.*

3 Work in groups of four. Take it in turns to be the pair of candidates and the pair of examiners. One pair should look at the pictures in Task A and the other pair should look at the pictures in Task B. After each pair of candidates has completed their task, the examiners should comment on the candidates' performance.

Task A (Examiner's questions)
Which two of the jobs below would you like to do least and which two most? Why?

Task B (Examiner's questions)
Discuss the different ways below that a school principal could use to choose a new teacher. Which procedure do you think would be most useful? Which would be least useful? Why?

Topic review

a What is your favourite place in your country?

b How is your country like Great Britain? How is it different?

c How far do you think people judge by appearances?

d What is the most romantic spot in the world for you? Why?

e How do you feel about flying?

f An increasing number of people are going on walking holidays. Why do you think this is?

g Which do you prefer: tests or continuous assessment? Why?

h Does wrapping children up in cotton wool protect them or harm them?

i When people are nervous in job interviews, how do they show it?

j What did you use to want to be when you were a child?

Vocabulary

1 For each of the sentences below, fill the gap with a word based on the word in brackets at the end of each sentence.

a The mountainous .... in Switzerland is particularly spectacular. (scene)

b The gardens were all south-facing to gain maximum .... to the sun. (expose)

c The Grand Canyon was created by millions of years of .... (erode)

d .... , her father wasn't too pleased when she said she'd scratched his new car. (predict)

e I was absolutely taken aback by such .... behaviour from him. (expect)

f From the airlines, you only get a small sum in compensation for lost luggage, ... of the value of the contents of your suitcases. (regard)

Reading

1 Answer these questions about the text. Choose the correct option, A, B, C or D.

1 What did interviews tend to be like more than five years ago?
   A friendly conversations
   B either very relaxed or deliberately stressful
   C accompanied by a cup of tea or lunch
   D a police interrogation

2 How do modern companies want to save money?
   A by not inviting so many people to interview
   B by interviewing people from a distance
   C by not choosing unsuitable employees
   D by using scientific interview techniques

3 Which part of the selection process now has most influence on who gets a job?
   A interview
   B aptitude test
   C personality questionnaire
   D evaluation at assessment centre

4 What is the main aim of interviews these days?
   A To check that you have the necessary skills for the job.
   B To discover whether your past experience is relevant for the job.
   C To determine whether you really want the job.
   D To establish that your values match those of the company.

5 What is special about a structured interview?
   A It includes psychological tests.
   B All candidates are asked the same questions.
   C Questions vary to match individual candidates.
   D It asks candidates what they would do in specific situations.

6 Why are interviews in some ways more relaxed now than they used to be?
   A Candidates talk more when they are relaxed.
   B Offices have simpler furniture these days.
   C Work hierarchies have no importance now.
   D The interview is seen as a meeting of equals.

7 How successful are modern interviews in helping employers to choose the right candidate?
   A very successful   **B** quite successful
   C not very successful **D** of no use at all

8 This article was probably published in
   A a magazine for employers.   **B** a psychology journal.
   C a general interest newspaper. **D** a magazine for students.

Making the best of a good job

Today's applicants need to run the gauntlet of modern interview techniques. Peter Baker reports.

If your last job interview took place five or more years ago, you could be in for some big surprises when you re-enter the employment market. Interviews are now much less likely to take the form of a cosy fireside chat. Neither, at the other extreme, should you expect an intimidating interrogation supposedly designed to test your ability to cope with stress. These traditional approaches have gone the way of tea-trolleys and two-hour lunch-breaks.

As lean modern companies have learned the costs of making bad appointments, interviews have become part of a multi-layered quasi-scientific selection process, and are increasingly likely to be conducted by managers trained in complex psychological techniques. They are also becoming high-tech: before too long, candidates can expect many interview panels to include at least one member who participates by means of video-conferencing technology from another site or even overseas.

One thing has not changed. It is still unusual to get a job without a face-to-face encounter with your boss-to-be. Interviews are used by 75 per cent of companies for every category of staff they employ, according to an Industrial Relations Services (IRS) survey published in September. The same proportion of firms believe that, of all the selection tools available, interviews have the most influence on their appointment decisions.

But these days you cannot rely just on your skills as an interviewee to get the job you want. There is a good chance that you will have to start proving yourself well before you reach the interview room.

A recent analysis of recruitment methods by the Institute of Personnel and Development found that 61 per cent of firms also used aptitude tests, 43 per cent sent out personality questionnaires and 30 per cent evaluated potential staff at assessment centres. Professional and managerial staff are especially likely to be put through a wide range of selection techniques before they reach the final interview with the employer.

'By the time you've reached this stage, you are 90 per cent there in terms of an acceptance by the employer that you can do the job,' says Bill Robbins, director of the senior executive centre at Drake Beam Morin.

'Although you may be tested further on the skills and experience the company thinks are especially important, the interview is likely to focus more on your motivation for the job and how well you will fit into the organisation and its culture.'

Selection panels are now putting increasing effort into probing candidates' inner values to see whether they match those of the company. Your values could even be assessed by psychological tests conducted during the interview itself.

A test devised by occupational psychology consultancy Criterion Partnership requires candidates to select, rank and then discuss cards containing value-reflecting headings or statements such as 'money and status', 'opportunity to make independent decisions' and 'I need approval in work'.

Criterion has also developed an interview exercise that assesses candidates by asking them to discuss what they believe to have been the causes of positive or negative past work experiences. Someone who is inclined to blame themselves for negative events may be judged not to have sufficient emotional stamina to take on a job dealing with customer complaints, for example.

In today's job marketplace, you can expect the interview to be a 'structured' event – each candidate will be asked the same predetermined questions – rather than a process guided by whatever questions happen to float into the minds of the panel. (This standardisation aims to provide a better basis for comparing candidates and reducing bias on the grounds of race or gender.) The IRS survey found that nine out of ten interviews are now structured, compared with seven out of ten two years ago.

An increasing number of interviews are also 'situational'. This means that candidates are asked questions such as 'What would you do if...?', an approach that lets them provide practical examples of how they would tackle particular situations, whether or not they have had any direct experience of them.

Despite their increasing rigour, interviews are generally becoming a lot less formal. Candidates and interviewers are now much more likely to sit on sofas than face each other across a large mahogany table. Fran Minogue of recruitment company Norman Broadbent believes that selection panels 'aim to relax people so they can open up and do as much talking as possible.' This new informality also reflects the decreasing importance attached to hierarchy within organisations.

The biggest change in the style of interviews will be noticed by senior staff with skills currently in short supply in the labour market. 'At this level, interviews are increasingly a conversation between equals,' suggests Bill Robbins. 'That's a big change.'

Yet despite all efforts to bring the interview process up-to-date, employers frequently make the wrong choice. Although the interview remains the centrepiece of organisations' selection procedures, it is in fact a highly unreliable predictor of a candidate's suitability. When Oxford Psychologists Press examined all the evidence, they found that interviewing came third from bottom in a list of eight methods of selection. Only astrology and graphology scored worse.

But you would be best advised not to point this out to a potential employer – at least not until you have definitely been offered the job.

Grammar

1 Write one word in each gap. The exercise begins with an example (0).

Testing ... testing ... testing

Is the nation's obsession with examining (0) .....*its*..... pupils placing a continuous burden of toil and stress on teachers, parents and children?

At Clapham Manor primary school in south London on Thursday, 24 children, all 10 or 11 years old, sit in silence completing, along with (1) .... estimated 599,976 children in classrooms around the country, a key stage 2 English writing test.

Some fidget, some look around the room, but most (2) .... diligently. They have to deliver one piece of writing from four choices.

Their teacher has read through the paper with them. They have had 15 minutes (3) .... plan and 45 minutes to write. They are in their normal classroom, but some parts of their walls have (4) .... to be covered – aides-to-learning like "explanation" words.

When the exam finishes there is no heavy sighing, (5) .... hint of tears. They just sit while their teacher gathers their papers, and wait (6) .... the next thing, which happens to be *The Guardian* asking them (7) .... it went. Four thought it was hard. Fourteen thought it was easy. Twelve (8) .... nervous before. Sixteen enjoyed it. Four thought their parents were worried about how they would (9) ....

"You don't have to look for things to write – it's just your imagination," said Ali.

"We have done (10) .... many practice tests before this that it was easy," said Rachel.

Speaking

1 Work with a partner. Allow each other one minute to talk without interruption on one of the following subjects:

- what I have particularly enjoyed during my CAE course
- what I shall always remember about the people in this class
- the unit that I enjoyed most from this book.

2 Now discuss with the class as a whole what your plans and hopes are for the next few months, for keeping up your English and for your life in general.

Grammar folder

Unit 1

Conditionals

Conditional sentences are often considered to be one of four main types:

- Zero conditional is used to talk about common states or events.
  if / when + present simple + present simple
  If she knows you well, she is more talkative.
  When we see each other in the street, we say hello.

- First conditional is used to talk about possible future states or events.
  if / when + present simple / continuous + *will / be going to*
  If you go away to study, you'll meet a lot of new people.
  I'm going to go without him if he doesn't come soon.

- Second conditional is used to talk about unlikely or imaginary states or events in the present or future.
  if + past simple / continuous + *would / could / should / might*
  If she spoke Spanish, she could apply for the job in Madrid.
  If they had the money, they would leave their jobs and travel the world.
  With *be*, the second conditional uses *were* instead of *was* in formal contexts.
  If I were / was good at languages, I'd learn Japanese.

- Third conditional is used to talk about imaginary states or events in the past.
  if + past perfect + *would / could / should / might* + *have* + past participle
  If we had studied other cultures at school, we might have been more confident about travelling.
  If you had arrived in Japan three months ago, you would have seen the cherry blossom.

Mixed conditionals

Different conditional forms are sometimes mixed, particularly second and third conditionals.

- A third conditional cause is sometimes linked to a second conditional result to show the imaginary present result of an imaginary past event or situation.
  If my parents had never met, I wouldn't be here now!

- A second conditional cause is sometimes linked to a third conditional result to show how an ongoing situation produced an effect in the past.
  If I knew anything about computers, I would have applied for a website design job.

Other conditionals

There are a number of other conditional sentences formed with different patterns of tenses to the four main types described above. Some common examples of alternative conditional structures are:

- *if / when* + present simple + imperative
  This is used to make suggestions or to give advice or instructions.
  If you need a translator, please let me know.
  Get off the train when you get to the third station.

- *if / when* + present simple / present perfect + *can / could / would / should / might*
  This is often used to make suggestions or offer advice.
  She could give Martin a message if she sees him in Italy.
  If you've studied English, you should try to speak it.

Notice that when the *if* clause is first in the sentence, it is followed by a comma. There is no comma when the main clause comes first.

- We can use *will* after *if* when we talk about the result of something in the main clause, or in polite requests.
  Post the parcel at the main post office if it will get there quicker.
  If you will just wait a moment, I'll tell Mr Jackson you're here.

- To make the request more polite, we can use *would*.
  If you would take a seat for a moment, I'll let Mr Jackson know you're here.

- We can leave out *if* and put *should* at the beginning of the clause, particularly in formal or literary English.
  Should you wish to extend your stay, please inform reception.

- We can use *was / were not for* or *had not been for* to say that one situation is dependent on another situation or person.
  If it hadn't been for the tour guide, we would never have seen those carvings in the caves.

- We can use *if* + *was / were* + *to* + infinitive to talk about imaginary future situations.
  If the technology were to become available, we would be able to travel across the world in just a couple of hours.

Unit 2

Prepositions and adverbs

- A preposition is a word that expresses the relation between the word(s) before it and the preposition's object which follows it. The object of a preposition is a noun or noun group. Prepositions in their most basic use indicate direction and position.
  Jane's moving to the Isle of Skye. (direction)
  Write the address on this envelope. (position)

- Many prepositions can also be adverbs and are used without an object.
  He went in. (*in* is an adverb)
  He went in the house. (*in* is a preposition)

- An adverb is a word that modifies or qualifies a clause. There are different types of adverbs, including adverbs of place, manner, time, frequency and duration.
  There's a good hotel nearby. (place)
  She writes entertainingly. (manner)
  My parents write to me regularly. (frequency)

Words which can be commonly used as both adverbs and prepositions include:

about   above   below   down   in   near   off   outside   up

A good dictionary will tell you if a word is a preposition or an adverb.

Unit 3

Wish and *if only*

Wish and *if only* is used to express wishes and regrets.

- *Wish* and *if only* + past simple is used to express a wish or regret about a general state that exists in the present, or a usual or regular event or habit.
  He wishes he was a photographer instead of an actor.
  If only we had longer holidays.
  If only driving to work didn't take so long.

- *Wish / if only* + *would* is also used to express a wish or regret about a usual or regular event or habit. We use *would* when the person or thing doing the action could change their behaviour if they chose to. It is often used to complain about someone's behaviour.
  If only the children would be quiet.
  I wish you would look for a job.

- *Wish / if only* + past perfect is used to express a wish or regret about the past by saying how we would like the past to be different.
  I wish I had trained as a doctor instead of as a teacher.
  If only she had thought more about her career while she was still at school.

- *Wish* + infinitive is used in very formal language to mean *want* + infinitive. It can be used to talk about the past, present or future.
  Napoleon wished to keep his battle plans a secret until the very last moment.
  Please be quiet. The Director wishes to say a few words.
  I'm sure she'll wish to thank you for your gift.

- Note that when people talk about their wishes for the future, it is unusual to use the verb *wish*; the verb *hope* is usually used.
  I hope you enjoy your stay in our town.
  She hopes to get a job in television.

It's time

There are several different structures that can be used with *it's time*. The meanings are very similar:

- *It's time* + infinitive
  It's time to go home now.

- *It's time for* + subject + infinitive
  It's time for us to go home now.

- *It's time* + subject + past simple (a little more formal)
  It's time we went home now.

- *It's time* + subject + past continuous (more colloquial)
  It's time we were going home now.

- To say that something should have been done already, *about time* and *high time* can be used.
  It's about time we went home.
  It's high time we went home.

Would rather / would sooner

Would rather and *would sooner* are used to express a preference for one situation or event over another. They mean the same as *prefer to* + infinitive.

- *Would rather / would sooner* + infinitive is used to express a preference about a general situation or event, or about a possible future situation or event.
  I'd sooner work days than nights.
  I'd rather / I'd sooner travel the world than go to university.

- *Would rather / would sooner* + subject + present simple / past simple is used to express a preference for another person (or thing) to do or not do something generally or in the future. The use of the past simple expresses the preference a little more tentatively or politely than the present simple.
  I would rather she works than does nothing.
  He'd sooner you didn't tell anyone about the interview yet.

- In formal contexts the subjunctive is used. Instead of present simple we use the infinitive without *to*; past subjunctive is the same as past simple except for *be*, where the past subjunctive always uses *were*.
  I'd rather he go now.
  I'd sooner she were happy in her work.

- *Would rather / would sooner* + *have* + past participle is used to express a preference for one situation or outcome in the past over another.
  When he was young, he'd rather have been a photographer than an actor. (But he is / was an actor.)

- *Would rather / would sooner* + subject + past perfect is used to express a wish or preference that actions or events in the past were different, and it is often used to talk about another person's actions.
  I'd rather you had asked me before you borrowed the car yesterday.
  I'd rather it hadn't rained all through the holiday.

Unit 4

Modals: *may, might, can, could*

Modal verbs give an indication of a speaker's attitude and of the relationship between the speaker and the person spoken to. Modals can indicate degrees of certainty, uncertainty, formality, informality, tentativeness, respect and politeness.

Ability

- *Can* expresses ability in the present; *could* expresses general ability in the past.
  He's lucky he can remember facts very easily.
  When I was a child I could speak Welsh but now I've forgotten it completely.

- To talk about an achievement or something that was done with difficulty, we do not use *could*. We can use *was / were able to*, *managed to* + infinitive or *succeeded in* + verb + *-ing*.
  She managed to / was able to memorise all the words before the test.
  On holiday, they succeeded in holding a conversation with a vocabulary of just 50 words.

- We can also use *was / were able to*, *managed to* + infinitive or *succeeded in* + verb + *-ing* to express that someone was successful in doing something on one occasion.
  Were you able to get his autograph after the concert?
  We managed to find my mobile phone by ringing my own number.
  After queuing for an hour, we succeeded in getting tickets for the show.

Permission

- *Can* is often used to express permission and *cannot / can't* is often used to express prohibition in the present and in general time. *Could* and *couldn't* are used to express permission and prohibition in the past.
  You can leave whenever you want. (permission)
  In the UK, children cannot leave school until they are 16. (prohibition)
  In the 1950s, children in the UK could leave school at 14. (permission)
  In the 1950s in the UK, young adults couldn't vote until they were 21. (prohibition)

- *May* is sometimes used to express permission and prohibition in the present. It is more formal and polite than *can*.
  Members may not wear jeans or T-shirts at formal ceremonies.

Requests, suggestions and polite orders

- *Can* and *could* are both used to make offers and requests and give polite orders and suggestions. *Can* is informal; *could* is neutral.
  Can / Could I help you with that? (offer)
  Can / Could you test me on these words? (request)
  You can / could check the recipe and find the ingredients while I wash up. (polite order / suggestion)

- *Might* is sometimes used to request permission very politely but is usually used only in highly formal situations.
  Might I be allowed to give an opinion on this matter?
  Might I suggest that we take a vote on this proposal?

Possibility and probability

- *May, might* and *could* are used to speculate about the possibility of events and situations in the present and future. *Might* indicates a lower probability or more uncertainty than *may* and *could*. In the negative, *could not / couldn't* indicates almost total certainty, much higher than *may not* or *might not / mightn't*. (In modern English *mayn't* is extremely unusual and should not be used.)
  They could decide to take the train. (possible)
  She may get here on time if she catches the early train. (possible)
  She might get here on time if she catches the later train. (less probable)
  She couldn't arrive before 10, it's impossible. (certain)

- *May, might* and *could* + *have* + past participle are used to speculate about events and situations in the past.
  They're late. They may have been held up in the rush hour traffic.
  I left a message at their hotel but they might not have got it yet.
  They couldn't have met by coincidence in London; it's too big.

- *May, might* and *could* + *have* + past participle are used to talk about possibilities in the past that we know didn't actually happen. The context has to be examined to decide whether the structure has this meaning or whether it expresses speculation about something that perhaps did actually happen as described above.
  Didn't you use a map? You might have got lost. (But you didn't.)
  She was very intelligent and could have gone to university. (But she didn't.)

- *Cannot / can't* is used to express negative certainty about the present based on evidence.
  This bill can't be right. We've only had two coffees!

- *Cannot / can't* + *have* + past participle is used to express negative certainty about the past based on evidence.
  This doesn't taste like pizza. She can't have followed the recipe.

- *Can* and *could* are used to talk about theoretical possibility. *Could* indicates less confidence than *can*.
  The school can take 1,000 pupils and it usually does.

  The school could take 1,000 pupils but it would be difficult in terms of space.

- *May, might* and *could* + *be* + verb + *-ing* are used to speculate about events and situations in the immediate present and in the future.
  Where's Sam? He might be studying in his room.
  Fiona could be managing her own company a year from now.

Unit 5
Relative clauses

Defining relative clauses

- Defining relative clauses give essential information so that we can identify who or what is being talked about. The relative clause follows immediately after the noun referring to the person(s) or thing(s) we are talking about.
  The woman who showed the most determination got the job.

- We do not put commas at the beginning and end of a defining relative clause.

- We can sometimes omit the relative pronoun. The relative pronoun must be used when it is the subject of the following verb.
  She showed me photos of the gorillas (which / that) she had studied.
  She showed me photos of the gorillas which / that lived nearby. (The relative pronoun must be used here because it is the subject of *lived*.)
  The letter (which / that) you received in September explains our position.
  The letter which / that arrived in September explains our position. (The relative pronoun must be used here because it is the subject of *arrived*.)

Non-defining relative clauses

- Non-defining relative clauses give non-essential, extra information about something or someone.
  Dian Fossey, who was born in the USA, made a major contribution to the study of primates.

- We use a comma before and immediately after the clause.

- We cannot omit the relative pronoun in non-defining relative clauses.

Relative pronouns

Many relative clauses are introduced by a relative pronoun.

- *Which* and *that* refer to things but *that* is not used in non-defining relative clauses.
  The study that she published last month is remarkable.
  Her most recent study, which she's just published, is her best yet.

- *Who* refers to people.
  Dian, who has specialised in primates, has spent a lot of time in Africa.

- *Whom* refers to people if they are the object of the clause. It is very formal and not commonly used in modern English.
  Professor West, whom I worked with recently, has won the Nobel prize.

- *Whose* can be used with things or people and expresses possession or belonging.
  She is a scientist whose work is world famous.
  The book, whose focus is African primates, is very influential.

- *When* refers to time.
  She described the moment when she first saw a wild gorilla.

- *Where* refers to place.
  She spent many years in Africa, where she observed gorillas in the wild.

Prepositions in relative clauses

- In neutral English, and sometimes in modern formal English, prepositions can be placed at the end of the sentence.

- In formal English, putting prepositions at the end of the sentence is sometimes considered bad style. Formal sentences are often constructed to place the preposition earlier in the sentence.
  That was the story which the film was based on.
  That was the story on which the film was based.

- When the preposition is placed earlier in the sentence, *that* cannot be used.
  That's the research that/which she received the award for.
  That is the research for which she received the award.

- When the preposition is placed earlier in the sentence, *whom* must be used as the relative pronoun when the object is a person.
  She spoke to a professor that / who / whom she is friendly with.
  She spoke to a professor with whom she is friendly.

Unit 6
Phrasal verbs

- Phrasal verbs are made up of more than one part. They are verbs with prepositional or adverbial particles. Some common examples are:
  put off   look up to   take in   do up   break out   get out of   turn down

- The meaning of a phrasal verb is often not obvious from the meaning of its components and so it is probably best to learn them as individual items.
  make off with = steal something and carry it away quickly

- There are many phrasal verbs in English and they are most frequently, though not exclusively, used in spoken English and in more informal writing. There is often a single word with the same meaning which is preferred in more formal writing.
  The football match has been put off until next week.
  The football match has been postponed until next week.
  The price of petrol has gone up three times already this year.
  The price of petrol has increased three times already this year.

- Many phrasal verbs have more than one meaning.
  He asked her to stop singing as it was putting him off. (distract)
  The football match has been put off until next week. (postpone)
  Don't be put off if you can't do it straight away. (cause someone to change their mind about doing something)
  Would you put off the light before you leave? (switch off)

Word order restrictions vary for different phrasal verbs.

- Some verbs can have their object before or after the particle.
  We did our bathroom up last year.
  We did up our bathroom last year.

- If the object is a pronoun, it must go between the two parts of the verb.
  We did it up by ourselves.

- Other verbs can only take an object after the preposition. With such verbs the pronoun also follows the second part of the verb.
  She has fallen for the boy who lives next door. Fortunately, he has also fallen for her.

There is more information about the grammar of phrasal verbs in the grammar folder for Unit 23.

Unit 7
Cause and effect

Cause and effect can be expressed in a number of different ways.

- Verbs and verb phrases
  The following verbs all introduce **effect**:

  bring about   generate   give rise to   lead to   produce   result in

  Summer clubs for school students in the UK have led to a decrease in the crime rate.
  A poor diet will result in health problems.

  The focus of the following verbs is **cause**:

  arise from   be based on   come from   lie behind   stem from

  Her attitude stems from her background.
  The employees' hard work and enthusiasm lie behind the success of the company.

- Conjunctions and adverbs
  The following conjunctions and adverbs show **relationships between cause and effect**:

  because   consequently   so   therefore

  She got to the top in her career because she spoke to all the right people.
  He is ambitious, so he doesn't mind staying late at work most evenings.

- **Prepositions**
  The following prepositions all introduce **cause**:

  because of   due to   for   owing to

  Rosy got the job because of her pleasant manner.
  Owing to the storms, all trains have been cancelled.
  I couldn't sleep for worrying.

- **Nouns and noun phrases**
  The following nouns refer to **cause and effect**:

  *aim   basis   consequence   explanation   motive
  outcome   purpose   reason   result*

  The aim of the programme was to give students work experience.
  His laziness is the reason why he is not as successful as he could be.

Unit 8
Modals: *must, should, ought to, shall, will, would*

Must

- *Must* can be used to express obligation. *Mustn't* expresses prohibition. The past form of *must* used to express obligation is *had to* and the negative is *wasn't / weren't allowed to*.
  You must do exactly what the exam questions ask you to do.
  You mustn't talk during the exam.
  We had to write two compositions in last week's exam.
  We weren't allowed to take any books into the exam.

- *Must* can also be used to make deductions from evidence and expresses certainty. The past form of *must* for deduction is *must + have* + past participle. We use *must be going to* + infinitive to make deductions about the future. The negative of *must* for this meaning is *can't* (see Unit 4).
  That must be John coming up the steps – I recognise his footsteps!
  The train is late – the heavy snow must have caused delays.
  They bought lots of paint – they must be going to decorate.

- *Must* and *mustn't* are used to give strong advice.
  You must stop smoking.

- *Must* and *mustn't* are used to make recommendations.
  You must see Spielberg's new film – it's brilliant!

- *Must* and *mustn't* are used to talk about strong necessity.
  We must have oxygen to survive.

Ought to and should

- *Ought to* and *should* are used to say that something seems likely because it is logical or normal.
  It's 6 o'clock. He ought to / should be home soon.

- *Ought to* and *should* can be used to give advice or suggest that something would be a good idea.
  You ought to / should tell her how you feel.
  Someone ought to / should open a café here because there isn't one for miles.

- *Ought to* and *should* are used to talk about duty and express weak obligation.
  People ought to / should wait in the queue and not push in.

- *Ought to* and *should* are used to criticise actions or attitudes.
  People ought to / should show more respect for old people.

- *Ought to* and *should* are used to talk about the importance of doing something.
  The manager suggested that we ought to / should leave the restaurant as quickly as possible.
  We ought to / should get back before the sun goes down.

- *Ought to* and *should* are used to talk about necessity.
  Sports clothes should be light and allow you to move easily.

- The negative forms are *ought not to* or *oughtn't to* and *should not* or *shouldn't*.
  You oughtn't to / shouldn't be late on your first day at work.

- The past forms are *ought to / should + have +* past participle.
  You ought to have / should have let us know you were coming.

Will and would

- *Will* and *would* are used to make polite invitations and requests. *Would* is more polite.
  Will / Would you sit here, please?

- *Will* and *won't* are used to describe habits and characteristic behaviour in the present and in general. If *will* is stressed, it indicates the speaker's irritation with or negative opinion of the habit.
  He will / he'll watch TV all evening. Sometimes he won't talk for hours.
  *He **will** play golf every weekend, instead of helping me in the garden.*

- *Would* and *wouldn't* are used to talk about past habits and characteristics. If *would* is stressed, it indicates the speaker's irritation with or negative opinion of the habit.
  Every evening she would / she'd sit in the garden reading her newspaper. She wouldn't stop until she'd read every page.
  *He **would** insist on smoking. It killed him in the end of course.*

- *Will* is used to express demands, insist that something happens in the future or express determination.
  You will do as I say immediately!
  I will / I'll go where I want and don't try to stop me!

There is more information about other uses of *will* and *would* in the grammar folders for Unit 1 (conditionals) and Unit 10 (future forms).

Unit 9
Participle clauses

The table below shows the different participle forms for the verb *wash*.

Participle	
Present active	*washing*
Present passive	*being washed*
Perfect active	*having washed*
Perfect passive	*having been washed*

- Participle clauses with a present participle can be used adjectivally.
  Look at that man sitting in the corner. (= who is sitting in the corner)
  Who is the girl being interviewed by the journalist? (= who is being interviewed)

- All participle clauses can be used adverbially.
  Feeling exhausted after the flight, I went to bed as soon as I got to the hotel. (= Because I felt exhausted …)
  Washed by hand, this jersey will keep its shape for years. (= If it is washed by hand …)

- Perfect participle clauses are often adverbial clauses showing when or why something happened.
  Having made your decision, it is not possible to change your mind. (= When you have made …)
  Having spent happy holidays in Spain as a child, she was keen to return there with her own family. (= Because she had spent …)

- The subject of the participle clause is usually the same as that of the main clause. However, it is possible to have participle clauses with a different subject.
  There being no money left, we had to start making our way home. (= Because there was no money left …)
  It being too late to get a bus, we took a taxi. (= Because it was too late …)

- When the participle clause describes a situation, a different subject is often introduced with the word *with*.
  I was beginning to get a headache with the children all talking at the same time.
  With it / It being Sunday in New Zealand, we couldn't find any shops open.

Unit 10

Future forms

The future in English can be expressed in many different ways.

Will

- *Will* is used to talk about a future action or event at the point of decision.
  I'll come to the cinema with you tonight, I think.

- *Will* is used to make predictions about the future.
  You will meet a tall, dark stranger.

- *Will* is used to make promises.
  I'll buy you a car for your birthday.

Going to

- *Going to* is used to talk about intentions. Sometimes it is used to talk about plans and arrangements based on intentions (but the present continuous is more commonly used for talking about arrangements).
  We're going to visit our friends in New Zealand next winter.

- *Going to* is also used to talk about future events and actions based on present evidence, especially when we can see the event is imminent.
  The way Brazil are playing at the moment, they're going to win the match.
  Watch out! We're going to hit that tree!

Present continuous

- The present continuous is used to talk about plans and arrangements for the future. A time reference often makes the future meaning clear.
  What are you doing tonight?
  We're meeting early tomorrow morning.

Present simple

- The present simple is used to talk about timetables and schedules.
  Our train leaves at 6.30 tomorrow morning.

- The present simple is used with future reference in subordinate clauses after time conjunctions such as *when, before, until, as soon as.*
  We'll reply when we hear from you.
  I hope you'll write to us as soon as you get home.

Be + infinitive

- *Be* + infinitive is formal. It is used in rules or instructions, or to talk about official plans. It is particularly common in news reports.
  Staff are not to use company telephones for personal calls.
  The Prime Minister is to visit South America next month.

Future continuous

- The future continuous focuses on an action or event in progress at a specific time in the future.
  This time next week I'll be lying on a beach in the sun.

Future perfect

- The future perfect looks forward to a future time and then looks back from that point.
  By the end of next year we'll have finished the project.

Future in the past: *was / were going to / would* + verb

- These forms are used to look back to a past time and talk about the future as it was at that past time.
  By the time I left school I knew I was going to / would become a doctor.

There is more information on first and second conditionals in the grammar folder for Unit 1.

Unit 11

Direct and reported speech

Grammatical changes

Some features of grammar in direct speech must be changed in reported speech.

- When we report what someone said, we tend to change the verb tense, which is called 'backshift'. Personal pronouns, demonstratives and other references to the 'here and now' may also need to be changed.
  'I've seen a bank clerk wearing a nose ring.'
  She said that she'd seen a bank clerk wearing a nose ring.
  'I'll be arriving at your house at 10 am tomorrow.'
  She said that she would be arriving at my house at 10 am the next day.

- Most modal verbs do not usually change, but *can* changes to *could* and *will* changes to *would*.
  'You must dress professionally at all times.'
  He told us we must dress professionally at all times.
  'You should have a dress code.'
  She suggested that we should have a dress code.
  'I can pay cash.'
  He said he could pay cash.
  'I'll pay by credit card.'
  He said he'd pay by credit card.

- When something is reported that is a general truth, or if the situation hasn't changed yet, there is often no tense change.
  She said that darker coloured clothes generally look smarter.
  My neighbour's 4-year-old told me she wants to be a dress designer when she grows up.

- In reported questions, the subject usually comes before the verb and the auxiliaries *do*, *does* and *did* are only used in negative reported questions. Yes / No questions are reported with *if* or *whether*. Question marks are not used in reported questions.
  'Which suit do you prefer?'
  She asked (me) which suit I preferred.
  'Why don't you like shopping?'
  He asked (me) why I didn't like shopping.
  'Could you help me choose some new shoes?'
  She asked (me) if / whether I could help her choose some new shoes.

Verbs used to report speech

We can use a wide variety of verbs to introduce reported speech. Different verbs are followed by different structures. The list below shows some common verbs and their dependent patterns. Note that *that* may be omitted after most of the common reporting verbs.

- *advise + to +* infinitive
  She advised us to check the contract carefully.

- *agree + that* (optional) */ + to +* infinitive
  He agreed (that) our money would be refunded.
  He agreed to refund our money.

- *ask + if/whether / + to +* infinitive
  We asked if we could have more training.
  We asked to have more training.

- *complain + that*
  We complained that the service was very slow.

- *deny + that* (optional) */ + -ing*
  She denied (that) she had taken the credit card.
  She denied taking the credit card.

- *insist + that* (optional) */ + on + -ing*
  He insisted (that) we stay at his house.
  He insisted on our staying at his house.

- *invite + to +* infinitive
  She invited us to visit any time.

- *offer + to +* infinitive
  They have offered to help.

- *promise + that* (optional) */ + to +* infinitive
  The management has promised (that) training will be provided.
  The management has promised to provide training.

- *recommend + that* (optional) */ + -ing*
  I recommend (that) you book well in advance.
  I recommend booking well in advance.

- *regret + that* (optional) */ + -ing*
  He regrets (that) he won't be able to attend the ceremony.
  He regrets not being able to attend the ceremony.

- *say + that* (optional)
  The manager said (that) we should arrange an appointment.

- *suggest + that* (optional) */ + -ing*
  She suggested (that) I bought the black jeans.
  She suggested that I should buy the black jeans.
  She suggested buying the black jeans.

- *tell + that* (optional) */ + to +* infinitive
  His sister told him (that) he should get a job.
  His sister told him to get a job.

- *threaten + that* (optional) */ + to +* infinitive
  The bank manager threatened (that) she would take away my credit card.
  The bank manager threatened to take away my credit card.

- *warn + that* (optional) */ + to +* infinitive */ about + -ing*
  She warned me (that) credit was expensive.
  She warned me not to use credit.
  She warned me about using credit.

Unit 12

Past tenses and the present perfect

Past time can be expressed in many different ways in English. Some examples of the different forms used to refer to the past are described below.

Past simple

- The past simple is used to talk about a completed action, event or situation at a particular time or over a particular time in the past.
  The train left at 8.30 am.
  We lived in London until I got a job in Oxford.

- The past simple is used to talk about repeated actions in the past.
  He read a chapter of the book every night before going to sleep.
  We went to the beach at weekends in the summer.

Past continuous

The past continuous cannot be used with stative verbs (*be, know, love*, etc.), which describe a state rather than an action. With stative verbs the past simple is used.

- The past continuous is used to talk about a situation or action in progress around a point in time in the past.
  I was living in London when Kennedy was assassinated.
  What were you doing at 9 on Tuesday evening?

- The past continuous is used to talk about a situation or action in progress that is interrupted by another event.
  While I was thinking about the problem I suddenly had the most amazing idea.
  The plane was coming in to land when it was struck by lightning.

- The past continuous is used to emphasise that two situations or events were happening simultaneously.
  While I was trying to phone her, she was trying to phone me!
  I was putting the toys away and the children were getting them back out again.

- The past continuous is used with *always* and *forever* to talk about repeated actions or behaviour.
  They were forever asking for favours, but they never did anything for anyone else.
  She was always offering to babysit so that my husband and I could go out.

Present perfect simple

- The present perfect simple is used to talk about past events or situations in a time period that extends from the past up to the present. It is often used to talk about experience. The specific time is unknown or unimportant and we cannot use words which mark the specific moment when the event happened (e.g. *yesterday, last year*).
  That shop has had three new managers and it's still losing money.
  I've been to Russia. – When did you go? – I went last June.

- It is also used to say how many times something has happened in that period.
  They've lived at three different addresses since June.

- The present perfect simple is used to talk about an event in the past that has a result in the present. In this use the focus is on the effect or importance of the past event at the present moment. The event is often, but not always, in the recent past. The specific time is unknown or unimportant and, again, we cannot use words which mark specific points in time like *yesterday* or *last year*.
  Cancel the skiing trip – I've broken my leg.
  Has he finished that report yet?

- The present perfect simple is used to talk about the duration of an event or situation which started in the past and extends up to the present. The specific starting point or the length of the period is given.
  How long have you worked here? – I've been here for two months.
  I've played the piano since I was four.

Present perfect continuous

The present perfect continuous cannot be used with stative verbs (*be, know, love*, etc.), which describe a state rather than an action. With stative verbs the present perfect simple is used.

- The present perfect continuous is used to talk about past events which continue up to the present or up to a time in the recent past.
  I've been watching this film on TV but I'm going to turn it off if something doesn't happen soon.
  She's been helping me with the housework but now she's got bored with it.

- The present perfect continuous is used to talk about repeated past events in a time period that extends up to the present.
  The car has been breaking down a lot recently.
  He's been seeing a new girlfriend most evenings.

- The present perfect continuous is used to talk about an event, action or behaviour in the recent past that has a result in the present. The action may be finished or unfinished. In this use, the focus is on the present evidence for the past event. The specific time is unknown or unimportant and we cannot use words which mark specific points in time.
  It's been raining. (The rain has stopped but the streets are wet.)
  You look exhausted. Have you been working hard? – Yes, but I've almost finished.

- The present perfect continuous is used to talk about the duration of an event or situation which started in the past and extends up to the present. The specific starting point or the length of the period is given.
  Has she been writing her novel for a long time?
  She's been working on it for about six years.

Past perfect simple

- The past perfect simple can be used in similar ways to the present perfect simple, but instead of referring to actions or events up to the present, it refers to actions or events before a particular time (or before another event or action at a particular time) in the past.
  I'd only just sat down at my desk and my boss was asking me where the letters were. (one event happening before another)
  Before I was 18, I hadn't been outside my home town. (experience)
  When I got home, I realised I had left my key at the office so I couldn't get into my flat. (result)
  I'd lived in the house since I was a child and was sorry to leave. (duration)

- Unlike the present perfect, the past perfect can refer to specific times in the past.
  We already felt like old friends even though we had only met that morning.
  He asked me when exactly I had first heard about the problem.

Past perfect continuous

The past perfect continuous cannot be used with stative verbs (*be, know, love*, etc.), which describe a state rather than an action. With stative verbs the past perfect simple is used.

- The past perfect continuous can be used in similar ways to the present perfect continuous, but instead of referring to actions or events up to the present, it refers to actions or events up to a particular time (or up to another event or action at a particular time) in the past.
  The government had been watching the situation closely and were considering whether to intervene. (continuous action)
  She'd been helping at a charity soup kitchen on and off for a few months. (repeated action)
  From the piles of books I knew she'd been working on her thesis again, and I could hear her typing frantically at the keyboard in the next room. (evidence)
  They had been planning their expedition for months before I joined their team. (duration)

- The past perfect continuous can be used in other similar ways to the present perfect continuous, but instead of referring to actions or events up to a recent past, it refers to actions or events up to just before a particular time (or just before another event or action at a particular time) in the past.
  The students had been protesting about the cuts all day, but when I arrived that evening everything was quiet. (continuous action)
  He'd been drinking. I could smell it on his breath. (evidence)

- Unlike the present perfect continuous, the past perfect continuous can refer to specific times in the past.
  At breakfast I wondered why I felt so tired, then I remembered that at 2 am I'd been listening to my neighbours arguing again.

Unit 13

-*ing* forms

With verbs

The -*ing* form occurs in various grammatical patterns and is used to perform different grammatical functions.

- The -*ing* form can be the subject of a verb or the object of a verb.
  Travelling broadens the mind. (subject)
  I dislike travelling by ship. (object)

- Common verbs which are followed by an -*ing* form include:

admit	avoid	begin*	come	consider	delay
deny	dislike	enjoy	forget**	hate*	imagine
intend*	like*	love*	mind	miss	practise
prefer*	remember**	resent	risk	start*	stop**
suggest	try**				

  I considered living in Ireland for a while.
  I don't remember telling anyone.

Verbs marked * can also be followed by an infinitive with no change in meaning. Verbs marked ** can also be followed by an infinitive, but the meaning is different. (For example *He tried to do it a different way* means he attempted it, but we don't know if he did it. *He tried doing it a different way* means he actually tested a different method, but we don't know if the new method was any better or worse.)

- Verbs which are followed by the -*ing* form can also be followed by the passive -*ing* form, which is *being* + past participle.
  She enjoys being looked after.

- The verbs *need, want* and *require* can be followed by -*ing*, but this has a passive meaning.
  The machine needs / wants / requires servicing. (The machine needs to be serviced.)

After prepositions

- The -*ing* form can be the object of a preposition. The -*ing* form (rather than the infinitive) always follows a preposition.
  He isn't interested in listening to stories.
  They apologised for being late.
  He never tires of listening to Mozart.
  You should spend more time on renovating the house.

After common phrases

The -*ing* form follows some common phrases.

- *it's (not) worth*
  It's worth getting a book about the country before you go.

- *as well as*
  I play the guitar as well as playing the saxophone.

- *it's no good / use*
  It's no use crying; it won't change anything.

- *there's no use / point in*
  There's no point in waiting because he's not coming.

- *instead of*
  Let's take the car instead of walking in the rain.

- *can't help*
  I can't help laughing whenever I see that film.

- *to be / get / become used to*
  After a few years of travelling by tube, I've got used to people ignoring each other.

After determiners

- The -*ing* form can be used after determiners in formal English to show the possessive.
  Does my listening to the radio bother you?

Unit 14

The passive

When to use the passive

- We use the passive when the action is more important than the person or thing doing the action (the agent).

- We often use the passive when the agent is unknown.

- The passive is often used in more formal situations, such as lectures, academic writing and news reports.

How to form the passive

- The passive is usually formed by moving the object to the front of the sentence. Because of this, usually only transitive verbs can become passives; transitive verbs are verbs which have an object. We cannot say *It has been happened* because *happen* is intransitive.

- However, some intransitive phrasal verbs can also be passives.
  He woke up because of the noise. (active)
  He was woken up by the noise. (passive)

- Passives use the appropriate form of the verb *to be* and the past participle of the main verb. The appropriate form of the verb *to be* is the form that you would use for the verb in the equivalent active sentence. For example:
  Someone is stealing it. – It is being stolen. (present continuous)
  Someone has stolen it. – It has been stolen. (present perfect)
  Someone stole it. – It was stolen. (past simple)
  Someone was stealing it. – It was being stolen. (past continuous)
  Someone had stolen it. – It had been stolen. (past perfect simple)
  Someone will steal it. – It will be stolen. (future simple)

- When a verb has two objects, either object can be the subject of a passive clause. The object that is more important to the message of the sentence is generally the subject.
  Active: *Jill gave her brother the money.*
  Passive: *Her brother was given the money. / The money was given to her brother.*

- We can use a passive construction + *by* + agent, when the agent is important to the message.
  Her portrait was painted by Picasso.
  She's been awarded a medal by the Queen.

- The passive with modals is formed with the modal + *be* + past participle. The past form is modal + *have been* + past participle.
  She might be interviewed on TV tonight.
  She should have been interviewed long before now.

The passive used for reporting information

We can use the passive form of reporting verbs to give ideas or opinions without saying exactly where the ideas come from.

- Verbs typically used in the passive for this purpose include:

  assume   believe   claim   consider   feel   hope
  report   say   think

- We can use *it* + passive (*that*) + active clause, where *it* is the impersonal pronoun that does not refer to a real subject (like in *It's raining.*).
  It is said (that) most computer users are women.
  It is thought (that) most computer users surf the net.

- We can use passive + *to* + infinitive.
  Most computer users are said to be women.
  Most computer users are thought to surf the net.

- We can use *there* + *to* + infinitive (usually *be*).
  There is reported to be an increasing threat to our ecosystem.
  There are believed to be more than 600 species of trees per hectare in tropical rain forests.

- We can use passive + perfect infinitive, which indicates that the event has already occurred.
  The president is known to have been involved in the incident.
  There is thought to have been a cover-up by her staff.

There is more information about the passive *-ing* form in the grammar folder for Unit 13.

To have / get something done

- subject + *have / get* + object + past participle. We use this construction to say that the subject arranges for something to be done by someone else.
  I'm going to get / have my hair cut.
  She's going to get / have her portrait painted.

- The same construction is used to say that something is done to a person or thing belonging to the subject of *have / get*.
  I had my passport stolen on holiday.
  I left my bag open and got my passport stolen.

Although both structures can be used in the above examples, there are some differences in meaning when using *have / get something done*.

- We use *have something done* to imply that the subject of the sentence is not responsible for or has no control over what happens.
  I had my passport stolen while I was away.
  She had her wisdom teeth taken out last year.
  However, *get* can also be used in sentences like these in informal spoken English. We also tend to use *have* to focus on the result of an action (rather than the action itself).
  I'll have the report finished by tomorrow morning.

- We use *get something done* to imply that the subject of the sentence causes something to happen (perhaps accidentally) or they are to blame for it.
  I'll get the letters sent out to you first class.
  I got my hand trapped in the door of the car.

Won't have

- *Won't have* + object + present participle / past participle. This can be used to say that we will not allow someone to do something, or something to happen.
  I won't have you watching TV all day.
  She won't have her holiday ruined by them.

Want it done

- *Want* + object + past participle. This can be used to say that we would like someone to do something or we would like something to happen.
  I want the report finished by next Monday.
  Put your car in my garage. We don't want it damaged in the street.

Unit 15

The infinitive

The infinitive in English is the base form of the verb. It is called the full infinitive when *to* is used before the verb and the bare infinitive when there is no *to*.
  I want to watch the film tonight. (full infinitive with *to*)
  Let me see the newspaper. (bare infinitive without *to*)

The full infinitive is used:

- after certain verbs. Common examples include:

  afford   agree   appear   ask   choose   expect
  help   hope   intend   prefer   pretend   promise
  seem   want

  I asked to see the head teacher.
  We expect to arrive by eight.

- after impersonal *it + be +* adjective where the adjective describes the event that follows.
  It was good to see her again.
  It's always interesting to hear your views on life.

- after verbs which follow the pattern verb + someone + *to do* something. Common examples include:

  allow   ask   beg   encouraged   force
  persuade   teach

  My mother persuaded me to buy a computer.

- after the verbs above when we use them in the passive.
  He was allowed to choose for himself.

- after *be* with the meaning of a formal instruction or information about the future.
  You are to report here at 8 tomorrow morning.

- to express purpose.
  She's saving her money to go on holiday.

The bare infinitive is used:

- after verbs which follow the pattern verb + someone + *do* something. Common examples include:

  have   let   make

  I'll have the waiter bring us more water.
  His father lets him play football.

- after modal auxiliary verbs (but remember that some modals contain *to* in themselves: *have to do, ought to do* and *need to do*).
  We might go to Italy on holiday this year.
  We should get some brochures.

Unit 16

Articles and determiners

There are many different rules about the use of articles and determiners in English. Here are some of the points which cause difficulty for advanced learners of English.

- No article is used before uncountable and plural nouns when used in a general sense.
  I like music.
  She's interested in animals and wants to be a vet.

- When there is a following phrase or clause specifying exactly what is being talked about, the definite article is required before uncountable and plural nouns.
  I like the music they play at the jazz club in town.
  Are the animals in the rain forest safe in their environment?

- *A* or *an* is used the first time a singular countable noun is mentioned but after this *the* is used since the reader or listener is clear about what is being referred to.
  A bird was trapped in the room and Anna called for her brother to help her free the poor creature.

- Singular countable nouns must always have an article or some other determiner (like *each, my, this*) except for a few fixed expressions like *by car, in hospital,* etc.

- *The* is not used with the names of most countries. It is, however, used with plural names or names of countries which contain a common noun.
  The Philippines (plural), *The United Kingdom* (kingdom = common noun), *The United States* (plural and state = common noun)
  (Note that these nouns behave like singular nouns with verbs: *The United States is a huge country.*)

- *The* is used with playing instruments but no article is used with playing games.
  Mary's hobby is playing the guitar and mine is playing chess.

- *The* can often be used before *car, train, bus, plane, ferry* or *boat* when talking about the use of different types of transport in general, even when the mode of transport has not previously been referred to. *A* is also used.
  Are you going to take the train / a train or the bus / a bus to London tomorrow?

- *Each* and *every* precede singular nouns.
  Every girl has her own locker and each class has its own cloakroom.

- Parts of the body are usually preceded by a possessive pronoun rather than an article when they are talked about in the context of their relation to a specific body or bodies. When parts of the body are talked about in general, *the* is normally used.
  Sally has sprained her ankle.
  The liver is the largest organ in the body.

- The word *own* must be preceded by a possessive pronoun rather than *the* or *a.*
  When did you first get your own car?

- When we talk about the units in which commodities are generally bought or sold, we often use *by + the.* When we talk about price, we usually use *a /an.*
  Her parents used to buy coal by the ton.
  Those chocolates are nearly $100 a kilo.

- If we miss out *a* before *few* and *little,* the meaning is changed to mean *less.*
  She had a few friends. (some)
  She had few friends. (less than you would expect)

- We use *a /an* when describing someone or something in a way that applies to others.
  Kim is an interesting character. (There are other interesting characters in the world.)

Unit 17

Language of persuasion

Listed below are some of the structures that can be useful for persuading people to do things. There are many other different expressions which could be added to each set. However, the lists provide an indication of the variety of language that is available. While language used for persuasion is very sensitive to register and context, there is overlap between the lists. Some more informal phrases may be used in formal situations and vice versa. Tone of voice, for example, can also help to make something more or less formal.

- Formal writing (e.g. discursive essay, business letter)
  It goes without saying that …
  One of the most successful ways of … is ….
  Most experts in the field agree that …
  It cannot be denied that …
  There is every reason to believe that …
  The advantages of … strongly outweigh the disadvantages.
  My opinion is borne out by research.
  The point I am making can be effectively illustrated by an example.
  There are three main reasons why I hold this view.

- Formal speech (e.g. at a business meeting)
  But surely the best course of action would be to …
  Surely the most sensible thing would be to …
  I really think it would be a pity if we didn't …
  But surely it's in our own interests to …
  How can I persuade you to …
  Can't I persuade you to …
  Couldn't you be persuaded …
  Are you quite sure you won't reconsider?
  Are you quite sure you've taken everything into account?
  I think you might regret it later if you didn't …

- Informal speech (e.g. to a friend)
  Come on!
  Go on!
  Don't be like that!
  Please!
  Go for it!
  Can't you just …
  Won't you …, please.
  Please let me …
  Why don't you …
  Do …
  It won't (hurt / take long / cost much)!
  Do it for my sake!
  Not even for me?
  Just this once!
  You're not going to let me down, are you?

- Neutral speech
  I really think you should …
  Are you really sure you can't …
  Surely you could …
  You'd do well to …
  You'd be well advised to …
  Think it over, at least.
  Give it some thought, please.
  How can I convince you?

Unit 18

Cleft sentences and other ways of emphasising

Cleft sentences create emphasis by using a relative clause.

- Cleft sentences often use *the thing / something* or *the person / someone*, etc. For more emphasis, *one thing / person*, etc. is used.
  The thing (that) I like about him is his honesty.
  One person (who) I can't understand is the Prime Minister.

- We can use *the only* or *all* to emphasise that we're excluding everything else.
  The only thing that interests me is your happiness.
  All (that) I want is your happiness.

- *The thing that* is often replaced with *what* (making a nominal relative clause).
  What I really liked was the climate.
  The climate was what I really liked.

- When we want to talk about actions in the main clause of cleft sentences, we use a *be* + infinitive clause.
  What I like to do on cold, dark winter nights is light a big fire.

- Cleft sentences are often formed with impersonal *it* + *be*.
  It was you that created this problem, not me.

- Cleft sentences can be used to emphasise the subject or the object of a sentence.
  My brother cut down the apple tree.
  It was my brother who cut down the apple tree. (not someone else)
  It was the apple tree that my brother cut down. (not another tree)

In addition to cleft structures, other ways of emphasising include the following:

- use of *so* and *such*
  He's such a nice man!

- use of exaggerated lexis
  We're starving!

- use of intensifying adverb
  She's absolutely wonderful.

- use of simile
  You're as cold as ice!

- use of *on earth*, after a question word
  Why on earth did you say that?

- use of inversion (exchanging the position of the subject and verb) after a negative adverbial
  Under no circumstances would he agree to that.

- use of inversion after a restricting adverbial
  Little did she guess what would happen next.

- Auxiliary verbs in spoken English are not usually stressed (except for modal auxiliaries), and are usually contracted, e.g. *I am* becomes *I'm*. If we stress them, it adds emphasis to the sentence. This emphasis is used in various ways, e.g. to show determination, to convince someone or to contradict someone.
  *I **will** finish this race, or I'll die trying.*
  *I **am** going to tell him. I promise.*
  *I don't think she's coming. – She **is** coming. I know for a fact.*

- In present and past simple forms, *do* and *did* are used as stressed auxiliaries before the main verb to give emphasis.
  I do enjoy a good detective novel!
  You did get permission for this, didn't you?

There is more information about inversions in the grammar folder for Unit 19.

Unit 19
Emphasis

For emphasis, certain adverbs and adverbial phrases can be put at the beginning of a sentence or clause with an inversion of the following verb; the position of the subject and verb is the same as in question forms. These structures are often used in literary or formal contexts. The adverbials are referred to as broad negatives and have negative or restricting meanings.

Forms of inversion

- When the verb is used in a form with an auxiliary, the structure is adverbial + auxiliary + subject + main verb.
  Hardly had I started speaking when he interrupted me.

- When the verb is used in a form with more than one auxiliary, the structure is adverbial + first auxiliary + subject + other auxiliaries + main verb.
  Never have I been introduced to so many people in a single night.

- With present / past simple, the structure is adverbial + *do* / *did* + subject + main verb.
  Never did he consider he might be discovered.

- With the simple form of *be*, the main verb is placed before the subject.
  Rarely was he at home.

Common examples of adverbials used in these structures are listed below:

- *hardly*
  Hardly had we set foot outside when it began to rain.

- *little*
  Little did I ever imagine that I would one day be working here myself.

- *never*
  Never have I seen anything more remarkable.

- *no sooner*
  No sooner had she walked in the room than everyone fell silent.

- *not only … but also*
  Not only did he cook dinner for everyone but he also tidied the kitchen after everyone had gone home.

- *on no account*
  On no account am I going to tell him what I think of him.

- *seldom*
  Seldom have I encountered such rudeness!

- *under no circumstances*
  Under no circumstances could we ever agree to such an arrangement.

There are other adverbials which are followed by different patterns of inversion to those listed above. These include:

- *so … that*
  The structure is *so* + adjective + *be* + subject + *that*.
  So alarmed was he that he fell from his horse.

- *only after / not until*
  Only after and *not until* introduce a clause. Consequently, the inversion comes after the whole *only after* or *not until* clause.
  Only after this project is completed could we contemplate taking on something new.
  Not until you convince me that you are committed will I give you my agreement.

Unit 20
Hypothesising

Listed below are some of the structures that can be useful for signalling a hypothesis. There are many other expressions which could be added to each set, but the lists provide an indication of the variety of language that is available.

While language used for hypothesising is sensitive to register and context, there is overlap between the lists. Some more informal phrases may be used in formal situations and vice versa. Tone of voice, for example, can also help to make something more or less formal.

- Formal writing and formal speech
  On the assumption (that) *oily fish is good for the heart, you should start eating it at least once a week.*
  Provided (that) *you are careful, your health problems should not recur.*
  Allowing for the fact (that) *eating a lot of fruit and vegetables is known to be healthy, what else might there be about these people's lifestyle that could explain their longevity?*
  Given that *he has been a heavy smoker since he was a teenager, it is not surprising that he is having respiratory problems now.*
  If we were to *go back to medieval times, we would probably be rather shocked at the level of hygiene we found.*
  Were we to *go more deeply into this subject, we should probably come to the conclusion that people in the past became immune to many of the germs that would have a devastating effect on the pampered modern body.*
  Had we *access to the documents that we now know were destroyed in the fire a hundred years ago, we could be much better informed about how things really were at that time.*

- Formal speech
  If I may speculate for a moment, *any new government would seem unlikely to put much more money into the health service, whatever their election promises.*
  Speculating for a moment, *I would like to consider what might happen if we encouraged garlic as part of everyone's everyday diet.*
  Let us take a hypothetical case: *two twins are separated at birth and are brought up in two very different homes, one in which a healthy and varied diet is the norm and the other in which the child is fed almost exclusively on junk food.*
  Let us imagine / consider / suppose / assume that *this house once belonged to a rich merchant, his wife and their four young children.*
  Let us imagine / consider *what life must have been like for women in the past.*

- Neutral speech and informal writing
  If we had more examples of women's writing from that period, we would be much more able to comment with confidence on how things really were for them then.
  I wonder whether people were basically more or less stressed in past times.
  Suppose you had the opportunity to go back to any period in the past, when would you choose?
  What if we could be transported back to Ancient Greece, wouldn't it be wonderful!
  Just imagine having the opportunity to listen to Socrates or Plato!
  If only we could know more about how ordinary people felt in the past!

Unit 21
Range of grammatical structures

- Making grammatical choices is more than simply a matter of choosing between correct and incorrect structures; you also choose from a range of structures, all of which are correct. In written English especially, too much repetition should be avoided for the sake of style, and variety is important in holding a reader's (or listener's) attention. In an exam situation, variety also allows the examiner to appreciate the breadth of knowledge the student has, but structures must be used in appropriate contexts and without errors.

- The intended meaning is the starting point of any communication. Before we can phrase our ideas, we must have a clear idea of the meaning we wish to express. Only then can we select a grammatical form that is appropriate to convey that meaning. Consider particular features of the situation you have in mind that may require the use of a particular form. For example, does it involve a relationship in time between two events, and, if so, should a perfect form be used? Or is it an event still in progress at that point, calling for the use of a continuous form? Is there some sort of cause and effect relationship that could be described using a participle clause? Using appropriate vocabulary is essential of course, but the choice of suitable grammatical forms is equally important.

- Bear in mind that in addition to meaning, aspects of register such as formality also need to be considered when putting an idea into words. Other features, like emphasis, may be important too.

- When a grammatical form has been selected, it is then necessary to pay close attention to how the form is constructed so as to avoid inaccuracies. It is here that small details, such as correct auxiliary verbs or choice of *-ing* forms versus infinitive, become important as they may change the apparent meaning entirely in unintended ways.

Unit 22
Linking devices

- We use *because* to indicate the cause of an event or situation. It is used to link two clauses together within a single sentence. We need a comma between the clauses only if the sentence begins with *because*, not when *because* is in the second clause. In informal English, it sometimes starts the sentence that explains the sentence before.
  Many animals sleep through winter because the temperature and light levels are so low.
  Because the temperature and light levels are so low, many animals sleep through winter.

- Where the cause is a noun or noun phrase, we use *because of.*
  Many animals sleep through winter because of the low temperature and light levels.
  Because of the low temperature and light levels, many animals sleep through winter.

- We use *however* to indicate that one fact or idea contrasts with another, which is usually in the preceding sentence(s). As a linking device, *however* must have punctuation before and after it. *However* tends to be less common in neutral English, where sentences with *but* are more commonly used.
  Some people feel low in energy when the light levels fall. However, it is believed that low light levels make people more creative. / It is believed, however, that low light levels make people more creative.

- We use *on the one hand* and *on the other hand* together to contrast or compare two facts or ideas. They are usually used in different sentences and can be several sentences apart. Used in this way, they must have punctuation before and after. Occasionally, they occur together in the same sentence with a conjunction.
  On the one hand, tanned skin can look very attractive. On the other hand, tanned skin tends to age faster.
  On the one hand, tanned skin can look very attractive, but on the other hand, it tends to age faster.

- We use *on the other hand* on its own to contrast or compare a fact or idea with something that was said previously.
  There would be lots of advantages to living somewhere that was hot all year round. On the other hand, I think I'd miss watching the seasons change.

- We use *contrary to* to indicate that a fact or an idea contrasts with another which is untrue. *Contrary to* is followed by a noun or noun phrase. It is often used in fixed expressions like *contrary to common belief / opinion …*
  Contrary to what is commonly thought, the world already produces enough food for everyone.
  The world, contrary to what is commonly thought, already produces enough food for everyone.

- We use *whereas* to indicate that a fact or idea contrasts with another in the same sentence. We often use it to talk about small differences between things that are quite similar. *Whereas* can come at the beginning of a clause, and a comma is needed between the clauses if this is the case.
  Whereas the hole in the ozone layer is largely the result of CFCs, global warming is caused mainly by carbon dioxide.
  Global warming is caused mainly by carbon dioxide whereas the hole in the ozone layer is largely the result of CFCs.

- We use *indeed*, followed by a comma, to introduce information that reinforces or extends a point just made. It is highly formal.
  Sunshine can be harmful to health. Indeed, it can be fatal.

- We use **in conclusion** to indicate the beginning of the final point or summary of what is being said.
  In conclusion, it can be said that unless the population as a whole pays more attention to atmospheric pollution, our grandchildren may face a very uncertain future.

- We use **on the whole** to indicate that we are speaking generally without taking account of unusual cases.
  On the whole, industry is trying to bring carbon emissions under control.

- We use **therefore** to indicate that something follows logically from what has been said, or to introduce a result of it.
  The climatic problem is immense. Therefore, we should encourage all countries to cooperate on this issue. / We should therefore encourage all countries to cooperate on this issue.

- We use **given this** to indicate that if we accept something is true, then what we are about to say follows logically from it.
  We know that overexposure to sunlight can cause skin cancer. Given this, the government should promote the use of sun creams.

- We use **despite** or **in spite of** to indicate that something is not influenced or prevented by something else. *Despite* or *in spite of* is followed by a noun phrase or *-ing* form.
  Despite warnings about global warming, we are not doing enough to reduce pollution.
  In spite of it being so cold, they walked further and crossed the frozen lake.
  Despite or *in spite of* cannot be followed by a finite verb (so we cannot say *Despite we have warnings about global warming, we are not doing enough to reduce pollution* or *In spite of we were so cold, we walked further and crossed the frozen lake*). However, *despite* or *in spite of* can be followed by a clause with a finite verb after *the fact that*.
  Despite the fact that we have all the information at our fingertips, we do not seem to listen to the warnings about global warming.
  In spite of the fact that they were so cold, they walked further and crossed the frozen lake.

- We use **in comparison** in formal language to examine the difference between two things.
  Britain has a moderate climate. In comparison, Poland experiences more extreme temperatures.

- We use **although** and **though** to indicate that there is an unexpected contrast between what happens in the main clause and what happens in the adverbial clause.
  Although / Though most people traditionally live along the coast, the kindest climate is not to be found in the coastal regions.
  Though is often less formal. *Though* (but not *although*) is also used as an adverb to indicate that the information in a clause contrasts with the information in a previous sentence.
  I like going there on holiday. I wouldn't like to live there, though.

Unit 23
Phrasal verbs

There are different types of phrasal verbs which are used in different ways. It is always useful to consult a good dictionary to check their meaning and structure.

Verb + adverb

- Some of these phrasal verbs have no object.
  The school is gearing up for sports day.
  His explanation just doesn't add up.
  I'll be there at 8 unless something crops up.
  The truth hasn't sunk in yet.

- Some of these phrasal verbs need an object. If the object is a noun, it can be placed before or after the adverb. If the object is a pronoun, it must be placed before the adverb. Verbs of this type in the unit are:

  carry out   jot down   make out   sift out   take out

  We need to sift out the good ones.
  We need to sift the good ones out.
  We need to sift them out.

- Some of these phrasal verbs have a very limited set of objects or are expressions. The noun comes after the adverb, and we do not use pronouns with them.
  You must pluck up courage and face the situation.
  We might get the contract, but I don't hold out much hope.

Verb + preposition

- These phrasal verbs need an object, which is always placed after the preposition.
  I could look at that picture for hours.

Verb + adverb + preposition

- Some of these phrasal verbs need an object, which is always placed after the preposition.
  I must get on with some work.
  You should always stick up for your friends.

- Some of these phrasal verbs need two objects. The first one is always placed after the verb and the other after the preposition.
  He didn't want to come, but I talked him into it.

There is more information about phrasal verbs in the grammar folder for Unit 6.

Unit 24
Linking devices

- We can use *as* to begin a subordinate clause to indicate that an event or situation happens or exists at the same time as another. In this use *as* is a conjunction joining two clauses in the same sentence. A comma is needed if the subordinate clause comes before the main clause.
  I saw my friends waving to me as I finished the marathon.
  As I finished the marathon, I saw my friends waving to me.

- We use *by then* to say that something happens before that point in time.
  I arrived late. By then, everyone had left and the place was deserted.

- We can begin subordinate clauses with *provided* to say that something is conditional. A comma is need if the subordinate clause comes before the main clause.
  Provided (that) it doesn't rain, the Fun Run should be a good day out.
  The Fun Run should be a good day out, provided (that) it doesn't rain.

- We use *result in* + noun to express cause and effect.
  The rain may result in the race being cancelled.

- We can use *so* as a conjunction to talk about the consequence of an event, and as an adverb to indicate a conclusion or realisation that is a consequence of previous events or information.
  I saw you so I know you were there. (conjunction)
  There's Lucy! So she did come! (adverb)

- We can use *even* to express that something seems surprising or beyond what we would expect.
  Even Lisa found the race hard, and she trains with the national team.

- We use *what is more* (*what's more* is informal) to add emphasis to a point which supports or extends a previous statement.
  She finished in record time. What's more, she didn't seem tired.

- We can use *to cap it all* to express that something is the final event in a sequence that is already becoming difficult to endure. It can begin a sentence or occur in the middle of one. It is an informal idiom.
  It was crowded, I couldn't see the runners, there were no hot dog vans about, and to cap it all it started raining.

Unit 25

Complex sentences and adverbial clauses

Complex sentences have at least two clauses: a main clause and at least one subordinate clause. Adverbial clauses are subordinate clauses which give information about the main clause, such as time, place, manner, reason, condition, concession, etc.

- Adverbial clauses of time are usually placed just after the main clause. They can be placed before the main clause, followed by a comma. They use conjunctions including:

  after   as   as soon as   before   every time
  since   until   when   while

  We used to eat baskets of strawberries every time we visited the farm in summer.
  Every time we visited the farm in summer, we used to eat baskets of strawberries.

- Adverbial clauses of place come after the main clause and usually begin with *where*.
  She still lives in the village where she was born.

- Adverbial clauses of manner tell us how something happens. They are often participle clauses with *by* or *from*.
  He made his living by / from painting pictures of the rich and famous.

- Adverbial clauses of reason tell us why something happens. If they come before the main clause, they are followed by a comma. They often use *because* but they can also use the conjunctions *as*, *for* and *since* (with the same meaning as *because*).
  She moved to the coast as she was told her health would benefit from the sea air.

- We use adverbial clauses of condition to talk about possible situations and their consequences. When placed before the main clause, they are followed by a comma. These clauses usually use *if* or *unless*.
  If you look at the website, you will find all the information you need.
  You won't find the information unless you check the website.

- We use adverbial clauses of concession to talk about information that contrasts with information in the main clause, or seems surprising in some way in relation to the main clause. These use conjunctions including *though*, *although* and *even though* (which is stronger). When placed before the main clause, they are followed by a comma.
  Although we felt we were being too ambitious, we all agreed to get the report finished by Friday.

Unit 26

Like, alike, as, so and *such*

Like, alike and *as*

- We use subject + verb + *like* + noun to talk about similarity. It can be used for emphasis, and is often used in idioms.
  She sounds just like her father, in fact she reminds me of him in many ways. (similarity)
  He eats like someone who hasn't seen food for a year. (emphasis)
  Dennis drinks like a fish. (idiom)

- We can use *alike* as an adjective meaning similar or identical.
  The twins are very alike in character as well as appearance.

- We use subject + verb + *as if / as though* + clause to give a description, or offer a possible explanation of something. It can also be used for emphasis. (In informal spoken English, we can use *like* instead of *as if / as though*.)
  He always talks to you as if / as though he were addressing a whole lecture theatre. (description / emphasis)
  Her essay looked as if / as though it had been written in a hurry. (description / possible explanation)

- We use *as* + adjective + *as* to make comparisons, but this structure can be used for emphasis, and is often used in common expressions.
  Our house is as old as theirs. (comparison)
  They've got a bath as big as a swimming pool. (emphasis)
  The room was as cold as ice. (expression)

- We can use *as* in different types of adverbial clauses, e.g. time, place, manner, but *like* is only used in clauses of manner. In clauses of manner, *as* is more formal.
  As (she is) the head of the department, Ann has her own assistant. (reason)
  As Ann arrived, I was typing a letter. (time)
  I always organise the meetings as / like Ann (does). (manner)

So and *such*

- We use *so* and *such* for emphasis. *So* is followed by an adjective or adjectival phrase (e.g. adverb + adjective). *Such* is followed by a noun or noun phrase (e.g. article + adjective + noun).
  The book was so good.
  It was such a good book.
  It was so good a book. (this is less common)

- The structures above can be followed by *that* to show the result.
  The book was so good that I couldn't put it down.
  It was such a good book that I couldn't put it down.
  It was so good a book that I couldn't put it down.

Unit 27
Emphasising

Cleft sentences and other ways of emphasising are also covered in Unit 18. Unit 19 looks at forms of inversion which are often used for emphatic effect and Unit 26 covers *so* and *such*, which also have a role to play in emphasis.

- We can use *what* + the part of the sentence that normally follows the verb + subject + verb.
  The ambassador has a remarkably informed view of world affairs.
  What a remarkably informed view of world affairs the ambassador has!
  What is usually followed by an adjective and often an adverb to modify the adjective. Even without an adjective or adverb, the structure still indicates something unusual about the noun, either good or bad.
  What a view of world affairs the ambassador has!

- *How* is often used at the beginning of exclamations.
  How lovely!
  How hot I am!
  How sweetly she sings!
  How he's aged!

- We can use a comparative structure for emphasis. The noun phrase used for comparison usually contains a negative and is placed at the beginning of the sentence. Sometimes set expressions are used, e.g. *nowhere on earth, nothing in the world.*
  No resort in Europe has a better beach than this.
  Nobody I know has as many holidays as she does.

- We can create emphasis by strengthening adjectives with adverbs.
  We've got bargains at unbelievably low prices.
  I hear the Taj Mahal is astoundingly beautiful.

- 'Fronting' means placing the information we want to emphasise at the front of the sentence.
  The best time to visit Paris is in spring in my opinion.
  Spring is the best time to visit Paris in my opinion.
  In my opinion, the best time to visit Paris is in spring.

Unit 28
Adverbials expressing opinion

There is a type of adverbial that is used to indicate the attitude of the speaker (or writer) to the entire event or situation described in the sentence as a whole. These are sometimes called sentence adverbs. Like certain other adverbials, this type can be placed in many positions in the sentence. The more common positions are:

- at the beginning of the sentence, usually separated by a comma:
  Evidently, he hadn't read the book or he would have understood what I was saying.

- before the main verb (except for the verb *be*. We place the adverbial after *be*):
  They've apparently decided to buy a house in Scotland.
  The east coast of Scotland is surprisingly warm in summer.

- at the end of the sentence, especially in spoken English:
  We arrived late, but the film started late, fortunately.

Some common adverbs which can be used to indicate the attitude of the speaker include:

*apparently   astonishingly   curiously   evidently
indisputably   inevitably   interestingly   predictably
regrettably   surprisingly   unbelievably   understandably
undoubtedly   unexpectedly*

Unit 29
Gerunds and infinitives

Gerunds and infinitives are dealt with separately in the grammar folders for Units 13 and 15. The following notes deal in more detail with those verbs which can be followed by both the gerund and the infinitive. These fall into three groups:

Verbs which can be followed by the gerund or the infinitive with no change in meaning.

- The choice is purely a matter of the user's stylistic preference. Such verbs include:

  *begin   can't bear   continue   hate   like   love
  prefer   start*

  She began unpacking her case as soon as she arrived.
  She began to unpack her case as soon as she arrived.

- Note that the *-ing* form is not used after *would like / love / hate / prefer.*
  I like / love / hate / prefer eating / to eat in Chinese restaurants.
  I'd like / love / hate / prefer to eat in a Chinese restaurant tonight.

Verbs which can be followed by either the gerund or the infinitive depending on whether there is a person after the verb.

- Where there is a person after the verb, these verbs are followed by *to* + infinitive. Where there is no person after the verb, these verbs are followed the gerund. Such verbs include:

  advise   allow   forbid   permit

  The rules didn't allow dancing. The rules didn't allow us to dance.
  He advised taking a vacation. He advised us to take a vacation.

Verbs which can be followed by either the gerund or the infinitive but the choice affects the meaning of the sentence.

- Such verbs include:

  forget   go on   mean   regret   remember   stop   try

- We use *forget*, *remember*, and *regret* + *to* + infinitive when we think about the action first and then do it (or don't do it). When these verbs are followed by the gerund, it means we think about the action afterwards. Note that *regret* is very formal when followed by infinitive + *to* and is usually used with verbs such as *inform* or *notify* to give information.
  I don't remember meeting her before, but she assures me that we met last year.
  I must remember to ask for her telephone number.
  I regretted missing the party.
  We regret to inform you that your contract with this company will not be renewed.

- We use *go on* + gerund to indicate that the same action or situation continues. *Go on* + *to* + infinitive introduces a new action or situation.
  The manager went on talking for nearly an hour.
  My teacher at high school went on to become a university lecturer.

- Followed by a gerund, *mean* is the same as *involve*. With *to* + infinitive it is the same as *intend*.
  If I want to pass the exam it will mean working hard.
  I mean to work hard and pass the exam.

- *Stop* followed by a gerund means *cease*. If *stop* is followed by *to* + infinitive, it means that some action that has not been mentioned has been stopped for the purpose of doing another action.
  We stopped (driving) to look at the scenery.

- Followed by *to* + infinitive, *try* means the same as *attempt*. Followed by a gerund, *try* means to experiment with something.
  I tried to contact him by phone but there was no answer. (I attempted to contact him but was unsuccessful.)
  I went to his house and tried knocking on his window, but there was still no answer. (I knocked on his window but it didn't help.)

Unit 30

Using a range of structures

As described in Unit 21, it is important to use a range of grammatical structures. Here are some further examples for the four functions discussed in Unit 30.

Advice

- conditionals
  If you didn't buy so many new clothes, you could save lots of money.

- modals
  You should / could spend less on luxuries.

- inversion
  Were I in your position, I think I'd try to find an evening job.

- present simple
  Taking it in turn to cook simple meals for friends is a cheap way of spending an evening.

Reminiscing

- *used to*
  I used to spend hours looking for shells on the beach.

- *would*
  I would build huge sand castles that were bigger than I was.

- past simple
  I once built a raft from old driftwood and some rope that I found.

- present perfect
  I've always loved going to the seaside.

Telling a story

- past simple
  Marlena looked up at the clouds moving quickly across the sky and felt a sense of envy.

- past continuous
  The Monday morning bus queue was waiting idly for its dreary future to arrive.

- past perfect
  She had often thought about escaping to a new life where nobody knew anything about her.

- inversion
  Never before had she felt this way.

Hypothesising

- conditionals
  If humans hadn't evolved to become the dominant species on the planet, the world would be a very different place.

- wish
  I wish we could go back and save from extinction all those species that we have wiped from the face of the earth.

- indirect questions
  I wonder how many new species might have appeared in the absence of humans.

- inversion
  Had evolution followed a different course, who knows what might have happened!